Mulatto
America

HarperCollins*Publishers*

Mulatto America

At the Crossroads of Black and White Culture:
A Social History

Stephan Talty

Grateful acknowledgment is made to the following for permission to reprint song lyrics:

"That's Heaven to Me" written by Sam Cooke. Published by ABKCO Music Inc. (BMI). Copyright © 1959, renewed 1987. All rights reserved. Reprinted by permission.

"Chain Gang" written by Sam Cooke. Published by ABKCO Music Inc. (BMI). Copyright © 1959, renewed 1987. All rights reserved. Reprinted by permission.

"Bring It On Home To Me" written by Sam Cooke. Published by ABKCO Music Inc. (BMI). Copyright © 1960, renewed 1988. All rights reserved. Reprinted by permission.

HarperCollins books may be purchased for educational, business, or sales promotional use. For information, please write: Special Markets Department, Harper-Collins Publishers Inc., 10 East 53rd Street, New York, NY 10022.

FIRST EDITION

DESIGNED BY SARAH MAYA GUBKIN

Printed on acid-free paper

Library of Congress Cataloging-in-Publication Data is available upon request.

ISBN 0-06-018517-1

02 03 04 05 06 WB/RRD 10 9 8 7 6 5 4 3 2 1

FOR MY MOTHER AND FATHER

"A man's life is dyed the color of his imagination."
—MARCUS AURELIUS

ACKNOWLEDGMENTS

I would like to thank individuals who contributed to the writing of this book more than they could know. Patricia St. Louis, there from day one, was an irreplaceable source of inspiration and encouragement. The old cliché—this book could not have been written without her—is in this case true. Karen Singleton and Suraiya Baluch provided sympathy and aspirin, as well as their friendship. My agent, Lisa Bankoff, worked diligently to get the book off the ground. The late Robert Jones saw the possibilities in a short proposal and brought me to HarperCollins. My editor, Gail Winston, lent her enthusiasm and sharp eye to the book, as well as her humor to its author; and her assistant, Christine Walsh, did the legwork with quiet skill.

Benj DeMott published an early version of the Sam Cooke chapter in *First of the Month* and urged me on, as did Jim Jagodzinski. K. K. Ottesen was kind enough to shoot the author photograph on her Brooklyn rooftop. And Marie Vilceus contributed her caring support, moral and otherwise.

Michael Vazquez accepted an early version of the first chapter for *Transition* magazine, and Kelefa Sanneh edited it. The staff at the Schomburg Center for Black Culture, with whom I spent many silent hours, was an indispensable resource.

In the way of old debts, my first mentor, Alfie Wright, guided me and several generations of Bishop Timon's students toward the literature to which he devoted the better part of his life. At Amherst College, Benjamin DeMott made it clear how much culture mattered in his astonishing classes, which are still clear in my mind. Jim Moser gave me my first job in New York and was more of a friend than a boss.

My parents, my brothers, Brendan and James, and my sister, Eileen, contributed years of understanding and love, for which I am deeply grateful.

CONTENTS

INTRODUCTION

Nearly four hundred years ago, two cultures were placed side by side on the American continent. One had been stolen away from Africa and yoked into place beside the more favored and powerful resident, and was soon forced not only to serve the white man but to look at him with longing, hatred, bitter admiration, and confusion about what drove these men and women. The other culture was at first largely indifferent to the black people among them, but the more perceptive whites soon had premonitions of disaster. Thomas Jefferson privately recorded some of the earliest when, in thinking about slavery, he wrote: "Indeed, I tremble for my country when I reflect that God is just." White society soothed its worries about slavery by finding biblical justifications for it, but that hardly stopped them wondering about the men and women caught in its net. Over the centuries, white Americans looked on their darker half brothers and sisters with indifference, with pity, with a genocidal wish that they would magically disappear, with respect for certain skills, or fear or envy or . . . well, fill in the blank. Almost every attitude and emotion has found a place in those deep sidelong glances, from white to black and back again.

The color line is not only a problem, as W. E. B. Du Bois famously said, not only a political issue or social dilemma, but a presence in American life, like the Rocky Mountains in the history of Tennessee, like Harlem or loneliness in the work of Langston Hughes. That's hardly a new idea, but that word "life" is taken literally here and is the subject of this book: more precisely, the most intense moments of that shared existence. Interactions between the races produced effects not measurable by residential statistics or employment data. Even the most famous chapter in the relationship—the civil rights struggle of the 1950s and 1960s, the central moral primer of the American twentieth century—is dwarfed by the full story. This chronicle places the reader at certain key moments of interracial mixing, and asks what the two races found in each other, what they loved and hated in the other, what they stole and refashioned. There have been a few awkward attempts to describe this phenomenon: cultural integration, mongrelization (very popular during the earliest days of rock and roll), and the blander "race relations." But Du Bois, typically, named the phenomenon best. He called it "deep contact."

The deep contact between the races was for many years conducted by people who were somehow at odds with the society itself: jazzmen or missionaries or early rhythm and blues fanatics. It wasn't until the late 1960s that knowing things about black people became actually desirable in a significant portion of white American society; before then, if you were white, it was most often a social liability. Information about how blacks lived and felt and thought was scarce or, at best, warped: Most nineteenth-century whites considered the minstrel shows to be precise and even sympathetic reports on black life, down to the last chicken-thief joke. If, on the other hand, knowing about white men and women in detail was often part of the job description of being a black American, and your information tended to be more accurate, still you were forced to keep any knowledge a secret from whites themselves, and only reveal your true feelings when you were certain you would not be betrayed. And the knowledge, hidden away, often turned corrosive.

But occasionally members of the races met in ways that produced a flash of recognition, and that recognition was often passed on to the general society in the form of musical notes, language, fashion, key bits and pieces of the American style. Sometimes, as with Christianity or rock and roll, the flash ignited a sustained series of detonations that remade the landscape forever. These interactions were almost always led by a small group of individuals, whether slaves or musicians or just ordinary Americans who crossed the color line and lingered awhile, for personal reasons that nevertheless reflected larger currents in the society. For the most part, I have relied on their experiences and their voices to relate this history. These individuals often experienced the effects of the era's contact more intensely than their fellow citizens. Indeed, their experiences often *resulted* in a new, dissenting view of American society in people who had previously thought of themselves as being completely in tune with it. The slave owner who has fallen in love with her slave can't pretend that she is the same loyal citizen she was before so stupidly allowing herself to become infatuated.

This is not a work of traditional, or academic, history. The chapters consider but do not focus on the forces that reshaped American race relations so profoundly: wars, economics (the thing that inspired the relationship between black and white, after all), questions of labor and management, political alliances. Those forces have their histories. This book is closer to literary journalism: concerned mostly with the dramatic realities of race, how the most significant interactions between blacks and whites produced results that spilled outside their own historical time and place—that is, how they revealed things that didn't have to do just with slavery or integration or jazz composition, but with the American character in general. If one imagines the American past as a drama with characters and themes, one can see that the story of these half brothers crowds to the footlights in era after era. The possibility that anything could happen between the two races, anything at all, from murder to mass social movements, heightened the drama. The fact that it often *did* happen made their meetings fraught with possibilities.

It's likely that we have seen the heyday of this particular relationship, which was, of course, never the only significant one in our history. The creative and destructive tension between blacks and whites may not be the primary spring providing American culture with its famous energy, but for extended periods of our history it certainly *felt* as if it was. What else could approach the relationship for illicit love, rage, desire, schizophrenic reactions, not to mention interesting literature and even greater music? It had an undeniability about it; it was impossible to be bored by it. But America in the twenty-first century is changing fast. The population grows more beige every day, as magazines never tire of telling us. Latinos and Asians are coming into their own as forces in society; prosperity, common sense, and plain boredom with the whole subject works silently at the roots of the black-white relationship. The ground beneath our feet is sloping gently downward, away from the peaks of Nat Turner's rebellion, the jazz revolution, Elvis and Dr. J.

The first four chapters of this book look at the chinks in the society's armor that allowed the races to see each other as human in a time when blacks were regarded as property. The last seven look at culture. But why these particular topics: Christianity in the 1700s, jazz in the 1920s, hip-hop in 2003? A complete account of such contacts would run to five or six volumes, so a few criteria were used to choose the topics that could be covered in a single book. These areas provided a vehicle for one race to see deeply into the other's life. They have not been among those few interactions that have been more than adequately covered (abolitionism, the civil rights leadership, and so on). They were transactions freely available to most people in the United States (which rules out specific institutions like the Army, and regional movements like populism). Their influence lingers today. Reading about the illicit affairs of slaves and whites in the 1700s, one is shocked by how current their dilemma seems. Time dissolves, and the emotions involved in those scandals are alarmingly familiar.

Though I have tried to paint in the often dark and violent background against which these rebels took their risks, the book looks most closely at those moments when something of value passed across the color line. The book does not focus on the distrust, ignorance, and the masked or unmasked hostility that ruled the relationship for so long. Though you could argue that Nat Turner saw further into white hearts than any Christian convert ever did, or that the speeches of George Wallace were more typical of the mood of the 1950s than the lyrics to "Chain Gang," Turner and Wallace are not the principal subjects. The book belongs to those who made out of the sometimes criminal trips to the other side of town a drama in the Greek sense: an experience that, after great pain, produced something close to wisdom, or emotions that retained their shape and power over time.

Mulatto
America

One of the near-white child slaves "auctioned" by the
Reverend Henry Ward Beecher. These light-complexioned
captives terrified some white Americans into
glimpsing slavery's hidden face.

*Courtesy of the Photographs and Prints Division, Schomburg Center for
Research in Black Culture, The New York Public Library,
Astor, Lenox and Tilden Foundations.*

1

THE LOST HISTORY
OF THE WHITE SLAVE

AS EVENING FELL, the prow of the Brooklyn ferry cut through the
dark surface of the East River, its waters whipped by an ice-tipped
October wind. The instant the boat touched the foot of Wall Street,
Henry Ward Beecher strode off and headed uptown. Hurrying
through the jostling crowds, the young preacher fought to stay alert.
He had been working long hours to build his Brooklyn Heights congregation, and had recently auctioned off the pews in his Plymouth
church for the princely sum of $8500.[1] Beecher's merchant parish-
ioners were as devout as they were eager for pride of place in New
York's most fashionable church. He was deeply satisfied by the
response and the fresh cash for his ministry. But tonight's event, also an
auction, would be far trickier.

In 1848, the 36-year-old Beecher was not yet the most famous religious spokesman of the century, "as much an embodiment of nineteenth century America as Walt Whitman,"[2] as he would accurately be
called. That would come within a few years, but his influence was
growing rapidly. A politician in vestments, the spokesman for a thriv-

ing American middle class, a brilliant cliché maker, and an egotist, Beecher was fighting his way out of the shadows of his famous father and eleven accomplished siblings by leading his flock away from his progenitor's steely Calvinism toward a more liberal Protestantism. And tonight at Manhattan's Broadway Tabernacle, he would again confront the most vexing social question that had nagged at him throughout his rise to prominence and would begin to tip him into unheard-of national fame: slavery. The auction he was hurrying to was of not of pews but of two human beings—light-skinned mulattos known as the Edmonson sisters.

The daughters of a slave mother and a white father, the Edmonsons had been offered for sale to a slave dealer for "exportation to New Orleans and the markets," but they had escaped to a northern-bound schooner and found their way to New York. Their case had been written up in the local newspapers, and tonight they would be the center of an anti-slavery auction, where Beecher would try to raise the slave owners' ransom price (around $2000) and buy their freedom.

The preacher had equivocated on slavery for years, much to the disgust of the still-marginalized abolitionist movement. Though he would come to be considered a radical by mainstream America, his stance was shot through with moral evasions. Slavery was wrong, Beecher believed, but it was inextricably bound up in the Union; therefore it could not be ended immediately, as William Lloyd Garrison and the other abolitionists were demanding. In fact, Beecher believed it would be literally "ages" before slavery died a slow, natural death. His view represented the opinion of most liberal-minded Americans—that is, if they gave any thought to the issue at all.

On arriving at the crowded Broadway Tabernacle, the preacher climbed to the podium; he would, as usual, be the center of attention, serving as auctioneer. He looked out on the eager faces of the Christian burghers and their wives, then called the Edmonson sisters to the front and began the proceedings. "A sale by a human flesh dealer of Christian girls!" Beecher cried. Painting scenes as "lurid as a Rembrandt,"[3] he enumerated the cruelties the girls would face on the plantation—lashings, endless work under a blazing sun, rape (Beecher paid special attention to the girls' virginity and the certainty of their rape). The preacher played his part with an enthusiasm that surprised even him; later he bragged that he would have made "a capital auctioneer."[4] He explained that the Edmonson sisters had accepted their immortal Redeemer, but if sold into the jungle of the South, they would be brutalized, de-Christianized, de-souled.

A masterful preacher, perhaps the greatest of his century, Beecher outdid himself that night. "Of all the meetings I have attended in my life," said the reverend, who would attend thousands, "for a panic of sympathy I never saw one that surpassed that." Women wailed, grew hysterical; descriptions of later Beecher auctions detailed how female audience members tore off their jewelry—rings, bracelets, brooches—and piled them in the collection plates that passed through the crowd. Men's hands trembled as they tore the money out of their pocketbooks or unhooked their gold watches. There was a kind of intoxication of the spirit, a bonding with the fate of the slaves that was unusual for the times.

Beecher, too, was moved, in his own way. Later, his biographer Paxton Hibben would write that the fact that the girls were Methodists had made him see the entire subject of slavery differently. But that is an evasion: Many, if not most, slaves in the mid-1800s were at least nominally Christian. Something else was at work. Hibben phrased it as a question confronting Beecher: "Shall this girl—almost as white as you are—be sold for money to the first comer to do as he likes with?" The answer had to be no. Beecher believed strongly that Africans did not have the same inborn love of freedom that whites did; mulattos, on the other hand, inherited some of that liberty-loving spirit through their European heritage—a transfusion of values, if you will, through a transfusion of blood. The Edmonsons' Anglo-Saxon bloodlines made them no longer appear as doomed heathens, and empathy surged through Beecher as the congregation shouted. "He sees all of this," says Hibben, re-creating the scene, "as if he were an actor in it, himself. It is more real to him than the crowded church filled with sobbing . . . women."[4]

The auction exceeded all expectations: $2200 was raised, enough to free the two girls, and the next morning, the newspapers were full of accounts from the Tabernacle. In the following years, Beecher grew more vocal, pressing the issue. And he staged more auctions, which grew into notorious passion plays of redemption, sexual purity, and emotionalism. The girls (all of them Christian and attractive) grew whiter and whiter, until in 1856 Beecher found and "auctioned" one slave who was completely indistinguishable from one of his parishioner's fairest daughters. He kept a collection of photographs of the girls he had set free, and toward the end of his life would leaf through it like one would pictures of old lovers: "white and beautiful," his son said of the girls, "flaxen-haired children born under the curse of slavery."[5] If Beecher ever auctioned off a chattel slave who was "very homely and very black,"[6] one critic acidly remarked, it was never recorded.

A war correspondent working in the Balkans during the spate of wars there in the 1990s once wrote that he had figured out the region's problem: the people, he had discovered, were brain-damaged. Their brains were, remarkably, all damaged in the same area; talk to them about wine or the movies or the local produce or American music, and they were the most charming and reasonable people. But turn to the subject of the local ethnic conflicts, and their faces changed. The words that came out of their mouths were heavy and twisted. The people had become retarded in this one area of life, and they could not be persuaded that they were spouting nonsense. Brain damage, the correspondent concluded. There really was no other explanation.

To apprehend in a fresh manner the original situation between blacks and whites in this country, and to put the Reverend Beecher's extraordinary auction in context, it is useful to extend the analogy back to our early history. By the time of Beecher's auction, slavery had sunk its hooks deep in the American mind. Citizens regarded it fatalistically; it had been bestowed upon them by their forefathers, and it was here to stay, a permanent feature of the landscape. Most whites looked on blacks with disgust or pity, but, mostly, indifference. It was not that they secretly knew blacks were human and chose to ignore it. Their blindness was so deep-seated as to be almost a function of brain chemistry; they simply could not look at blacks and see creatures like themselves.

For whites, then, black men and women in chains were as much a part of the southern landscape as magnolia trees or livestock. But lighter-skinned captives stood out; they could disrupt slave auctions and unnerve an entire town. In 1821, the auction of a woman and her children who were "as white as any of our citizens" scandalized Louisville, and no one would bid for them, although the dark-complected slaves were quickly snapped up. There was "something so revolting to the feelings at the sight" of white captives, a local newspaper observed, that it prevented their purchase.[7] Light-skinned mulattos were prized auction items, so long as their African blood was clear. Experienced traders knew, however, that a slave whose coloring was too close to that of the buyers was often impossible to sell. Few Americans wanted to own a slave paler than themselves. Who would want to live with that shock to the optic nerve?

Beecher's speech in the Broadway Tabernacle enables us to measure the psychological impact of the white slave on a small sample group: the preacher's well-off congregation. But Beecher's auctions were not only strange and notorious displays, they also point up a wider abolitionist strategy, a psychological tactic that was best articulated by its leader, the great William Lloyd Garrison. If the abolition movement had a formal beginning, it came with Garrison's speech at the Park Street Church in Boston on July 4, 1829. In this address, which stunned the Boston crowd with its ferocity, Garrison threw down the gauntlet against the slave power. And toward the end of the speech there was a remarkable foretelling of the method Beecher would employ twenty years later. To cut through the fatalism of American whites, their jaded acceptance of the racial status quo, Garrison used a rhetorical device he called "imaginative substitution": Imagine that the slaves' skin suddenly became white, he instructed the rapt audience; would you then ignore their suffering and continue to talk about constitutional guarantees and slave owners' rights? No, he said, something very different would happen: "Your voice would peal in the ears of the taskmasters like deep thunder." Garrison used this device because he believed moral suasion and political participation would not be enough to destroy slavery; instead, "a most tremendous excitement" would be required to move the souls of white folks. For the nation to be willing to risk disunion and civil war, white Americans had to imagine the life of the black captives from the inside.

Garrison and other leaders used imaginative substitution both literally and figuratively. The leader of the Underground Railroad, Levi Coffin, once introduced some apathetic midwesterners to a "curiosity from the South": a white female slave named Rose. The crowd was exactly the kind of rock-ribbed small-town citizenry that Coffin and the other abolitionists knew must be won over for abolition to have a chance. Rose was "as delicate as a lady," remembered Coffin, her hair long and dark and, importantly, quite straight. The sight had the desired effect on the audience. "Can it be possible," the gentlemen called to Coffin, "that they are . . . liable to be bought and sold? It is a shame."[8]

So Beecher's performance becomes interesting in its attempt to overcome the inherited blindness of white Americans. The sheer effort he puts into painting a picture of the Edmonsons' fate in the South is instructive. Imagining that blacks are actually affected by daily degradations and even rape in the same way whites are isn't natural for Beecher or his parishioners; it's hard work in unfamiliar territory. Beecher has to create a "panic of sympathy": not just ordinary sympathy for a fellow parishioner who has fallen into alcoholism or lost his business to gambling, but a heightened state that will carry these white businessmen and their wives over the very high wall of race into the day-to-day life of a black woman on a plantation in the South. And one has to believe, along with Beecher's critics, that the white blood visible in the Edmonsons' faces was essential to his success.

The Edmonson sisters were mulattos, but it is now clear that there were a small number of whites who were kidnapped or sold into slavery in the years before the Civil War, actual white slaves. We will never know the exact number; most of the evidence is anecdotal, and some of the testimony comes from abolitionists, who sometimes let truth suffer in pursuit of racial justice. But certainly it happened: white children were kidnapped, white immigrants were sold, orphans were shipped south, and adults were caught and even "dyed" and sent into bondage. These "unfortunates" would later tell their tales in memoirs or testify in spectacular trials in the heart of slave country.

Critics might reasonably ask: why focus on their stories when millions of blacks suffered the same fate? Because these captives played a special and often overlooked psychological role, adding wrenching personal narratives to the abolitionist cause and inducing what might be called a creative nervousness about slavery itself.

In the early days of the republic, there were different levels of what one white kidnappee called "the shocking life" of slavery, and the distinctions were mostly psychological. From the beginning, European indentured servants arrived by the thousands in northern ports, and as far as discipline, work hours and diet went, lived under conditions similar to African slaves who were being trundled off ships in Virginia and points south. They were lashed and starved and abused like black slaves, but there were at least two crucial differences: the Europeans had agreed to their servitude in hopes of a better life in the New World, and they were released after terms of two or seven years with a new suit, a bushel of corn, and a plot of land. It was volunteer cruelty, and it was popular: from the mid-1600s to the mid-1700s, between half and two-thirds of all European settlers arriving in the colonies came as indentured servants.

But among this class of volunteers the first true white slaves emerged. They were kidnapped on the high seas or sold against their will by their cunning (or starving) relatives. Or they were snatched off country lanes by slave traders. Children were especially vulnerable; uncounted numbers of them were forced into black slavery. The exact amounts are hard to ascertain: one historian estimated that most of the thirty children that were "stolen yearly" from New York City ended up in "the markets of the south."[9] The slave-turned-abolitionist William Wells Brown reported that the enslavement of white children was "not an uncommon experience."[10] William Craft recalled speaking personally to several slaves who had been abducted from their Caucasian parents and estimated the number of slaves "as white as anyone" as being "very large."[11] Garrison himself wrote in 1835 that there were "thousands in bondage in the south far whiter" than the dark-complected Massachusetts senator Daniel Webster, although he was including very fair mulattos in that count.

The flitting of the white slave through the American landscape can be grouped into three categories, each of which fed the other until at the end these captives attained a fugitive importance in American culture. Some of the recovered narratives about these captives are on the level of ghost stories. One common scenario would begin with the child (often female) being snatched from some lonely country lane, a plaster stuck over her mouth and eyes and her body hidden under blankets in the back of a wagon. After a furious gallop into the back country, the kidnappee would feel the blankets being thrown off and her body being lifted from the wagon. The plasters would be stripped away, along with the child's clothes, and the terrified youngster would be carried to a rectangular pit filled with water and boarded by thin plywood, which looked like a small grave. The child would be thrown into the water by one slave catcher and held there; one contemporary illustration (in Bourne's *Picture of Slavery*, 1834) shows a slave catcher using a pole that resembled a bishop's miter. Another conspirator would pour a dye into the water—aqua fortis (nitric acid) and walnut bark were reportedly used[12]—and the girl would be turned slowly as the dye dispersed through the water and leached into the pores of her skin.

Children were the preferred targets; adults had documents, voting records, and memories that could come back to haunt the slave catcher in court. A young child's skin could be dyed for auction; even when the dye wore off or faded, he or she was now regarded as black, and only rarely were they able to convince courts of their Caucasian origins. There were even cases of abducted white slaves who had to be convinced that they were actually Caucasian, against their strenuous objections. Black slaves who escaped to freedom reported meeting white fellow captives who knew that they had Caucasian parents, but could not remember their addresses or hometowns, possessing only fading memories of home. Some were sold by their desperate families; better the child should become a chattel than starve to death. Others were illegitimate, given to black families to raise. In the 1830s, a Georgia clergyman discovered this practice was not uncommon in his parish, a revelation that left the community "hysterical."[13]

Newspapers reported one shocking case after another. The 14-year-old daughter of a prominent Pennsylvanian was snatched from a road near her home and driven south. The *Philadelphia Ledger* noted a particular irony: she was rescued by two black men.[14] A white boy was grabbed and actually tattooed (a much rarer method used by slave traders) until he was "a genuine nondescript, neither of the white, Indian nor African species."[15] Abolitionists managed to free him only after he had grown into an adult. Some parents recognized the dangers: one New Hampshire minister told William Lloyd Garrison that, because of the slave catchers, he would no more dare to send his child to play outside alone than he would send her into a "forest full of tigers and hyenas."[16] But even family didn't always protect a victim. An Alabaman named James Wilson married a white woman, then sold her and her children to a Georgia preacher named Guilford as slaves. Later, the wife's 15-year-old brother was also auctioned off.[17] The incident was reported in the staunchly pro-slavery Abbeville *Banner*, "and therefore," the *Anglo-African Magazine* commented, "cannot be set down as an abolitionist lie."

One young man, who actually had an undetectable trace of African blood in his veins (a fact his mother had never revealed to him), was kidnapped in the North. His face was slathered with a tan "ooze" and he was tied to a stake in the sun to darken; his hair was then cut short and seared with a hot iron. When the process was complete, he was sold into Georgia. The man later escaped, returned north to find that his wife had died (partly from the shock of his disappearance, neighbors told him) and that his six children had been scattered. His heart broken, he died shortly before the court date that would have determined his fate.[18]

The villains were not always individuals; institutions took part in the trade, with orphans sometimes being sold out of northern asylums. The New York *Journal of Commerce* in 1858 reported that a selection of boys and girls, chosen from a larger lot of 400, were to be examined and sold at the House of Reception, No. 23 West 13th Street.[19] Cash was put down, a bill of sale drawn up, and the purchasers were free to take their new property home. In Jamestown, Wisconsin, a local paper ran an account of an all-female, all-white auction at a place called, ironically, The Free Church; the price of each child was $10 cash.[20] Customers walked among the ranks of children "with perfect coolness," examining their condition: checking teeth, kneading muscles between thumb and index finger. These castaways were probably offered as indentured servants, but the line between servitude and slavery sometimes blurred in pre–Civil War America. Inevitably some owners bought the children as lifelong slaves, and professional traders purchased them, carried them to the South, and sold them as light-skinned blacks at a much higher price than they could get for an indentured servant. Immigrants also fell prey to the dealers. One trader confessed on his deathbed that, in August 1774, he had purchased an entire boat-load of Irish natives and sold them in the South, advertising them as light-skinned blacks.[21]

The gothic-horror-story nature of the phenomena is best captured in a story recorded by abolitionist Lydia Marie Child in her *Anti-Slavery Catechism* (1839). A young physician from the North moved to the deep South and made friends with a prominent Alabama family. During his visits, he noticed one of their maids, a beautiful, modest white girl. Despite the difference in their social positions, he fell in love and proposed marriage; she accepted and the two set up home. About a year after the wedding, the doctor received a visit from a gentleman known only as "Mr. J. of Mobile." "I have a trifling affair of business to settle with you," Mr. J. announced. "You have married a slave of mine." The physician, who had never even entertained the thought that his wife could have any African blood, was about to throw the man out of his house when Mr. J. produced irrefutable proof of his claim. The doctor was presented with a choice: pay $800 or see his wife auctioned off in the local slave market. The doctor came up with the ransom price but, dazed by the encounter, immediately found his wife and told her the entire story. On hearing it, she broke down. Mr. J., it turned out, was her own father.

Cue the organ music! It is a scene straight out of Victorian melodrama, and one suspects the work of a talented abolitionist writer in its details especially in the dialogue: Mr. J.'s "I have a trifling affair of business to settle with you" is simply too delicious to be quite real. And yet, such things really did happen: they were amply documented in court records of divorce cases and newspaper accounts of disputed wills or mysterious suicides. The story of Mr. J. and his daughter could be considered the folktale of a public phenomenon, the version that circulated in drawing rooms and taverns—heightened, yes, but still rich in truth. In an age where local legend and memory were more influential than newspapers or other media, these kidnappings and disappearances seeded the white imagination of townspeople with a new idea: that the slave empire was now consuming its own.

One could also say the white captive contributed a new kind of specter to American culture. Though we would like to imagine that whites thought about blacks in the slavery era, dreamed about them, were obsessed, there is really very little evidence of such fascination. Until the abolitionist agitations of the 1830s and onward, the black slave had faded into the scenery, like cattle glimpsed along a roadside. Southern plantation owners were often intimately involved with the slaves—seeing to their clothes and meals and health, regulating their work, intervening in disputes, exhausting themselves with their care and punishment. But this was drudgery, necessary farm maintenance. There were legends of masters who became obsessed with their slaves' behavior and obedience, but the only widespread psychological disturbance among the slave-owning population with a substantial literature is what might be called the Nat Turner dream: southern plantation owners were convinced that their slaves would someday rise up and cut their throats. Their diaries are filled with rumors and hysterical outbursts about plotters in their midst, and many slave owners slept with pistols by their beds. Rumors of an uprising could keep entire towns awake for days on end. "The danger of a conflict between the white and the black inhabitants," wrote Alexis de Tocqueville in 1830, "perpetually haunts the imagination of the Americans, like a painful dream." The white slave added another kind of bad dream to the repertoire, of which these reports and these folktales were evidence. One might call them humanizing nightmares.

In the second phase of the phenomenon, whites actually gained some insight into the details of the slave's life through the white bondsmen. Instead of the flashes of terror imparted by the kidnapping stories, these accounts had some official public role: they were contained in court transcripts, memoirs, and travelogues. The "trials of whiteness" are an obvious example. Court cases in which slaves attempted to prove they were Caucasians who had been tricked or sold into slavery were "a regular occurrence in Southern country courts."[22] In 1845, a New Orleans woman named Sally Miller claimed she was an Alsacian girl sold off when an unscrupulous travel agent stole her family's passage money. The crux of the trial occurred in the testimony of a New Orleans man who had somehow acquired the reputation of a racial expert. (His justification of the term: "People who live where there are many colored people acquire an instinctive means of judging that cannot be well explained.") Once his bona fides had been established, the expert was asked if, should he see Sally among a group of European ladies, he would not think that she was white. "I cannot say," the witness replied. "There are in New Orleans many white persons of dark complexion and many colored persons of light complexion." One can only marvel at the perfection of the enigma: Here was neatly summarized the core of the South's looking-glass world: race-divining was a voodoo art, dark was light and light was dark and only a true son of the South could measure the difference. It left no standard but that of power. "Legal determinations of race could not simply reflect community consensus," writes legal scholar Ariela Gross, "because there was no consensus to reflect."[23]

The uneasy mystery also registered in literature. Frederick Law Olmstead, the great urban planner and designer of Central Park, was riding one day through a large gang of workers during the travels for his 1862 book, *The Cotton Kingdom.* One of the overseers he was riding with called to Olmstead over the slave's song: "That one is pure white," he told the northerner. "You see her hair?" Olmstead stopped and studied the pale-skinned girl; her hair was straight and sandy, her complexion as light as his friends' daughters back home. "Every plantation has at least one," the overseer told him. To Olmstead, the slave was indistinguishable from an ordinary poor white girl, and most likely, that's exactly what she was—the overseer's description of her as "pure white" implied that she had no African blood at all. Startled, Olmstead asked the drivers if the girl should dress herself in respectable clothes and run away, would she be suspected of being a slave? Oh, yes, one of the overseers replied. A northerner could never tell the difference, but he would know her as a slave immediately; her language and manners would give her away—the exact same answer given in the Sally Miller trial. But what if she was raised among white people as a house servant, Olmstead asked, and learned white inflections thoroughly? Another overseer considered this for a moment and then replied: In that case, the only way to tell that she was a runaway was how she reacted when a white man "looked her in the eyes."[24] An escaped slave might change her clothes and even her dialect, but not the terror of her situation.

Europeans provided an even more revealing picture. In the late 1850s, a liberal-minded young English writer, Charles Mackay, visited the United States and made his way to New Orleans for the obligatory chapter on the South. With pro- and anti-slavery feelings at a fever pitch, he hovered near the doorway of a slave depot, afraid to go in lest he be suspected as an anti-slavery spy and jailed or even killed, as some abolitionists were during this period. But Mackay spotted a slave trader he knew from his stay in New York, and the man escorted him through the line of slaves (men on one side, women on the other) being offered for sale. The blacks called out to him, asking him to buy them and detailing their skills as nursemaids, carpenters, or waiters. Mackay soon regretted his curiosity; the display made him physically sick. He vowed that if "by the mere expression of my will"[25] slavery could be abolished, he would snap his fingers and release these people from bondage in a flash. But he was powerless to do so, and the slaves—learning he was just a writer absorbing some local color—gave him a dismissive look and returned to their vigil.

A few minutes later, Mackay spotted one man standing toward the end of the line. He slowly approached the slave; as he drew closer, he saw that the man was as white as himself, and looked to Mackay's well-traveled eye like a pure-blooded Irishman. The man stepped forward and announced that he was an excellent gardener who could also do some carpentry and look after horses, his voice rising and falling in the soft lilt of County Cork.

"But you are joking," said Mackay. "You are an Irishman?"

The slave replied, "My father was an Irishman."

The slave dealer and owner of the depot approached and Mackay pointed out the pale-skinned man, asking if some horrible mistake had been made: "This is a white man," he cried. The trader, probably amused by the foreigner's hysterical reaction, calmly replied that the man's mother was "a nigger" and that he himself had sold much whiter men. The nausea returned and Mackay fervently wished he could run out of the depot into the fresh air. But before he did, he made an extraordinary offer, one that did not occur to him when he was inspecting the other, darker-complected slaves. He wanted to buy the gardener—a very expensive proposition—and set him free in New York City. The trader refused to take his money, telling the Englishman that he would be doing the slave a disservice: freed slaves had no energy or self-confidence, and in New York this one would soon fall to the lowest levels of degradation. Reluctantly, Mackay allowed himself to be convinced and left the Corkman to his fate. But his incomprehension and his offer to free the man at the cost of around $900, a small fortune, shows that he sees himself in the alleged Corkman. As with Beecher, his good wishes have been sharpened to action.

Mackay's was the isolated experience of a tourist, but it fleshes out reports that we have from native sources. In his autobiography, William Wells Brown recalled one trip he took on a steamboat loaded with slaves for the New Orleans market. "A drove of slaves on a southern steamboat, bound for the cotton or sugar regions," he remembered, "is an occurrence so common, that no one, not even the passengers, appear to notice it, though they clank their chains at every step." Among this particular load, however, there was one woman, around 20 years old, beautiful, with blue eyes and fair hair, "perfectly white." The passengers felt the same morbid pull toward the captive that Mackay described. "She had been on the boat but a short time," Brown wrote, "before the attention of all the passengers, including the ladies, had been called to her, and the common topic of conversation was about [her]. . . . There was a general anxiety among the passengers and crew to learn the history of the girl."

Bits and pieces of the slave's inner life filter out in these narratives. Some of the more remarkable insights come early on with the story of Lord Altham of England, one of the most famous of the lost children. Lord Altham—or "the Chevalier James," as he dashingly refers to himself in his book—was an only child, a rich heir who was to inherit not one, but three baronies, along with thousands of prime acres in the English countryside and hundreds of tenants. But in the mid-1720s, the family's affairs were in crisis: the father was a drunk and a gambler; his wife was decent and clear-headed but thwarted by her jealous mother-in-law; and the father's younger brother—the decadent Richard, a monster straight out of Shakespeare—was greedy. For Richard to get his hands on his nephew's land and titles, however, the boy had to disappear; and the first thing that needed to happen was for James to acquire a new identity. Richard dreamed one up. "The Story he invented to bring the Master of the Vessel into this Project," recorded the Chevalier's memoir of 1743, "was, that the Boy being the natural Son of a Person of Condition, and not meriting the Protection of his Father on account of a Propensity to vile Actions, it was thought proper to send him where he might have less Opportunity of following his Inclinations."[26] In order to become a slave, it was best if one first become a sociopath, a heathen, or a captive of war. James fell under the first category.

In the memoirs, James is tricked into boarding a ship supposedly headed for Paris, and the captain soon reveals what's in store for him. The boy lets loose "piteous Cries and . . . violent Exclamations"; he goes on a hunger strike, and is put on a suicide watch in the hold, actions that were not uncommon on the African slave ships in their first days at sea. When the captain calls him to his quarters, James protests: "But I shall . . . be a Slave!" The officer cheerfully lies to him: "Yes, yes. There is [nothing] so terrible in the Name of Slave as you imagine—'tis only another name for Apprentice."

The Chevalier soon loses his rakish title and becomes, simply, "the Slave," though he is formally an indentured servant, serving out a long term of seven years. He is sold to a master named Drumon in Pennsylvania and enters "the House of Bondage." He is put to work in the virgin American forest, cutting wood for pipe-staves, hard labor that earns him beatings for his awkwardness. The Slave suffers terribly. He tries to escape and is whipped. He experiences night visions: the scales of justice descending to crush him; burning arrows shoot toward his head; a huge sword slices at his neck, "the blade blue with keenness." Freud would have little trouble reading those dream-symbols: the Slave feels that the combined forces of law and political power, his rightful inheritances, have turned against him. And he is right.

After months of this treatment, the Slave manages a description of the chattel's state of mind that will not be improved upon until the later slave narratives. No white man would equal it for its power until Garrison and John Brown:

> *Instead of his fresh and rosy Color, a livid Paleness overspread his Cheeks—his eyes lost [a] great part of their former Luster, and were continually cast down—his Sprightliness was converted into a kind of dead Sloth—a Melancholy which is not to be express'd hung upon his heart. . . . He knew what he* ought *to be, and to think he never* cou'd be *what he ought . . . was a Dagger to his Soul, which gave Wounds too severe for anything in the Power of those he was among to heal.*

James has entered the inner life of the slave and brought his white readers with him. But still, he is blind to the obvious similarities between his situation and black slavery; he never makes the connection with African princes who have taken the same middle passage. Blacks hardly appear in the Slave's narrative; he is aware only of his own tragedy. Instead of empathy across racial lines, James is infatuated with the idea of his own noble lineage; he wraps the knowledge of his true beginnings around him like a cloak, fantasizing about returning home and holding sway over *his* inferiors. The Slave's dreams at night are full of "the welcomes of Tenants, Dependents and Servants blended with the gay Show of Equipage and the Pomp of titles." He brushes off an Indian girl who falls in love with him, explaining that marriages between nobles and poor Iroquois girls just aren't done in his country. The girl doesn't comprehend the argument and eventually throws herself into a river. James soldiers on.

Finally, he is released from his bondage after thirteen years, almost twice his original term. Now a young man of 25, he boards a ship back to England and finally reverts back to "the Chevalier"; the Slave is left in America. As James looks back toward his noble home in England, he claims that he has not been changed by the experience: "So wonderfully did Providence interpose in favor of this young Innocent, that his pure and florid Blood flow'd through his Veins untainted, and his Mind imbibed nothing of the Principles of those he was among, not the least Tincture of their Manners." "Tincture" is an interesting choice here; its first definition is "a substance that colors, dyes, or stains." Though the Chevalier has barely mentioned black bondage before, here he throws his readers an unmistakable hint: he wants them to know that he might have been a slave, but he never became *black*.

But the ending of the Chevalier's first memoir (another was to follow) shows that he did, in fact, become psychologically black, if part of eighteenth-century American negritude could be said to involve a clear understanding of suffering and caste. When he arrives back on his native soil, the Chevalier finds that, despite his protests of being "untainted," he had been mysteriously altered by his time in America. After thirteen years of dreaming about the welcome of his serfs and the pomp of the British court, he dawdles about reclaiming his throne and marries a woman beneath his social station, appalling his friends. Then one day, while hunting with a friend—typically, not a noble but a gameskeeper—the other man spots two peasants poaching trout from his master's lake. They chase the pair, and during the pursuit the Chevalier's gun goes off and kills the older man. In mid-1700s England, an accidental shooting of a commoner by a lord (even a lord whose title was disputed) would have probably resulted in some kind of monetary gift to the family; a harsh jail sentence would have been highly unlikely. But the Chevalier is stunned into a trance very much like the one he experienced years before when the ship's captain revealed his fate. He cannot move or speak, standing "like one transfixed with thunder." The Chevalier goes into a kind of fugue state, running from house to house, hiding from the man's relatives. He flashes back to his terrifying hours as a runaway slave, memories he must have thought he had exorcised. When the relatives catch him, he breaks down completely, crying, "Oh, if any one among you is my Friend, have Compassion on what I feel, and kill me instantly." The plea, so inappropriate to an English lord of the time, stuns even the man's relatives. They release him; the accident is explained, and the lord gets off after a trial. There the memoir ends. The Chevalier's history, years before the abolitionists arrived on the scene, is a first step in the fusing of black and white experience. He is the master who has been taken through the slave underworld and emerged with different eyes.

Though it provided excellent copy for the abolitionist cause, human theft was, of course, not the main cause of the whitening of the slave population; sexual intercourse was. Mixed children, some of them as light-skinned as any free white, were commonplace in the South and figured prominently in Confederate racial theories (as described later in the chapter) and the plantations' hierarchies (light-skinned slaves became the favored house servants; darker bondsmen went to the fields). Southerners were well aware that illicit sex had caused the color line to blur. In 1859, the Charleston correspondent of the New York *Police Gazette* wrote that "if the morals of the city continue as at present, in a century there will be no Negroes here."[27] The Virginia *Sentinel* chimed in, saying that the South was becoming "so mixed up" that a man could not feel safe in marrying there for fear his wife would have black ancestry.[28] Scandalized Europeans agreed: the English travel writer Anne Royall visited Virginia in 1823 and wrote in *Sketches of History of Life and Manners in the United States* that "it appears that these people, instead of abolishing slavery, are gradually not only becoming slaves but themselves changing color."

The issue needed to be addressed. Even in the 1850s, slave owners believed that slavery would be with them for many generations; but how was one to deal with the lightening of the slaves' complexions? A man named George Fitzhugh provided the answer. Fitzhugh was the leading philosopher of slavery, possessed of a brilliant mind and a dark sensibility, and in his writings he came up with a solution. Basing slavery on color alone was clearly problematic in the long term: some slaves already resembled their masters and others escaped by passing as white. Fitzhugh suggested that socioeconomic condition become the new criteria for enslavement: the nation's poor whites would then become chattel alongside blacks. Fitzhugh's argument was simple: the strong were meant to rule the weak (of all colors), but also to care for them and include them in the plantation's extended family. Feudalism, not democratic capitalism, was the ideal human system. "Some were born with saddles on their backs," the

Tidewater planter wrote in his buccaneering style, "and others booted and spurred to ride them." Fitzhugh wanted to transcend race by creating a completely integrated house of bondage, ruled by the American elite.

Fitzhugh's modest proposal found supporters among the southern ruling class. Senator James Mason of Virginia, author of 1850 Slave Fugitive Act, affirmed on the Senate floor that slavery was "ennobling" to both races. Newspapers reprinted Fitzhugh's essays and ran serious editorials in favor of his views. "While it is far more obvious that Negroes should be slaves than whites," the Richmond *Inquirer* wrote, "the principle of slavery is, itself, right and does not depend on difference of complexion."[29] Spurred on by the knowledge that time would only bleach the slave population further, dooming a slavery based on color to irrelevancy, some southerners saw that Fitzhugh provided a way out.

The radical idea soon reached the ears of a young lawyer and aspiring politician in Illinois. Abraham Lincoln read Fitzhugh's influential 1854 book *Sociology of the South* and followed the white-slavery issue closely. What he read disturbed him. "The clamor for white slavery seemed to be in all the papers I read from the deep South," he wrote in 1855, the year before he joined the anti-slavery Republican Party in Illinois. Lincoln wrote a memoranda countering the planter's arguments; in them, the danger that underlies the stories of kidnapped white children is made explicit: "You are to be slave," Lincoln concluded, "to the first man you meet with a fairer skin than your own."[30] But even as he contended with Fitzhugh's essays, Lincoln sensed that the deep psychosis that lay just beneath their surface had already carried the issue beyond all rational argument. "The sentiments pouring forth from Dixie made me ever despair that slavery could ever be removed from this country by peaceful means," he wrote a friend soon after reading *Sociology*.[31] The promotion of white bondage completed for Lincoln the South's vision of a coast-to-coast slave paradise where simple poverty (like that of Lincoln's own parents) would replace race as the governing standard.

Fitzhugh was not in the mainstream of southern thinking on slavery; he was a brilliant eccentric in the southern tradition who ended up penniless and forgotten in his later years. But his ideas got a serious hearing in the southern press because he provided an intellectually serious solution to the whitening of the slave population. What his argument points up is the pressure that miscegenation was placing on the system; the slave owners' lust undercut the idea that white blood was sacrosanct. To modern readers, Fitzhugh's ideas provide a glimpse into a grotesque alternative future, as seen by the slaveholding mind. It was one in which race has been superseded not by colorblindness, but by a new medieval order.

One hundred years after the publication of Lord Altham's memoir, another equally strange book answered it. The first abolitionist novel published in the United States, preceding *Uncle Tom's Cabin* by twenty years, it was entitled *The Slave* (1836); a longer 1852 version was called *The White Slave*. Now forgotten, *The Slave* is the story of a near-white mulatto, part Nat Turner, part embryonic Malcolm X, who escapes from slavery and returns to the country disguised as a white man. The novel is a turbulent expression of all the rage that Harriet Beecher Stowe suppressed or transformed into Christian forbearance in *Uncle Tom's Cabin*. It is the culmination of the white slave's impact.

Written by the anti-slavery activist and historian Richard Hildreth but published anonymously (to give the impression that it was a real-life account), *The Slave* begins with a dedication to its future reader. From the first sentence, the tone is seething: The narrator imagines his story piercing through the "triple steel"[32] that encircles the oppressor's heart—penetrating into his conscience and teaching it "how to torture him with the picture of himself."

Archy, the book's hero, is the son of a beautiful mulatto slave and a Virginia aristocrat, Colonel Moore; the combination of backgrounds means that Archy has "the best blood in Virginia" running through his veins. He feels himself to be the equal of any man he encounters, and a superior to many, including his rich half brothers. "I prided myself on my color as much as any Virginian," he boasts in the beginning. As a young boy, he becomes the playmate for the master's son and learns to read and write. This gives him ideas: he demands that his father recognize him as a son. Though Archy is the brightest of the Colonel's offspring, it is considered an unpardonable crime for a white father to acknowledge his illicit children in any way, and the Colonel—angered at Archy's demand—sends him into the fields to be lashed by the overseer. "My love for Colonel Moore turned into hate," Archy says. "I trembled for the future, and cursed the country and the hour that gave me birth!"

As he grows older, Archy graduates from childhood pet to worker; he becomes just another common field nigger. He falls in love with a fellow slave and runs away and has a son with her before they are separated. When he holds his boy in his arms, he considers killing the child—better dead than chattel, is his reasoning. But he resists the temptation and eventually escapes, alone, to England, where he is accepted as a white man. With papers establishing him as a British subject, he returns to the United States and becomes a kind of double agent, circulating through the top ranks of southern society; he's welcomed into the mansions of plantation owners and observes slavery from the other side of the looking glass. Planters gossip to him about miscegenation among the Founding Fathers, one recounting how he had once seen a woman sold who claimed to be a direct descendant of Thomas Jefferson, and "as far as resemblance goes, her face and figure sustained her pretensions." They whisper about Martin Van Buren, whose relationship with a black maid was hot gossip in the 1830s; some Yankees accompanying Archy cannot believe they will have an "amalgamator" as vice president, but one planter defends him. There is nothing wrong with having a black lover or mulatto children, he explains, so long as you don't treat them as human beings.

Archy's tour among whites deepens his understanding of the slave owner's mind, and sharpens his hatred. "Were I inclined to superstition, I should believe they were not men, but rather demons incarnate, evil spirits who had assumed the human shape, who falsely put on a semblance of human feelings in order the more secretly and securely to prosecute their grand conspiracy against mankind." There are times when Hildreth's language shocks with its modernity; that is a sentiment that could have rung out from a 1960s Black Muslim meeting or a 1990s Bronx streetcorner.

Near the end, Archy delivers a remarkable monologue aimed at the true white slaves of America, which are "far more numerous than the black ones: not white slaves such as I was, pronounced so by the law," Archy explains, but those millions of Americans who either support slavery or, cowed by southern threats, stand by and let it continue. "Those chains which you have helped to rivet on the limbs of others, you now find have imperceptibly been twined about yourselves and drawn so tightly that even your hearts are not longer able to beat freely."

Even though it was written by a white man, *The Slave* is a surprisingly convincing portrait of a volatile, sensitive, haughty, unfooled, murderously witty captive. It introduces a new type of character onto the scene: the angry mulatto as a kind of historical inevitability. The passive white slaves that Beecher auctioned off, who bowed their heads and spoke not a word to their saviors, are replaced by an insurrectionist. Archy says things you simply weren't allowed to say in 1830s America; he calls slave owners devils, the Constitution a fraud, and America a nation on the brink of cataclysm. Hildreth's decision to make Archy a near-white mulatto may have been prompted by his own unconscious racism; perhaps he couldn't envision a coal-black hero being as icily brilliant as Archy sometimes is. But there was clearly more to it. Hildreth attempted to create an American changeling who can testify to details in the lives of both chattel and master; he wanted Archy's unappeasable anger to emerge from a man who looked very much like the reader. Like Beecher, he was throwing slavery's voice, so that it would be heard clearly.

The White Slave did not become a bestseller, but it scored a moderate success, going through at least seven printings and becoming a cult novel, passed from hand to hand even in the South. Garrison biographer Henry Mayer reports how "throughout the 1830s and 1840s abolitionists and their friends wept over the book," believing it to be a true story. It became a bible for a movement that had no bibles (except for the original), and it paved the way for the actual slave narratives to do their important work. If the Chevalier's narrative a hundred years before had begun the process of bringing the white imagination into black slavery, *The Slave* (and not *Uncle Tom's Cabin*, for all its merits) completed the task in the pre–Civil War era.

Like Archy, the figure of the white slave existed at the fringe of the society, in the corner of the eye, as it were, moving there like some restless, aggrieved ghost. Its early place in the society was that of a fugitive symbol, a reminder that slavery was not morally or even physically containable. Its presence brought white America close to the experience of black slavery, far closer than it ever wished to come.

A typical Protestant "camp meeting" in the South.
The stories of the Bible provided slaves their first entryway into the Western
tradition, and an antidote to the whites' inexplicable power over them.

*Courtesy of the Photographs and Prints Division, Schomburg Center for Research in Black Culture,
The New York Public Library, Astor, Lenox and Tilden Foundations.*

2

HUSH HARBOR:
SLAVES AND THE CHRISTIAN REVIVALS

IN THE ANTEBELLUM American South, blacks and whites, slaves and masters, freedmen and dirt-poor Scotch-Irish farmers, free and bond, lived in communities more integrated than most middle-class suburban neighborhoods today. Religious services on the plantation or in the Piedmont backcountry were far more racially mixed than they are in present-day Charleston or Clarksville. Southern whites and blacks often spoke to a member of the opposite race at least once a day, every day, for the length of their lives. Life in the lower depths—at cockfights, fistfights, juke joints, horse races, town fairs—was noted for its racial egalitarianism. White indentured servants plunged into the Mississippi thickets or Louisiana swamps alongside black slaves, after teaming up in a dash for freedom (and were whipped with equal vigor when caught, as most were). In terms of physical life, the pre–Civil War South was a shining example of integration; in it, folk culture passed through the biracial crowd, mutating like a virus.

But this sometimes profound familiarity with the faces and pas-times and habits and moods of the other race (often more profound on the black side than on the white) was deceptive. It didn't mean that slaves let masters see their innermost selves, or vice versa. Familiarity expressed through culture was preparing the way for whites and blacks to see each other clearly, but not yet: it could not dissolve the distance created by slavery and racial animus, which mandated that whites believe blacks were, as one historian put it, "ignoble savages who were innately barbaric, imitative, passive, cheerful, childish, lazy, cowardly, superstitious, polygamous, submissive, immoral and stupid."[1] And this was true even for those masters who *loved* their slaves, in their own minds. For blacks, the smile of the decent white person still begged the question: How can you profess to love someone and still keep blacks as property? The first complaint of most slaves was their master's cruelty: families being split up, whippings. In the second rank was one that lingers to this day: hypocrisy.

The masks slowly perfected in slavery times still reappear today, but then they were welded in place. Overseers who got too familiar with their slaves were often dismissed, or they moved on by their own volition, knowing a line had been crossed. One southern driver wrote that his class must "hide all of his faults" from blacks; if not, "the overseer is unmanned, better to retire at once from such a place he can but disgrace."[2] Some masters forbid slaves to look them in the eye; most restricted their contact to matters that touched on their livelihoods. And the code at the heart of culture, the written word, was often guarded as fastidiously as the Enigma machine in World War II; whites could and did serve prison time for breaking the code and teaching slaves to read. Slaves could pick up the words needed to plant and reap with, but the insights into freedom, law, and the Anglo-Saxon heart were not to be broadcast in the South.

On the other side, slaves were actors restricted to a few roles (the white stereotypes of the good-natured "Sambo," the rebellious "Nat," and "Jezebel," the flashing-eyed temptress, could almost be considered parts played by blacks looking to survive). They spent their days under the eyes of an overseer or yeoman farmer, their real selves shoved deep inside a layer of sullenness or clownish stupidity. Masking became a cultural trait. Children learned it. Masters would bribe them to spy on their parents; in one famous case, a female slave learned her daughter was a snitch and took her to the river to drown her, but was persuaded against it by an older hand. The child had betrayed a central belief in Negro life, as captured in a slave song:

> *Got one mind for white folks to see,*
> *'Nother for what I know is me;*
> *He don't know, he don't know my mind.*[3]

Whites recognized this: The Reverend C. C. Jones saw the slaves' dissembling as something that "descends from generation to generation. . . . They are one thing before the whites and another before their own color."[4] And most accepted it almost as a natural part of the eternal game between slave and master: "It is their business to deceive us," wrote J. S. Brisbane, the president of a southern agricultural association, "and ours to detect the deceit."[5]

For blacks, it was less of a sport to infiltrate the inner workings of whites. They studied the master, the overseer, and the missus and knew them intimately as individuals, their pressure points and foibles. But the larger question perplexed them: the controlling depths of the white soul were a mystery, one with lethal power over their lives, which makes it, in some way, a spiritual mystery. For those slaves who were not debased into believing that they were meant to be chattel, there was one central enigma at the center of their relations to whites: What enabled the Anglo-Saxons to win so much of the world's favor (money, land, freedom) and enslave African-descended human beings? Slaves asked this question again and again throughout their history and their bewilderment can be measured by the extremes of their conclusions: a few came away believing that whites were literally divine, others that they were devils in human form (that idea would last far longer, slipping into the Black Muslim ideology). Some accepted that blacks had indeed fallen under the biblical curse of Ham, so often cited by proslavery ideologues. Most slaves, as the scholar Mia Bay has written, equated whiteness with power and oppression, without distinguishing between plantation owners and poor farmers, and subtracting from the mass of whites those individuals whom they knew to be kind or good. They were less fascinated by color itself, but more concerned with the shades of white authority. If they had one stereotype that might encompass the white figure in the black mind, it would be, in a biblical sense, that of Pharaoh.

If the white slave tore the veil aside for the whites who brushed up against him, there was one institution that did the same for blacks, but on a much larger scale: Christianity.

Religion came to the slaves, to most Americans, slowly. Americans are familiar with the missionaries sent to Africa and the Orient, but few remember that the colonies were once on the European list of heathen nations that needed conversion. The Society for the Propagation of the Gospel was formed in England by the Anglican Church in 1701 with the mission of bringing the Word to America. By 1734, it had priests in all the Atlantic seaboard colonies. The SPG was the most ambitious missionary scheme to focus on the new territories and, later, the new nation.

It was hardly a plum assignment. Especially in the younger, rougher southern colonies, distances between worshippers were great, the heat intense, disease rampant, and the population otherwise occupied, mostly in acquiring land and working it from dawn to dusk, often seven days a week. In 1708, Commissary Gideon Johnston was sent to Charles Town (later Charleston), South Carolina, to head up St. Philip's Parish; on arrival, he began reporting back to the bishop of London, like a novitiate sent to Sodom. After only one year, he wrote the bishop: "The People here, generally speaking, are the Vilest race of Men upon the Earth. They have neither honour, nor honesty nor releigioun enough to entitle them to any tolerable Character, being a perfect Medly or Hotch potch made up of Bankrupts, pirates, decayed Libertines, Sectaries and Enthusiasts."[6] Johnson eventually drowned in Charles Town Harbor in 1716 after his boat tipped over during a public ceremony, swallowed up by the waters of the unruly colony. He had barely begun his missionary work.

If he was being colorful in his reports, Johnson was telling the truth about the new Americans. Especially among poor southern whites and blacks, children went unbaptized, churches went unattended basic catechism (the foundation of Anglican teaching) was rare, the holy sacrament was administered less than five times a year, and burial was not in a consecrated churchyard but in the local fruit orchard or backyard, without benefit of clergy. One priest, the Reverend John Lang, wrote in 1724 that he often rushed to the bedsides of dying men and found the nominal Christian "so woefully ignorant that . . . they could not rehearse the Articles of our Christian Faith, nor the Lord's prayer and Commandments, nor give any solid accounts of the nature and use of the holy Sacrament."

Christianity, when it came, did not have virgin soil to colonize. Folk spirituality—Celtic superstition, magic, African hoodoo—was strong, and it got stronger the farther you traveled from established towns. This belief was multiracial; whites had carried their own pagan survivals from Ireland and Scotland as slaves had brought theirs from Africa, though the slaves' belief in a spirit world that pervaded the physical world was more powerful. As Mark Twain would make clear in *Huckleberry Finn*, to ordinary men and women the American back-country, its springs, thickets, hollows, and especially its rivers and graveyards, was a haunted landscape. Healing with herbs and incantations was common, and masters often had to hire root doctors from other plantations to cure their sick Africans, who weren't satisfied with white doctors. On May 14, 1750, the *Gazette of South Carolina* carried a front-page story on "The Negro Caesar's Cure for Poison and Rattlesnake Bite." The antidote was so effective that South Carolina purchased Caesar's freedom and guaranteed him 100 pounds a year for life. It wasn't as magnanimous as it sounds. So many slaves were poisoning their masters with African-derived potions that a native pharmacist had to be found.

This interpenetration of magical thinking was so complete that it is difficult to locate which beliefs were originally African and which were European. But blacks did have one specialty never approached by whites: work with charms and poisons. Black conjurers often gained the respect of nearby whites, who sought them out. Young white ladies visited fortune-tellers to test out their power over lovers; one white even enlisted a slave conjurer to help murder his wife. For the slave, though the African spirit world was long-lasting and powerful, it had limitations. It could not explain, nor could it overpower, white supremacy. Hoodoo was understood to be effective only if you believed in it; most whites were outside its cosmos. Blacks learned this the hard way: Slaves sought out spirit-workers for protection from lashings, carried out the medicine man's instructions to the letter, and returned to the plantation in high spirits, only to be whipped for being "sassy." They blamed the spirit-worker. (One ingeniously replied that he had also given the man a charm for speed; so why had he not run away?) Some then looked to a competitor, but when that man's potion failed as well, the magic itself became suspect. Though African-American folktales record the small victories of black conjurers over white masters, the victory in real life was rarely complete. So in the broadest sense, African magic had no answer for the deepest question: Why am I a slave?

What began to alter the religious state of the country was what would come to be known as the First Great Awakening, initiated by the Reverend George Whitefield of Oxford, England. Whitefield was a rebellious Anglican priest who created a stir when he began his evangelical tours of England and Scotland, drawing huge crowds (as large as 100,000) who screamed and moaned, wept, prayed, and sometimes thrashed about in a "Phrenzy." His work might be seen as an emotional reformation of Protestantism; the sober Anglican ritual, where even singing was strictly curtailed, was burst from the inside by radical preachers advertising the power of the Holy Ghost.

The whole notion of a "Great Awakening" or wholesale revival of Christian practice is now disputed by historians, who see separate revivals connected by Whitefield's publicity machine. But the preacher's work certainly laid the groundwork for the successful evangelization of the colonies (especially the South) by Protestant sects. Whitefield and his fellow travelers remade Protestantism in several ways. They took a book-bound faith that required literate believers and months if not years of study and compressed the basic conversion process into something that could strike in a split second. They preached that individuals, not the church, possessed the means of confirming authentic conversions. They focused on the behavior of men instead of on deciphering the will of God. And they adopted a dramatic style of preaching that was designed to rouse the emotions of their hearers. Whitefield's proper upbringing and almost laughable experience of the dark side of life (his great regrets as a youth were "attending plays and spending money on sweets"[7]) could never give him an understanding of the everyday lives of his poor, despised, "sin-sick" American listeners, both black and white. But his Calvinist message, newly packaged, would set them ablaze.

Whitefield arrived in America in 1739. Using Benjamin Franklin's printing presses to shape and promote his message, he stormed the colonies hoping to "transform the nation." He attracted crowds of 20,000 or more, inspired lay preachers to take up the evangelical cause, and left new congregations in his wake like mushrooms after rain. The detractors of the Whitefield movement, mostly in the established Anglican Church, mocked the revivals. One said of an especially vigorous one in Boston where the "madman" preacher James Davenport led his singing followers through the streets: "They look'd more like a Company of Bacchanalians after a mad Frolick, than sober Christians."[8] If the revivals happened today, one would remark almost routinely on the near-sexual nature of the excitement; but the favorite metaphor for contemporary observers was mental derangement.

Americans have always responded to millennial, ecstatic faith, and Whitefield was the first mass example of that phenomenon. His movement, moreover, became the first crossover event in American history, in which slaves left their cabins and immersed themselves in a founding ritual of European life, and were received, quite often, as individuals worthy of being saved.

The 1740 diary of one representative Connecticut farmer sets the scene for Whitefield's arrival.

Like most colonists, Nathan Cole had always believed that he would be saved by his own prayers and good deeds; it was a practical faith that placed the American dream ahead of religious duty. But word of Whitefield's message created a taste for something beyond the mercantile semi-frontier existence men like Cole led, fanatically focused on money and survival. (Slaves recognized this drive as the motivating factor in most of the whites with whom they came in contact, from yeoman farmers to mistresses intent on the plantation books.) Everyone was talking about Whitefield, though no one as yet had seen or heard him. Cole's diary recalls the intense anticipation, the almost electrical taste in the mouths of those who passed the word from farm to farm about the young preacher. Then one day, in his field, Cole heard that Whitefield had arrived in the town of Middletown, 12 miles away.

His response was immediate; the first gesture was sacrilegious to the life he had been leading. "I was in my field at workd [and] *I dropt my tool that I had in my hand* and run home and run thru my house and bade my wife get ready quick," he wrote.[9] The couple gathered their things and set out, running their horse ragged "as if we was fleeing for our lives." Nearing the town along rough country paths, Cole and his wife heard over the hills a low, rumbling thunder (they had never heard crowds stampeding before and could not place the sound) and saw a rising cloud of dust caused by the advancing throng. Soon they came upon other farmers on the roads, their horses "all of a lather and fome with swet, ther breth rooling out of their noistrels." On the river, ferry boats were packed, and the land was black with people. "Everything— men, horses and boats—all seamed to be struglin' for life."

After the crowd had filled the countryside, Whitefield appeared and immediately launched into his sermon, which was not filled with pleasant messages about God's love but stories of man's sinfulness, at maximum volume. Benjamin Franklin, who was in the crowd at one of the preacher's first revivals, speculated on why Whitefield had such a powerful effect on his listeners when he was "assuring them they were naturally half Beasts and half Devils."[10] But the Americans followed closely the pattern of his English crowds: listeners toppled to the ground, thrashed about, cried out to God for mercy, and generally behaved as if the day of judgment had arrived. The reaction was generally one of heart over mind. There were no theological surprises; only new emphasis and delivery. Nevertheless, his listeners felt physically *pierced* by Whitefield's words: "My hearing him preach gave me a heart wound, by God's blessing," Cole remembered, and many other white revivalists describe the same feeling; "pricked to the heart" was a common expression. (Whitefield varied the bodily theme slightly by characterizing his style "touching as with a coal.") When, after a few hours, Whitefield left for his next meeting, the process continued. You could walk through nearby villages for weeks afterward and hear families singing psalms from inside their houses.

At first, slaves apparently went to the revivals for entertainment— to drink, gossip, and participate in an old tradition: watching white folks making fools of themselves. But, as would happen so often in the future, one race was seduced by what it had come to mock.

What struck slaves right off was the evangelist's *manner*. Whitefield and the others were unrestrained; they yelled, they acted out the Old Testament, they perspired, they went "a howlin." In a word, they were emotion-struck in a way that few whites were in front of blacks. Furthermore, the emotion was a spiritual fervor, not drunken rage or lust. One of Whitefield's sermons reveals his ability to animate biblical stories—here, Peter after his denial of Christ—by imagining the shifting inner life of its characters, like a good actor:

> *Methinks I see him wringing his hands, rending his garments, stamping on the ground and, with the self-condemned publican, smiting his breast. See how it heaves! Oh what piteous sighs and groans are those which come from the very bottom of his heart! Alas! It is too big to speak; but his tears, his briny, bitter repenting tears, plainly bespeak this to be the language of the awakened soul. Alas! Where have I been? On the devil's ground. With who have I been conversing? The devil's children.*

One must imagine Whitefield performing *as Peter* to get the full impact of the passage.

Many slaves remarked upon this behavior. In his famous slave narrative, Olaudah Equiano said Whitefield "sweat[ed] as much as I ever did while in slavery on Montserrat beach."[11] Slave Samuel Poynter testified about Whitefield's "earnest manner of giving out the text . . . it struck [him] that there was something more implied in the words than [Whitefield] was aware of."[12] What Poynter is hinting at is that Whitefield seemed to have been transported, possessed even, by the word of God. A black woman stated it plainly: "Jesus Christ had told him what to speak to the people, or else . . . he could not speak as he did."[13] Blacks had had some small chance to become consumers of different religions: Catholics, Quakers, Moravians, and even Mormons proselytized among them, without much success. Theology was essential to their failure—one can imagine the Quakers' quietism falling flat before a slave audience—but so was the lack of high emotion.

Some of Whitefield's impact was awakened cultural memory: As many historians have pointed out, there is a direct correlation between the style of Whitefield and his followers and the African belief in spirit entering the individual. In Africa, "possession by the God was the supreme religious experience," anthropologist M. Herskovits wrote. For Africans, spirit could and did inhabit everything in their world: it flowed through animate and inanimate matter as jazz riffs would flow through song structure. "Animism" is a poor translation of this feeling for god-in-everything; "voodoo," as commonly understood, is worse. In African religious ceremonies, possession was the peak moment of contact between gods and men and, clearly, the evangelicals hit that nerve directly and hard.

But perhaps there was something else, something entirely American, as well. Seeing whites overpowered by the spirit of a terrible God whose command to love was surely being flouted with the institution of slavery must have been a revelation to the slaves. The spectacle of thousands of whites moaning and being reborn gave many blacks their first chance to see whites unmanned, recumbent before a higher power, and speaking in heartfelt terms of brotherhood and sinfulness. In their hearts, blacks must have asked the question: Who was this God that could make masters drop to their knees?

Unlike voodoo, Christianity had a demonstrable effect on some whites. Occasionally, blacks witnessed a true miracle, such as a master freeing his slaves. Beginning in 1791, Robert Carter freed nearly 500 slaves on his Virginia Nomini Hall plantation after hearing a Baptist preacher rail against the institution. And Whitefield, who did support slavery, was nevertheless outspoken on the issue of black suffering: "As I lately passed through your provinces, I was touched with a fellow-feeling of the miseries of the poor negroes," he wrote American slaveholders. Whitefield asked the slaves to pray *for him*, turning the tables on masters. Finally, he issued a blistering condemnation of cruelty against blacks: "Think you, your children are in any way better by nature . . . ? No! In no wise! Blacks are just as much, and no more, conceived . . . in sin, as white men are; and both, if born and bred up here . . . are naturally capable of the same improvement." Ministers told plantation owners to study the faces of their slaves carefully, because they would be seeing them again on Judgment Day, when servants would testify about their treatment on Earth.

The two southern sects that grew strong after the First Great Awakening, the Baptists and Methodists, thrived on the margins; most prosperous whites considered them subversive or low-down. The red-hot Baptists, who founded nearly 150 new churches during the Awakening, outstripped everyone. They were strict Calvinists whose faith was loud, bodily, and ecstatic; renegades from the authority of the Anglican Church, they were famously disputative and intent on converting slaves and the poorest of the poor whites. Baptist imagery was earthily poetic, violent, proto-southern, their image of Christ as raw and badly used as the bodies of listeners:

> *Reaking with sweat and gore!*
> *See his side sprout a stream of blood*
> *And water through the wound.*

The devout white southern Baptist with a Klan hood under his pickup seat would become a cliché in the 1950s, but in the beginning, poor blacks and whites were fused in Christ. Preachers like the workhorse Shubal Stearns (who ordained 125 ministers in his church) sought out slaves and brought them to the interracial gatherings in shacks and "Baptist taverns," to midweek prayer meetings and "love feasts." At some revivals, blacks and whites would be separated into two "camps" (with the blacks delegated to the area behind the pulpit, the worst seats). The preacher would address the segregated meeting until at the emotional peak of the revival, at the sound of a horn, the two camps would rush together and shout, pray, and weep as one. It was a rehearsal for Judgment Day, when Gabriel and his trumpet would usher in a time where there would be no separation between colored and white, only between the sinners and the righteous. But at most of the early camp meetings, the two races mingled together freely from the beginning. In fact, many white preachers gauged the effectiveness of their sermons by the slaves' response; when it came to emoting, whites were already ceding ground to black taste.

The rolls of the new Baptist and Methodist congregations confirm that they were almost all biracial: in Virginia, the Hartwood Church was founded in 1771 with 24 blacks and 134 whites; the Dan River Church had 63 whites and 11 blacks; in the Morattico Church, blacks actually outnumbered whites, and the slaves were able to criticize their masters's treatment of them as part of the regular proceedings. Unlike northern congregations, where individual blacks were often welcomed until their number reached a tipping point and they were cast out, southern whites mixed more intimately with black worshippers. In the North, partitions were erected in churches to separate black from white congregants, or blacks split off to form their own churches; in one famous instance, three black deacons mistakenly sat in the white section of a Protestant church and were dragged from their knees by white congregants, a sort of preview of the Woolworth lunch counter scenes of two centuries later. It occurred, however, in Massachusetts, not Alabama.

Blacks and whites experienced God's grace as a bolt of lightning: "It split me," one worshipper remembered. This God ravished people, tore them up or "killed" them outright to be born again in glory. Slaves and half-starved white peasants stood shoulder to shoulder and cried out, crashed to the pinewood floors together. They reached out without knowing who caught their hand, ushering each other through the visions of hell so real believers felt its heat. They traveled over mountains of sin, past naked, grinning devils. The final conversion (if, that is, it ever came—some waited their whole lives without getting the call) occurred at the end of a long, rugged process of fasting, praying, self-mortification, and inner journeying, and it most often occurred while the sinner was alone. Weakened by hunger, they would hear God's voice, calling them by their name, and the covenant was sealed; after their rebirth, the newly born worshippers returned to the fold to celebrate with their brothers and sisters. White preachers blessed black children, anointed sick slaves, washed the feet of black believers, and doused black converts in creeks and rivers; black preachers did the same for whites. (Even the Baptist exhorter Nat Turner would baptize a white man, years before his uprising.) With bodies and minds went folkways. As historian Donald Matthews wrote: "'African' and 'European' practices and expressions interacted in such a way as to make difficult any attempt to distinguish the culture of origin."

Believers also entered a shadow government. Suspicious of all authority, some backwoods churches created a biracial Christian democracy where slaves were very nearly equals; at the monthly business meetings, everything was put out on the table: backsliding members, sexual irregularities, gambling, "tale-bearing," drunkenness, and unjust whippings by masters. Blacks voted and plantation owners were reprimanded on petitions brought by their slaves and fellow Baptists; they had to recognize Christ's authority. Slaves who could not legally testify in court could and did accuse their owners in church, and they often received satisfaction. And this principle of citizenship in God extended to the Baptist policy, hammered out at yearly state associational meetings. One resolution passed at the 1789 Virginia meeting read: "Resolved that slavery is a violent deprivation of the rights of nature, and inconsistent with a republican government; and we, therefore, recommend it to our brethren, to make use of every legal measure to extirpate this horrid evil from the land." Methodist circuit riders, or traveling preachers, were required to free their slaves before they could be ordained, and early Baptist churches lobbied their members to manumit their bondsmen. There was in these churches the first institution in which slaves could expect a modicum of justice and respect.

This is not to say that Christian slaves entered a racial paradise. Some whites reverted to abusive behavior once the spell of good preaching had worn off; Christian masters often acquired bad reputations by becoming far more interfering in the cabins (and prone to the whip for sinning slaves); and the world outside the church did not disappear. White ministers recall gangs of white men bursting into their cabin churches and whipping slaves. But despite all this, the early Baptist Church was a place of rare moral recognition between black and white. A slave could enter it as a human being.

But in this near-ideal Christianity, this brief holiday from cruelty, a controversy awaits us. There was at least one key difference in black and white conversion experiences, as the scholar Mechal Sobel has pointed out.[14] Unlike whites, blacks saw heaven as a vision in ivory: the angel's garments, the believer's robes, the walls of Heaven were white. Jesus was almost blindingly white: "He looked like he had been dipped in snow," recalled one black Baptist. "Then Jesus came to me just as white as dripping snow," another told an interviewer.[15] A small white man—the descendant of a guide common in African spiritual visions—would come and take the slave's hand, bringing him from Hell to greet the Lord. Some of the converts even "became" white as they entered heaven: "I saw myself a little body, pure white, and flying along a beautiful stream that flowed from the east," was one representative description. This insistence on white visions became a tradition in black conversions.

In Africa, the arrival of white merchants and slavers sometimes tainted the color white and resulted in a widespread revulsion for pale skin. The Ibo tribe, as one fifteenth-century European observed, "in their native beauty most delight / And in contempt doe pain the Divell white." But in other African cultures, the color retained its original connotation, that of being holy and pure, probably because of its association with the sun and the coming of day.

So the convert's visions may have echoed traditional themes. Despite this, the question of their remarkable whiteness remains a loaded one. How could it not be? Many African Americans have looked at the slaves' devotion to the white Jesus as an embarrassment, if not a curse: Malcolm X summed up the argument when he stated that white Christians brainwashed Negroes to "look for his pie in the sky, and for his heaven in the hereafter, while right here on Earth the slavemaster white man enjoyed his heaven." The Negro with hands clasped, praying to a snow-white Jesus with ice-blue eyes, the very image of his master, is a symbol of the slave Christian as dupe.

But perhaps the slaves were cannier than we know. Two examples of the conversion experience in action give a different flavor: One slave, Amanda Smith, was at a "camp meeting," or countryside revival, when she believed she heard the devil talking to her. "Look, look at the white people, mind they will put you out," he whispered in her ear.[16] Smith had always been afraid of whites, and Satan's words brought her terror to a pitch. But then Jesus answered; she heard her Redeemer coolly refute the devil in the words of Paul from Galatians 3:28: "There is neither Jew nor Greek, there is neither bond nor free, there is neither male nor female, for ye are all one in Christ." Smith felt fear drop away from her, and the dimensions of her world alter; one consequence was a dramatic change in how whites appeared to her. "Now they looked so small," she wrote in her autobiography. "The great mountain had become a molehill." There were many such stories in slave testimonies.

The case of Morte, who got saved while plowing his master's field one day, is one example of how Christian life could remake a slave's mind in a flash; few would have witnessed anything so dramatic, but it marks off the far end of the possible. Working the fields, Morte saw a vision of God in the east, who told him without moving his lips, "My little one, be not afraid, for lo! Many wondrous works will I perform through thee . . . I am with you always." When Morte came to himself, he realized his odd behavior and moaning had scared the horse off, and it had plowed up an entire field of corn. He feared that his master would whip him "most unmercifully" for his carelessness and, sure enough, heard the man shouting at him for ignoring his work.

Morte had changed; he didn't cringe, he didn't shuffle his feet and lie when his master called. He *shouted*.

> *I told him I had been talking with God almighty and that it was God who had plowed up the corn. He looked at me very strangely, and suddenly I fell for shouting, and I shouted and began to preach. The words seemed to flow from my lips. When I had finished I had a deep feeling of satisfaction and no longer dreaded the whipping I knew I would get.*

Morte's master told him to catch the horse and bring him to the barn (where punishment would traditionally be delivered) and turned away. On the way to the barn, Morte fell into a trance, and took an hour to make the short trip; on arriving at the barn, the spirit welled up again and he began preaching. His master watched him intently, then "began to cry." In a broken voice, he said simply, "Morte, I believe you are a preacher." He allowed the man to preach to the other slaves, and to his own family.

Slaves spoke again and again not only of the Lord's gentleness but his willfulness. They delighted in the way their God interrupted anything at all to "strike them dead." They got saved in the oddest places: plowing a field, drinking, "playing in a crap game out at the Harding pike," or fixing supper. For blacks, whose days were not their own, the fact that God did not respect earthly schedules gave Him a kind of conjurer's power over their lives. The Holy Spirit even struck those who ran from it. "I don't know why it was I got converted," one slave with a gambling problem recalled, "because I had been doing nearly everything they told me I ought not to do."[17] As magical as all this sounds, it was also strategic: getting saved was a muscular display of free will.

Much of the power that slaves gave to Jesus, then, was stolen away from whites. That is, the slavemaster and the white man in general lost his final importance; there was now a higher source, one that knew of injustice and hatred and misery and could speak about them in the Gospels with a lyrical anger. If the whiteness of Jesus in the slaves' vision is uncomfortable to us today, we may be misinterpreting it; for those slaves who retained their dignity, those visions were simply an image of power freshly aligned with righteousness. They were not a glorification of the slavemaster's color; they were an *indictment* of it.

There is no more important moment in black American history, and few in American culture. Before the coming of Christianity, slaves stood on the threshold of the Western world; they were physically present, but they were outsiders in most other ways. When they accepted the Gospels, the slaves consciously entered the Western tradition. It was an irreversible decision: blacks committed their minds to the new world and began to focus much of their lives and their strategies for liberation in the church. Theoretically, they could have rejected Christianity, waited, held themselves back from American beliefs, and eventually developed a Afro-centric religion of their own, as happened in the twentieth century with Rastafarianism in Jamaica and the Black Muslim faith in the United States. But they chose a different way.

We are encouraged in modern-day life to stand in silent awe of the slaves' faith; their ability to love in the face of great torment is almost beyond human understanding. But perhaps we do not give enough credit to the demands that many of them made upon the religion, and the implied demand on white society, before accepting it. It was not a naïve choice: The slaves made a negotiated entrance into American life, just as in the early 1920s whites would make their first significant entrance into deep black culture when they decided to fall in love with jazz. These were events that could not be predicted, and they became vitally important for the society. For the slave's vision of the blond Christ was an acknowledgment that not only their own situation but also their oppressors' souls might just, perhaps, be redeemable. It was a large gamble based on scant evidence.

This vanguard of biracial Christians was brave and important, but it was still a vanguard; in 1775, there were 500,000 slaves in the colonies, but less than 5 percent were churchgoers, and among those, not all were members of the congregation.[18] Black Christians were often persecuted from both sides: whipped by masters (Christian and atheists) who had bought them, as one put it, to serve him and not God; and mocked by their fellow slaves for following that "white man's religion." (Black Christians, along with house servants, were the first large group of Negroes to be accused of selling out.) There were some turncoats: one Negro Virginia minister received a packet of "inflammatory pamphlets" that advocated freedom for the enslaved and immediately handed them over to the mayor, ensuring a whipping or perhaps death for whoever sent them. Others would parrot the master's instructions that the Bible told slaves only one thing: not to steal from the plantation. Some pastors used the job as a way to escape the fields, which was perfectly understandable.

The evangelical furor fanned by George Whitefield died out and then caught fire again around the turn of the century, again beginning in the Northeast and spreading south. The crucial decades were the 1820s to the 1840s, when thousands upon thousands of southerners were converted. From 1790 to 1830, the number of Methodists went from 57,361 to 511,153, and the Baptists from 65,000 to 320,000.[19]

This second and much larger wave of Protestant revivalism was much different from the first. In many areas, masters' attitudes toward Christianizing their slaves had hardened, especially since the major revolts (at Stono, Gabriel Prosser's revolt, and Nat Turner's rebellion) were all led by Christian preachers of one sort or another. Ministers and worshippers shared in the danger. Circuit riders were threatened, beaten, and killed; some were tarred or spent the night in jail. One Georgia "itinerant" named Daniel Marshall converted and baptized the policeman who arrested him and the magistrate who sentenced him, but many others weren't so fortunate.

The early and admirable resistance of the Protestant churches to slavery had now evaporated; Baptist and Methodist churches had succumbed to the South's ideology and supported chattel slavery. They had absorbed the establishment that had once despised them. Dirt-poor white farmers grew more respectable, less enamored of spiritual visions, and embarrassed by the charismatic church, and they quietly divorced themselves from their black brethren. Black worshippers who felt undervalued, patronized, or hemmed in spiritually split off to form their own churches, or were simply forced out by white congregations. Though there was still constant intermingling between exceptional white preachers and white masters who allowed the full word of God—with its promises of freedom hidden like underwater mines in the text—most often Christianity was now used as a tool of social control.

By the time of the Second Great Awakening, the slaves often had two masses on Sunday: the white mass, in which a white or compliant black preacher would give the "don't steal, don't lie, don't sass your master" lecture to the slaves, and a later, often secret, blacks-only mass. The chasm between the two is best caught in the catechisms prepared specifically for slaves, which dated back to the Anglican missionaries of the 1700s, and which contained question-and-answer sessions that would make clear what a good Christian slave should think:

> PREACHER: Do you think you are happier than [your master]?
> SLAVE: Yes. When I come in from my work; eat my hearty
>   supper, worship my maker; lie down without care on my
>   mind; sleep sound; get up in the morning strong and fresh;
>   and hear that my master could not sleep, for thinking on his
>   debts and taxes, and how he shall provide victuals and
>   clothes for his family, or what he shall do for them when
>   they are sick—then I bless God that he has placed me in my
>   humble station; I pity my master, and feel myself happier
>   than he is.
> PREACHER: Then it seems everybody is best, just where God
>   has placed them?
> SLAVE: Yes.[20]

In retrospect, the attempt to force-feed the slaves this line seems more pathetic than sinister, especially since slaves, though illiterate, knew of the more revolutionary aspects of Christian teachings. Black worshippers often recalled these lessons with outrage or laughter: Not only were they being served up an obvious fraud, but it was done in such a careless, two-faced way that it became an insult to their intelligence. Slaves would roll their eyes at mistresses who preached the same verse to them every week ("Servants, obey your masters") as if the Bible consisted of only that one sentence. They nodded, but in their minds, they responded with "Break every yoke and let the oppressed go free." One white traveler to the South wrote how remarkably common this topic was among the slaves.

The blacks pantomimed agreement with the white world, but, come nightfall, they would steal away and either gather themselves in a prayer house or in the woods for an "arbor mass." If the masses were forbidden, slaves might alert one another that they were to occur that night by singing the spiritual "Steal Away to Jesus" in the fields. When darkness fell, the slaves would slip out of the quarters one by one, ducking the patrollers who roamed the lanes and byways looking to catch a slave out without a pass and "beat the blood" out of him. If there was a hollow or thicket (called a "hush harbor") that gave maximum protection from the roaming bands, or that had acquired a reputation as a sacred place, every fugitive worshipper knew that was the spot to meet. If the mass was to be held in a new place, broken twigs on tree branches would point the way. Coded songs, movement in darkness, markers left by an invisible hand: everything spoke of secrecy, brotherhood.

Once gathered, the brothers and sisters would greet one another joyfully, their exhaustion from twelve hours under the southern sun slowly turning to anticipation. Often an iron pot would be turned upside down and placed at the center of the meeting; it was reputed to deaden the sound. There was no need for ministers here; suffering was the ticket of admission, and journeying to God's grace the matter at hand. The worshippers would begin by asking each how they felt, "the state of their mind." Then one member would begin testifying about his sin-sick life, his unworthiness; the pace at the beginning halting and heavy, the absence of the spirit clear to everyone. (One almost has to wonder if this almost ritualized opening was, in part, a subtle commentary on the white masses they had attended earlier, which were noted for their dullness and lack of emotion.) The others would moan along, but it wouldn't be long before the air changed and people began shouting and singing of Jesus and *to* Jesus. They would feel the edges of a trance—God had come to their thicket—and shout louder, stamp and fall senseless before the Holy Spirit, traveling inwardly and visiting Heaven. This was the old-time religion, before it had become respectable; now the mass became theirs, truly black. They recognized themselves as men and women in Christ, individuals with souls and responsibilities in a harsh land. They tasted freedom and reveled in it until the meeting broke.

Again and again, former slaves remembered the intensity of those secret gatherings. "Meetings back there meant more than they do now," remembered one ex-slave. "Then everybody's heart was in tune and when they called on God they made heaven ring."

From the 1830s onward, the harshness of the slave empire intensified in the face of sectional conflicts, northern abolitionism, and slave revolts. The connection with honorable whiteness was, in many areas, severed; the need for masks increased. But in these sanctuaries, slaves showed their true faces to God. That bond they had formed with Jesus, that privileged conversation, had gone underground. Here was a case of life imitating Scripture: what was their situation if not a reenactment of the Old Testament description of the Jews in Egypt, slaves wondered? Blacks began to think of themselves as the new Israelites: Martin Luther King Jr.'s final speech (with himself as Moses) can be traced to this era and the slaves' sense of themselves as living out the prophecies of the Bible; even their songs were spiked with references to themselves as "de people dat is born of God." They did not have to create prophecy, as did the Rastafarians and the Black Muslims much later; it had all been foretold. They had not only entered the Western tradition—they now claimed the role of its redeemer.

In the slaves' eyes, the masters had committed a mind-boggling and wonderful error by revealing Christ to them; they believed their eyes saw deeper into the Bible and discovered a secret message. Whites simply did not understand the true meaning of their own religion. "That ol' white preachin' wasn't nothin'" said the slave Nancy Williams. "Ol' white preacher used to talk with their tongues without saying nothin', but Jesus told us slaves to talk with our hearts." And no theological sophistication was necessary; many slaves scorned "book religion" of the masters and talked about a "heart religion."

This is a crucial development. All the sense of difference in small and large things that blacks felt between themselves and whites was poured into this gap. Christianity gave a name to that indefinable *thing* that blacks knew was unique to them. A secular parallel occurred when slaves would gather around and watch their masters dance European reels, shottisches, and minuets, steps that they immediately recognized as too "sedate and formalized" for their taste. A slave describes what happened next: "The slaves became proficient in such dances and could play a tune with their feet, dancing largely to an inward music, a music that was felt, not heard."[21] Call it what you will—negritude, "soul"— that inarticulable feeling that had marked them off from the Anglo-Saxon now acquired a moral narrative.

Aunt Aggy, a Virginia slave in the 1840s, revealed the secret to an interviewer. One can almost hear the whispering delight in her voice:

> *You t'inks I'm mistaken, honey! But I know t'ings dat de wite folks wid all dar larnin' nebber fin's out, an' nebber sarches fo' nudder. . . . No, honey! De good Lawd doan gib ebery'ting to his wite chilluns. He's gib 'em de wite skin, an' larnin', an' he's made 'em rich an' free. But de brack folks is his chilluns, too, an' he gibs us de brack skin an' no larnin', an' hab make us t' work fo' de wite folks. But de good Lawd gibs us eyes t's see t'ings dey doan see, an' he comes t' me, a poor brack slave woman, an' tells me be patient, 'cause dar's no wite nor brack in hebben. An' de time's comin' when he'll make his brack chilluns free in dis yere worl', and gib 'em larnin, an good homes, an' good times. Ah! Honey, I knows! I knows!*[22]

The republic did not recognize the slaves as human, but this new God did. Slaves trusted Jesus enough to reveal their true selves to him. In the spirituals, he was a "bosom friend"; Harriet Tubman remembered talking to him as she would to her closest companion, a completely natural and human conversation. After Emancipation, one white observer, Harris Barrett of Hampton Institute, was struck by the intimacy he observed in black churches, a tradition that stretched back to slavery days: "I have seen men and women . . . look and express themselves as if they were conversing with their Lord and Master, with their hands in His."

Originally, Christianity had brought the two races together; by the mid-1800s, it made clear the gulf between them. Whites often regarded blacks as horribly insincere Christians (which is exactly what blacks thought about them), always getting drunk, stealing their master's chickens, fornicating, acting like heathens, and then somehow declaring that they were sure beyond the sliver of a doubt that Jesus loved them. Once they had been saved, most blacks could not be convinced that Christ would not abandon them on Judgment Day, an idea that drove white preachers wild. But blacks considered their transgressions minor compared to the great crime committed against them. With this new confidence, the teachings of white preachers were edited, tailored, wholly remade to the slaves' dilemma. One Liberty County, Georgia, preacher named C. C. Jones learned this when he was preaching to a large black congregation on Paul's Epistle to Philemon. The reverend argued that the Bible was here instructing servants in fidelity and obedience and forbidding them to run away. This argument was a commonplace, the bedrock on which slave Christianization was allowed to take place. As soon as his listeners heard it, half of them abruptly stood and "walked off with themselves." The other slaves glared at him, and after the ceremony surrounded him and protested that there was no such epistle in the Bible, or that he was a stooge for the masters. The black worshippers informed him that they "did not care if they never heard me preach again." One is struck by how confident this second generation of black Christians felt in their faith. They were now the authorities on Christian tradition, and only their hearts could discern God's true intent.

The black masks perfected in the years of slavery came off briefly after Emancipation. Historian Eugene Genovese has written powerfully about the shock whites felt when their most trusted and loved servants abandoned them the moment the Civil War ended; the resulting bitterness poisoned their lives, as they realized they had never known their servants at all. On the other hand, after Emancipation slaves could express their feeling of religious superiority for the first time to their old masters. Often they condemned their owners for the treatment they'd received, but there are also numerous instances in the slave narratives of men and women forgiving their former owners. One, named Charlie, told the owner who had whipped him on the plantation: "I love you as though you never hit me a lick, for the God I serve is a God of love and I can't go to his Kingdom with hate in my heart." But Charlie also told the man of driving him to church and then sneaking to the door and peeping in to see the elite worship. His conclusion was simple: "You ain't right, yet, Marster," Charlie told him. "What is in me . . . is not in you."

The Christian church was the first, lasting place of his own the black American had made in America, outside of his family: and it would become, as Leonard E. Barrett has written, "his school, his forum, his political arena, his social club, his art gallery, his conservatory of music . . . his lyceum and gymnasium as well as sanctum sanctorum." Blacks had seized the white Protestant tradition in a moment of flux, and saw straight to the core of its moral story. Part of this new life they inherited from white culture, what might be called its accumulated wisdom of suffering and transcendence. Part of it they built hand-in-hand with whites. Part of it they created in conscious opposition to white failings. The last of it they built alone, in secret, under threat of death.

"The African Prince." This popular print hints at the
sexual curiosity that resulted in untold suffering for
black women in the South—but which also forced
some slave owners to see their lovers as
full-fledged individuals.

Author's collection.

3

The Mulatto Flag: Interracial Love in Antebellum America

THERE ARE IN America two ideas between which the issue of race has been strung like a wire, tightening and releasing along with the spikes in racial tension. They are both equally old. The first is a vision of a snow-white nation cleansed of the black race; its long history continues today in the philosophies of neo-Nazis and Black Muslims, both of whom would like to see separate homelands for their people. In the early and mid-1800s, the idea had strong mainstream appeal. Everything from schemes to send the slaves back to Africa to violent pogroms revealed, in the words of historian George Fredrickson, "the persistence in the white imagination of the impossible dream of absolute racial homogeneity."[1] Both those outwardly friendly and those inimical to black people have indulged in the dream. The former group supported the colonization movement of the early 1800s, in which they politely asked blacks to go back to Africa or, if that was too far, Haiti. Even Lincoln wanted to create an Anglo-Saxon utopia—he dreamt of the ship carrying the last of the ex-slaves sailing for Port-au-Prince—

and before his death he called free black leaders together to tell them about it. The Negro notables were appalled: this from their hero.

When others fantasized about a monochromatic nation, it was usually of blacks flocking to spots along the Gulf of Mexico (nineteenth-century "thermal" laws posited that they could survive only in warm climates) and pining away there from scrofula, syphilis, consumption, or advanced shiftlessness. Finally, they would fade into extinction. Even some of the fiercest abolitionists believed they were setting free a people that would not exist in a hundred years' time: Africans were believed to be a weak race, and Darwin had proved what happened to weak races. Active extermination was another option. Everyone from Jefferson to de Tocqueville saw war as a likely outcome to the race problem, and this was one vision that made sense to some blacks, few of whom wanted to return to Africa. Nat Turner dreamt the reverse dream, of white extermination, and he saw it literally: in one of his last visions before the uprising, he witnessed black phantoms conquering their white enemies. For Turner and many others, racial tension was so strong that it could never be lessened through peaceful means. The wire hummed, loud or soft, in the nation's ears.

At the other extreme from the idea of a race-pure America was the tiny minority opinion that sex would solve everything: The mixing of black, white, red, and yellow peoples would produce a physically new American. This theory was put into action even before it was coherently stated. Black men had accompanied the Spanish explorers, and later, black indentured servants (not slaves, as is often stated) landed in Virginia in 1619 and mingled and married freely with Native American women. But it was Daniel Elfrye who initiated the black-white mulatto experience in America. The English captain who is reputed to have brought the first shipload of Negros into Virginia afterward received an extraordinary letter from his employer, the London Company, on May 10, 1632. In it, they reprimanded him for "too freely entertaining" a mulatto woman onboard.[2] The British euphemism disguised the first recorded instance of a sexual encounter between blacks and whites in the New World.

The standard defense of men like Elfrye was to blame the incidents on aggressive black women. In *New Voyage to Guinea* (1744), William Smith marveled at the black female slaves who possess a "temper hot and lascivious, making no scruple to prostitute themselves to the Europeans for a very slender profit, so great is their inclination to white men." In a case of guilty transference, the black woman became a succubus.

Blacks and whites mixed their blood from the mid-1600s onward, but amalgamation became official American policy only when it involved Native Americans. Pocahontas, who saved the Plymouth colony and married the Englishman John Smith, became the model. When she abandoned her culture and embraced English values, her blood became the ingredient that enriched the nation's stock. In the 1800s, there was a full-fledged Pocahontas craze: warships and villages were named after her; manufacturers of cigars, perfumes, and flour slapped her name on their products, perhaps the ultimate American compliment. Poets sang her praises:

> *Know'st what thou has done, thou dark-hair'd child?*
> *Thou wert the saviour of the Saxon vine,*
> *And for this deed alone our praise and love are thine.*[3]

On the frontier, this copper-ivory mix was a necessity; there were so few white women that single male pioneers often married local Native American women (the reverse was much less common). Jefferson amalgamated with Sally Hemmings, but it was to the native chiefs that he offered his race as a bridegroom. "You will unite yourselves with us . . . and we shall all be Americans," he wrote five years after leaving the White House. "You will mix with us by marriage, your blood will run in our veins, and will spread with us over this great land." In the end, Native Americans often withered before the whites' embrace, which turned violent. But there was at least an original willingness to become one people.

The merging of black and white was more contentious; there were laws against interracial unions from as early as 1664. Virginia restricted intermarriage in 1691, Massachusetts in 1705, North Carolina in 1715, South Carolina and Delaware in 1717.[4] But sentiment varied; if a mixed couple traveled beyond a local hollow or across a medium-sized river in any of those states, they might be met with either a mounted vigilante or quiet tolerance. The ferocious responses to unions of black men and white women that have become a cliché of southern "honor"—the lynchings, the castrations, the pathological obsession with black rapists—date mostly from the Civil War period and onward; the institutionalized terror that ruled the South after the war was not the rule. Whites in some communities defended blacks accused of rape, hired famous defense lawyers, and signed petitions. A black's good reputation could trump prejudice. And it was white women (or, rarely, white men) who bore the brunt of the society's disapproval when they strayed from their assigned beds.

Still, there was a core of prejudice distinguishable from one end of the country to the other: if laws varied, social sentiment was overwhelmingly negative. There was a feeling that the union was literally against nature, as God had made blacks a separate and unequal race. The mind-set was revealed at the very first interracial marriage on record, the 1681 nuptials of an Irish servant girl named Nell Butler and a black slave named Charles on the lower western shore of Maryland. The event also brings us a small, but legendary, act of resistance.

The day of the wedding, Nell's master, Lord Baltimore, who had brought her with him from England, apparently decided he must do the paternal thing and warn Nell against her foolishness.[5] By a 1664 law, she and her children would become slaves if she went ahead with marrying Charles. Not only that, there was a shortage of white women in the colony at the time, making even illiterate female servants sought-after marriage material. After Nell served out her term of servitude, she would become a catch for a rising planter or a yeoman farmer. (Handbills passed around London's poor quarters at the time promised women that they would find rich husbands in the colonies.) Nell was choosing misery and social death over a comfortable life, status, and respect for her children. In going to her, Baltimore was acting as a substitute father, and there is evidence he was a tolerant man. He had arranged and paid for a ceremony and asked his well-to-do friends to attend. (They came, and gossiped like crazy about the match. "They could not imagine why Nell had chosen to marry Charles," writes historian Martha Hodes.) All in all, Baltimore clearly felt he had to gauge Nell's state of mind, perhaps even whether she was in full possession of her faculties. There are various reports of exactly what he said that morning—some reported he posed a straightforward question, others that he asked her rudely "how she would like to go to bed to a Negro."

Nell was stung to the quick. Flaring up, she told the aristocrat that the choice was her own and that she would choose Charles over Lord Baltimore himself. (In another version, Nell answers that she would rather sleep with Charles than with him.) Either way, she answered with extravagant feeling.

Nell had a great deal to lose; she still had four or five years' service left with Baltimore and he could have made them miserable by working her half to death or by selling her contract and breaking up her marriage. So why did she lash out? Perhaps, knowing what was before her, we can guess that this poor servant had a premonition of her own fate. Nell knew the price of her love would be high; she must have agonized over it, especially the knowledge that her children by Charles could be whipped before her eyes or auctioned on a whim. She was, in effect, selling her own children into slavery. Indeed, the worst scenario came true: Nell did become a slave, as did her several children by Charles. She spent her days as a "hard laboring body" in the fields, grueling work that left her "a much broken and an old woman," a different figure from the middle-class matron she could have easily become. In her answer is anguish at what awaits her. (She may have even known that it was aristocrats like Baltimore who crafted the law that sealed her fate.) Nell must have made her peace with her decision at some cost, and put it out of her mind at least for this one day, only to have it thrown in her face by Baltimore's blundering condescension.

Nell died a broken-down slave, but Maryland remembered her. After her marriage, Lord Baltimore led a fight in the legislature to change the law that decreed bondage for white women who married slaves; he argued that masters were forcing their poor white servants to marry blacks in order to keep the women in lifelong slavery. (What effect Nell's marriage had on his thinking is unknown, but the timing is intriguing.) The law passed, but it did not affect his Irish servant. Eighty years later, however, her grandchildren asked the Maryland courts to free them, as descendants of a white woman. The courts ruled against them, but Nell's great-granddaughter did win her freedom twenty years later with the same argument. As soon as the decision was handed down, other slaves began to claim Nell. Notices of runaways appeared in Maryland's western shore newspapers, seeking slaves who "pretend to be of the Butler family, who have lately obtained their freedom in the general court." One Steven Butler, a skilled worker, ran away from his master and justified his actions by saying he was a descendent of "famous Nell." In marrying Charles, Nell gave her neighbors an example of love that was stronger than the near-primal American instinct for segregation. And she mothered a flock of rebels who petitioned for freedom in her name.

Throughout America's early history there are Nell Butlers startling local prejudice with their inexplicable romances. Most were women; white men could have a black woman on the side and never pay a social cost. But one class of white lovers went further than Nell with a curious ritual made famous by novelist Edna Ferber in her sprawling novel *Showboat*. In it, the husband of the tragic mulatto Julie La Verne drinks a few drops of her blood, thus becoming black under the "one drop" rule. Jerome Kern and Oscar Hammerstein kept the gesture in their 1927 Broadway masterpiece, and generations have witnessed the gesture, without knowing that it was based on actual cases.

The first on record is a British soldier in the Revolutionary War in 1781. Fighting with Cornwallis's army in the North Carolina hills, the redcoat was wounded and became separated from his unit, a dangerous situation for any man in a war in which mercy was not always shown to the enemy. Somehow he found his way to the cabin of a mulatto woman and her daughter; instead of reporting him to the local rebels, they took him in and treated his wounds. After peace was declared, he decided he had fallen in love with the woman and announced he wanted to marry her; but the law prevented it. While watching a doctor bleed her for a minor illness, inspiration struck: He drank a few drops of his beloved's blood, marched off to the town hall, declared himself a Negro under the law, and came back with a marriage license.[6] The novelist Mayne Reid, a former frontiersman and literary acquaintance of Edgar Allan Poe, could have been speaking for the soldier when he had his hero declare his willingness to nick the vein of his black lover and drink her blood in his 1856 novel *Quadroon: or, a Lover's Adventure in Louisiana:* "What was it to me?" the hero asks. "Why should I care for customs and conventionalities which I at heart despised?"

Tempie James, a planter's daughter in the rich Roanoke Valley of

North Carolina, also remade herself through a transfusion. In the 1840s, Tempie fell in love with her father's coachman, Squire James. Her parents "raved, begged and pleaded" with her to forget the slave, but she was adamant. "You haven't given me Squire," she told them. "He's all I want." If one can detect the fury of a spoiled child in her voice, Tempie proved herself to be something more than that. When her father sold Squire to get him out of the valley, she tracked him down, bought him, and freed him. In the coup de grace, she took a tumbler, mixed in whiskey with several drops of Squire's blood, and drank it down. Then she swore to officials that "she had Negro blood in her." Faced with such a total renunciation of whiteness, the authorities agreed with her, and registered the couple's marriage, listing Tempie in the next census as a mulatto. Her family had had enough: they disowned her. But she stayed with Squire and bore him fifteen children.[7]

There are other cases on record of lovers drinking or injecting their partner's blood. But as heartwarming as these moments are, why should we even bring them to light when they were so exceptional in a country that grew, decade by decade, more and more hostile to the idea of black and white union, physical or otherwise? Certainly these were isolated incidents, and the very idea of interracial love was almost derisory in the context of slavery. But beyond seeding local legend with examples of successful unions, they also established what might be called a revolutionary tone. The blood-drinking gesture, for example, had enough iconic power to be resurrected in *Showboat* and in several novels. But we must also listen to the lovers' words. In them, we hear white people who have seen all the way through popular lies.

Example: E. S. Abdy, an Englishman, who toured America in 1831–1832 and wrote the requisite memoir. In it, he tells of a Vermont Irishman, perhaps a tradesman, who knocked on the door of a stranger's house and, when a white woman answered the door, asked her a question. Unable to answer him, she sent for her husband, and the Irishman received the shock of his life when the man of the house turned out to be a Negro. Insulted by the match (and, perhaps, by her lack of embarrassment over it), the visitor turned back to the wife and asked if "her family had met with any misfortune so that you should so far disgrace it to make such a degrading alliance." The woman, we can safely imagine, looked him up and down. "Yes," she replied. "My poor sister met with a misfortune that brought irreparable disgrace upon us. She married an Irishman."[8]

This came at a time when abolitionists, scientists, rich white bene-factors, and even free blacks were often apologizing for the black race. Despairing of the educational and cultural attainments of African Amer-icans, they insisted that emancipation did not mean social equality and dared not even speak the name of interracial love. In this atmosphere of shame, the Irishwoman's quip was a model of leveling rhetoric.

In the mid-1800s, this defiance often came from the Irish, who were schizophrenically cast as both the Negroes' fiercest enemies and their brothers in poverty. Year in and year out, "narrowbacks" and Negroes ran neck-and-neck for the title of most despised population in the country. "To be called an Irishman," one English traveler noted around midcentury, "is almost as great an insult as to be stigmatized as a 'nigger feller' and in a street row, both appellations are flung off among the combatants with great zeal and vigour."[9] Southern states such as Maryland imposed a heavy tax on any Irish person trying to enter the state; they were mobbed, beaten, rioted against, and denied work in much of the country. Many of them turned on blacks, but oth-ers became some of the first Americans to graduate from individual acts of defiance to something resembling an organized rebellion.

In the early nineteenth century, in the notorious Five Points section of New York City, the exiled tribes of Eire and Africa came together. This Bowery hellhole became the byword for everything that was wrong in urban America: crime, child neglect, inadequate housing, and alco-holism. It was a factory for criminal outfits like the Plug Uglies, who killed each other at a rate that would appall the modern-day Crip. But writers of the time were obsessed with another feature of the neigh-borhood: its complete racial integration. "Black and white, white and black, all hug-'em-smug-'em together, happy as lords and ladies, sit-ting sometimes round in a ring, with a jug of liquor between them," wrote the appalled Davy Crockett, home from the Indian Wars, in 1835. Blacks and whites lived side by side in the same awesomely decrepit houses (one census found 1,000 living in a single structure), even in the same rooms. Interracial couples were commonplace; no less than a scion of a rich New York society family, the Blennerhassetts, made his home here with his black wife. Black men were in a commanding position in the community as landlords, crime bosses, husbands, and sought-after lovers. The largest and most infamous dance hall in the Five Points was owned by a "coal-black Negro" named Pete Williams, and black and white prostitutes prowled the nearby lanes for eager customers, some of them young bucks from the best New York families looking for "adventures." In this fetid atmosphere, the Points became the place where the amalgamation horror was displayed, a national stage carefully lit and decorated for maximum effect by crusading journalists.

The only reason Davy Crockett or anyone else paid attention to the Bowery was the emergence of the abolitionists and the American Anti-Slavery Society in the 1820s. Their calls for the immediate ending of slavery shocked the city, ushering in a period in which the nation grew more and more obsessed and polarized on the subject of race. The flashpoint was the rhetoric of William Lloyd Garrison, and his new way of speaking to blacks. Garrison would tell black audiences that he came before them "as a black man," as "one of you." It would be difficult to underestimate how upsetting this was to whites, who in their own minds quickly reshaped the slavery debate partly into an argument about amalgamation and social equality. Debate is too polite a word, as whites quickly turned violent; in 1834, riots rocked New York City. Skilled workers terrified of the competition from freed blacks became the shock troops of white resistance. The riots forced the American Anti-Slavery Society to run a disclaimer in the New York *Times* and other publications, stating that "we entirely disclaim any desire to promote or encourage intermarriages between white and colored persons."[10] The mobs had made their point.

As soon as the rubble cleared, penny-press rags like the New York *Transcript* discovered the Five Points. They published regular police blotter accounts of their goings-on for their working-class readership. In November 1834, the *Transcript* reported the arrest of fourteen black and white prostitutes by "the indefatigable inspector of the Sixth Ward, M'Grath." The women worked as a kind of interracial sex gang, "enticing sailors into their haunt" in the Five Points, "making them drunk, and robbing them." Another blotter item concerned Samuell

Dunn and Dan Turner, two white workers who began their night on the town by "blackguarding some black beauties whom chance placed in their path," while John Curry, a sailor accused of "striking a female with his fist," blurted out a kind of amalgamator's manifesto. He adored women, Curry said, all women: "black or white, red or brown." His intoxication with the female sex inspired him to Shakespearean heights: "I love 'em all," he told a reporter, "and wish they'd all only got one mouth, and I had the kissing on't."[11]

Blacks often came off better than whites in this running drama. It was the Anglo-Saxon dregs at which the *Transcript* and the other working-class institutions shook their heads. "The negroes of the Five Points are 50% in advance of the Irish in sobriety and decency," testified one reformer. Blacks were often portrayed as model citizens accosted by drunken "amalgamators" who went looking for trouble and forced themselves on the Negro population. This was one point the fledgling black press could agree on: *The Freedmen's Journal* reported that "our streets and places of public amusement are nightly crowded" with prostitutes and Caucasian men on the prowl.

In 1842, the Five Points graduated from national to international eyesore when Charles Dickens described the neighborhood in his *American Notes*. The great humanizer of the English underclass visited the neighborhood in an attempt to get to the real New York, and pioneered the place for his many readers. His assessment was a mix of crude racism and fascination, a response that would set the tone for future generations of slumming whites. "Many . . . pigs live here," Dickens wrote. "Do they ever wonder why their masters walk upright in lieu of going on all-fours? And why they talk instead of grunting?" Only a black dancer that caught Dickens' eye could partly redeem the place.

> *The dance commences. . . . Single shuffle, double shuffle, cut and cross-cut; snapping his fingers, rolling his eyes, turning in his knees, presenting the backs of his legs in front, spinning about on his toes and heels like nothing. . . . In what walk of life, or dance of life, does man ever get such stimulating applause as thunders about him [here]?*

The reformers followed the British author into what soon had become known as "Dickens' Hole." Missionary Benjamin Barlow, accompanied by a policeman, toured the slums in 1861 and reported back to the *Independent* newspaper. In a garret, next to an apartment where weeks before "a millionaire's beautiful daughter" had been found "lying on the bare floor with a drunken negro," Barlow and the cop looked through a doorway. In a filthy room they saw "old Sambo over his brazier of coals, toasting his hands, and in the corner of the den is a long pile of rags. . . . It moves at one end; and an Irish woman lifts her tangled mop of a head out of the heap, and with a jolly voice, bids us 'good evenin'.'" The woman proceeded to horrify Barlow even further. "Look here, gentlemen, look at this little codfish," she called to them. Reaching into a pile of rags, she lifted up "a diminutive mulatto child of a few weeks old, to the great delight of Sambo, who reveals all his ivory." Barlow later wrote that the four stages of the child's future were clear to him: rum, theft, prison, and Potter's Field.[12]

The reformer despaired; what hope was there when the woman was so far gone she couldn't be ashamed of her own depravity? But looking at the visit through the eyes of the Irishwoman and her husband, one might assume that the woman delighted in playing the amalgamating Irish wench. *I know exactly what you're thinking*, her gesture says, *and I know how wrong you are*. The accompanying laughter is the sound of escape.

This spirit was writ large during the insurrections that rocked New York City two years later. The 1863 Draft Riots were unusually murderous. Gangs of Irish men, furious that they were being drafted into a "War of Amalgamation" (i.e., the Civil War), hunted up and down Manhattan streets for blacks and their progressive friends. They shot, hanged, roasted, or lynched blacks in neighborhood after neighborhood. It was only in the Five Points where they met significant resistance. When they attacked the drugstore owned by Philip White, a black man who often sold medicine on credit to his Irish customers, the mob found White's Celtic neighbors guarding the premises. When they ventured down into the notorious Hart's Alley and became trapped at its dead end, they looked up to see boiling starch being poured on their heads; black and white residents were bombarding them from windows above. The Five Points was the only neighborhood not to suffer a single black murder.

Arguing that the Five Points was a heroic outpost has its bizarre aspects. Certainly, Democratic politicians used it to press a racist agenda, and many of its residents were too soused, whipped-down, or brain-damaged to think very hard about racial justice. Their defiance wasn't intellectual, it was instinctive. But the neighborhood that these poor blacks and whites created was a place that defied the rest of the country with an unprecedented directness. Almost completely lawless and beyond the pale, the Five Points was a demilitarized zone in which race almost didn't matter, a kind of free state where New Yorkers came to explore the most American of taboos. And where the despised and the written-off became some of the first Americans to raise their own mulatto flag.

In the South, of course, there was no Five Points, or anything approaching it. Amalgamation was a private affair with its own code: one could joke about one's black mistress with other men, but it was a clandestine thing never to be brought out in public. In many areas, affairs with black women were de rigueur; in New Orleans, they were a test of manhood. Some slave owners saw black females as receptacles, to be used when their wives were pregnant or obstreperous.

Most of the relationships between southern black men and white women appeared to have been consensual; once you enter the 1800s, those relationships became increasingly dangerous for both parties. The record with black women and white men, however, is much murkier and more controversial. Some pro-southern historians in the early decades of the 1900's argued that black women initiated most affairs as a sought-after badge of superiority; though affairs did sometimes bring gifts and status, the argument is touched with the leftover image of the black succubus. Others argue that all interracial relationships under slavery were de facto rape, pure and simple. Angela Davis staked out this line over thirty years ago when she wrote that it was "as oppressors . . . or agents of domination that white men approached black women's bodies."[13] In *Darkwater* (1920), W. E. B. Du Bois spoke for generations of black men when he wrote that he would forgive the South for many painful things—slavery, the Civil War, its "hot blood," and its myths—but he would never forgive, "neither in this world or the world to come, its wanton and continued and persistent insulting of the black womanhood which it sought and seeks to prostitute to its lust." The extent of the crime, or the depth of the unappeased anger, should not be underestimated.

But the old South was a world of relationships ranging from the brutal to the sublime. In his massive study of life on the plantations, *Roll, Jordan, Roll,* Eugene Genovese came to several conclusions about the nature of interracial sex. Among them: There were enough assaults on slave women to "make life hell for a discernible minority" of female slaves; married black women and their husbands took these sexual violations very seriously and put up significant resistance; and most of the miscegenation on the plantations "occurred with single girls under circumstances that varied from seduction to rape and typically fell between the two."

The rapes were terrible enough, but they brought in their wake a lasting psychological divide between black men and women, as well as murders (most often of white masters by black husbands or fathers), suicides, and betrayals, perhaps the most common being the mulatto child who resembled the master too closely being sold away from its mother. In many cases, Davis's assessment is correct: white men approached black women as soldiers approach the women of their enemy. But what were the consequences of these relationships? There is, in fact, evidence that in a substantial amount of cases the men were converted to a new view of black humanity.

Wealthy landowners freed their lovers and their mulatto children, educated them, and asked anyone who disagreed to leave their houses. One ex-slave recalled that his white father told him he cared equally for him and his white sons, that he "should call no man master." Rich men left fortunes to mixed children, and southern men moved to the North to find breathing room for their multiracial families. These cases are sprinkled throughout southern law records, often in suits brought by the families of white lovers, who in court documents argued that their relative's affection and his bequests to his black mate were the product of "undue influence" or madness. Scholar Joel Williamson found that a highly significant number of white masters engaged in long-term relationships with domestic slaves, and many of these matches were marked by clear evidence of devotion.[14]

We have heard mostly from the whites in these relationships; there are very few records of black voices. Only one full-length memoir of a master-slave relationship has come down to us, but it is a classic. Harriet Jacobs's *Incidents in the Life of a Slave Girl* (1861) leans very much toward the dark side of the phenomenon, telling Jacobs's extraordinary story of her attempts to escape a master, Dr. Flint, who is intent on a sexual relationship. On the face of it, Jacobs's story would seem to prove Davis's point conclusively: Harriet saw her only true love affair aborted by Flint; her belief in human goodness was virtually destroyed; and she was forced to hide for seven years in the tiny attic of a relative's house to escape him. Jacobs's willpower and her acute writing style have made her into one of the most important black woman writers of the nineteenth century; she is studied intently in black studies and American history courses. Her spell in the attic suggests her place in the literature: She has become, in some ways, the Anne Frank of slavery. And Dr. Flint has taken up the role of her Nazi.

Incidents is written along the lines of the sentimental English novel of female experience: the heroine's introduction to the world—most specifically, the world of white people and slavery—form the book's main subject. Like any self-respecting woman out of Jane Austen, Harriet begins by searching for love. Her relatives embody it, especially her tough-willed grandmother, who works relentlessly to recover her family from slavery. But Harriet loves whites, too, especially her first mistress, who becomes like a mother to her, spoiling and comforting Harriet, treating her more like her own child than a slave. So when her mistress suddenly dies, a grief-stricken Harriet expects to be freed; indeed, her mother had been promised it. But both of them are shocked when the will names Harriet not as a beloved foster child but as an itemized piece of property to be passed on to her mistress's 5-year-old niece.

Harriet is hurt by the deception, but she still manages to shower affection on her new mistress, until the child's mother suggests that what the young white girl feels for Harriet is not love but fear. Overhearing her, Harriet plays the old game of guessing white folks' hearts. "This put unpleasant doubts in my mind," she writes. "Did the child feign what she did not feel? Or was her mother jealous of the mite of love she bestowed on me? I concluded it must be the latter. I said to myself, 'Surely, little children are true.' "

When she reaches puberty, Harriet immediately claims the attention of the master of the household, Dr. Flint, now well into his fifties and portrayed by Harriet as a sly and volatile obsessive. He probes her reactions for an opening and follows patterns that would today identify him as a classic batterer. "Sometimes he had stormy, terrific ways, that made his victims tremble," Jacobs reports. "Sometimes he assumed a gentleness that he thought must surely subdue." (Some scholars believe he actually did rape Harriet, but that she simply could not include such a shocking admission in her memoir.) In the many academic essays written on the narrative, Flint is an afterthought, a figure whose meaning—white male power on the rampage—is too obvious to need explaining. But Jacobs's hatred sharpened her pen; she captures Flint in exquisite detail. If you look at her portrait closely, the image of a monster slowly dissipates and is replaced by something that is more mercurial, almost affecting, and in terms of his treatment of Jacobs, much more reprehensible.

Dr. Flint was in love.

Perhaps not in the beginning. From Jacobs's description of his behavior, she was probably the latest in a line of servants he has turned into concubines. He is skilled, confident, casually lewd. (Not coincidentally, Flint is trapped in a loveless marriage to a suspicious, stone-faced wife.) The master whispers his vile intentions into Harriet's ear, somehow convincing himself that a teenage girl raised by a strict and loving grandmother would share in them. Rebuffed, he falls back on a standard line: "He told me I was his property," Harriet recalls of the first overtures. "That I must be subject to his will in all things."

But Harriet resists Flint, and he is annoyed. Clearly, he does not want this to be rape; he doesn't see himself as a beast. When Harriet asks to be sold to get away from him, however, he can't believe her ingratitude. "Have I ever treated you like a negro?" Flint asks. "I have never allowed you to be punished, even to please your mistress. And this is the recompense I get." Harriet calmly points out that his protection was only a deposit on later favors, and her acuity, the high valuation she puts on herself, begins to make her over in Flint's eyes. She is not docile or hysterical; she must be approached carefully as an intelligence instead of an object. Harriet writes that when she wept, he would say, "Poor child! Don't cry! Don't cry! I will make peace for you with your mistress. . . . Poor, foolish girl! You don't know what is for your own good. I would cherish you. I would make a lady of you." Seeing that he will have to coax Harriet along, Flint treats her as a delicious child, to be coddled and then seduced, little realizing that he is being changed by his own approach.

Over the years, the seduction turns into a duel, and Harriet makes Flint revise his estimate of her once again. She falls in love with a young free black carpenter and asks Flint to allow the carpenter to buy her. Harriet waits for a response, dreading a confrontation but still believing that he will do the only decent thing and let her go. Finally, a message comes. She is instructed to see the master in his study.

Standing at the study door, Harriet pauses for a moment of luxuriant hate, "gazing at the . . . man who claimed a right to rule me, body and soul." Flint finally senses her presence, turns and shoots her a smoldering glance. "He looked fixedly at me, with an expression which seemed to say, 'I have half a mind to kill you on the spot.'" Both are intent on hiding the emotions they feel, conducting themselves as if they were transacting business; she even uses "sir" in mock respect. In a clipped voice, Flint asks her if she wants to be married; she confirms it. He makes her a counteroffer; marriage to one of his slaves, matching her as he would a prize steer. She refuses. Finally, he can stand the game no longer and lets slip the question he has been studiously avoiding.

"Do you love this nigger?" he asks, abruptly.

Harriet replies with steel. "Yes, sir."

Flint blazes up. "How dare you tell me so!" he cries out "in a great wrath," then strikes her "a stunning blow." It is the first time he has hit her. Shocked, she cries out that she despises him. Flint, his hand still stinging, returns to his seat and grows unexpectedly quiet. Harriet watches him, waiting for his next move. Is he plotting some new punishment or is he genuinely upset? Even she does not understand what is happening inside her tormentor.

What *is* happening in Flint's mind? One must remember that he could ravish Harriet at any moment, as countless other masters did their helpless female slaves. No court will convict him, no fellow planter would cut him socially. But sex and a display of his own power are clearly not all he wants. Flint has been wounded by Harriet's confession of love for another; for him, this is a romantic crisis. One could transpose this passage into a Brontë novel where the heroine and the inarticulate master of the house, whose fits of anger conceal other, gentler emotions, rage at each other as gales moan in the windowpanes. If only Harriet would see him as he wishes her to, as her protector and—dare we say it?—her true love. Instead, he is trapped in an unplayable role as the hated master. For Flint, the irony must have been acute: Southern society has given him complete license to regard Harriet as a piece of chattel and to use her like one. But he can't quite do it. The fact that she is a thinking, feeling creature with individual strengths and vulnerabilities, her own stubborn desires, has risen before his eyes like some horrifying apparition.

For any reasonable observer and for Harriet, of course, this is no romance. Flint's "love" is delusional and obscene, a far worse scenario for Harriet than the normal terror the typical master would engage in. His affection is her bad luck; if only Flint *weren't* quite so human! Like most female Victorian memoirists, Harriet had begun her story hoping to learn about life and to achieve adulthood through the experience of love. Instead, she is given her education through one poisoned humiliation after another.

Finally, his frustration erupts: "Are you mad?" Flint cries at Harriet's latest insolent remark. "Do you think any other master would bear what I have borne from you this morning? Many masters would have killed you on the spot." (*Yes*, he must be thinking, *but why can't I?*) In Jacobs's narrative, he searches for his old authority again and again, but he cannot recover it. What he finds instead is something that feels suspiciously like jealousy.

Flint is no Brontë hero, of course; he doesn't turn away and mutter a few words releasing Harriet to her beloved, thus salvaging a bit of nobility for himself. His love is not unselfish; he will grant that Harriet is a human being, but he still wants to devour her. Flint refuses to sell her away, probably hoping that Harriet will somehow discern the secret message hidden inside his possessiveness (*Love me—or suffer*). In the months following their confrontation, the war rages on, and Harriet reluctantly learns the slave arts of deceit and attack, with a special twist: she begins to torture Flint as only a beloved can. The coup d'état comes when she sleeps with another white man and throws the affair in her master's face. "I knew nothing would enrage Dr. Flint so much as to know I favored another," she says. Flint responds by stalking her every move: "No jealous lover ever watched a rival more closely than he watched me."

They meet again to discuss her new paramour, with Dr. Flint again starting in a businesslike way but quickly arriving at the old question. "He sprang upon me like a wolf, and grabbed my arm as if he would have broken it. 'Do you love him?' said he in a hissing tone." Harriet answers that she is thankful she doesn't despise her new lover. Flint raises his hand to strike her, but it falls to his side. He sinks into his chair, his lips "tightly compressed." Finally, he recovers his voice and tells her that he has come to her with good intentions, but that her ingratitude has driven him to distraction. "I don't know what it is that keeps me from killing you," he says, as if caught in some dream.

The scene illustrates graphically our earlier metaphor for white racism: Flint's society-damaged brain is fighting for control with the part of his mind that now sees Harriet all too clearly. When he raises his arm to strike her, it is a response that American culture has almost managed to hard-wire into him—this is how the majority of masters have been taught to control their chattel for decades. It is as instinctive as pulling his hand from a hot stove. But the arm freezes and then falls to his side, useless; a new conception unknown to most of his class is short-circuiting his rage. This deep confusion is what these particular relationships introduced to the society before the abolitionists popularized the purely moral approach to slavery: an internal, dissenting voice powerful enough to counteract primal emotions.

Harriet finally gets away from Flint by sealing herself in a tiny attic in a relative's house. He searches frantically for her and sends agents and friends to pursue her when, after seven years in her living grave, she flees to the North. There Harriet finds freedom but little contentment; Flint has killed her "love-dream" of marriage to the carpenter and her talent for happiness. But Flint does not go away unaltered either. In one of their last meetings, he tells Harriet: "You have been the plague of my life," and by all indications, he is being sincere. She has made mastery hateful to him in those moments when it should have been most delicious. After Harriet disappears, he spends enormous sums on trips north to find her.

Jacobs's heroically honest memoir is the best account of the special terrors inflicted by slavery on black women. But it is also a test case of miscegenation, of what really passed between white men and black women in the antebellum South. *Narrative* makes clear the middle ground that Genovese speaks of, not the heart-warming exceptions that resulted in manumissions and long lives together, nor the thoughtless rapes in which white men treated black women as animals who did not even need to be called by their own names, but the dangerously alive relationships in between. Flint's torments suggests that sexual contact often brought white men face-to-face with the realization that the chattel under their command was not the half-child, half-savage of southern legend. Sartre once said that there was "an aura of rape and massacre" in all relationships between master and slave, but he missed the second sight that so many of these unions gave to the masters. Sometimes that revelation led to far harsher treatment than indifference would have brought, as was the case with Harriet. But when one considers that a significant portion of southern slave owners engaged in sustained relationships with their female slaves, one must conclude that there was a transfer of intimate knowledge that dwarfs what took place in the mixed wards of the Five Points.

Amalgamation did occasionally leap from personal drama into the political discourse, as in New York—and then it was usually ugly. As the Civil War approached, pro-slavery Democrats tarred Lincoln's Republicans with the dark brush. One "Black Republican Prayer" passed around in 1863 was typical for its day: "May . . . the illustrious, sweet-scented Sambo nestle in the bosom of every Abolition woman," the pamphlet read. "That she may be quickened by the pure blood of the majestic African, and the Spirit of amalgamation shine forth in all its splendor and glory, that we may become a regenerated nation of half-breeds and mongrel . . . and that we may live in bonds of fraternal love, union and equality with the Almighty Nigger . . . Amen."[15] Sniggling, vicious, and filled with animal imagery, this was a typical production. But in December 1863, a different kind of anonymous pamphlet was advertised in the New York papers, one that would not only give the interracial phenomenon a new name, but would become the most enigmatic and the most important political pamphlet to be produced in the United States.

The title was "Miscegenation: The Theory of the Blending of the Races, Applied to the American White Man and Negro." Seventy-two pages long and costing 25 cents, the pamphlet argued that the mixing of the races was a worldwide phenomenon that was producing the strongest nations on Earth, and that America should abandon its backward notions of racial purity and embrace amalgamation. Its prose was rich, futuristic, exulting in its own boldness: Its opening sentence, "The word is spoken at last," set the tone. With its title the pamphlet coined a new word, combining the Latin *misce*, "to mix," and "*gene*" "race," the result was quickly inducted into the working language.

Most of the booklet was taken up with clear parodies of then-current theories of racial superiority: physiology, anthropology, and dual genesis (the belief that there were two Creations, one for blacks and the other for whites). It got carried away at times, advising Lincoln to add a pro-miscegenation plank to the Republican platform, and it made salacious references to the southern woman's obsession with black men, pandering to myths that were strengthening in the South by the month. But it tried hard to convince, arguing that the advantages of race-mixing were clear: the English were a great people "because they are a composite race"; the Sardinians controlled the Italian peninsula because they had been overrun by the French and Austrians; France's "most brilliant" writer, Alexander Dumas, was of mixed heritage. The pamphlet pointed to the oxidization of the Statue of Liberty's metal skin to "a rich and uniform bronze tint" as a sign that Liberty herself was "not white, symbolizing but one race, nor black, typifying another, but a statue representing the composite race, whose sway will extend from the Atlantic to the Pacific Ocean, from the Equator to the North Pole—the Miscegens of the Future!" The writer is smirking, but there is something elusive, a tone beyond parody, in his writing.

The pamphlet was advertised prominently in the abolition papers and caused an immediate effect. The new word "miscegenation" filled newspaper columns, tripped off the tongue at society dinners, and became the leading topic of rumor mills. The writer was believed to be a "highly intelligent and educated mulatto girl." The Union League Club had installed a night bell at its Union Square offices, which would summon a black minister available around the clock to marry interracial couples on demand. The New York press, exhausted with the procession of bloody war news from the Union front, treated the pamphlet like a smash Broadway show: "A NEW SENSATION—'MISCEGENATION'" broadcast the New York *World.* The *Sunday Mercury* analyzed it in a front-page column: "A very curious work . . . argued with a singular power of language. . . . If his views prevail, mahogany-colored babies will become quite the fashion."[16]

Nothing like it had been spoken out loud before in such a public way. The pamphlet is a poem to the interracial instinct, and though some suspected from the beginning that it was a farce, its arguments still carried surprising power. In fact, some of its arguments stand the test of time: "The superiority of the slaveholding classes of the South," wrote the authors, "arises from their intimate communication, from birth to death, with the colored race. . . . The emotional power, fervid oratory and intensity which distinguishes all thoroughbred slaveholders is due to their intimate association with the most charming and intelligent of their slave girls." This could have been meant to enrage southerners, but it was also a serious and perceptive claim that W. J. Cash could have made in his classic study of southern society, *The Mind of the South.*

"Miscegenation" won praise from anti-slavery notables. Parker Pillsbury, editor of the *National Anti-Slavery Standard,* called it "a true prophecy." The influential Grimke sisters, daughters of the South who had gone abolitionist, were "wholly at one" with the author's sentiments, though they thought his scientific claims shaky and the wisdom of publishing the pamphlet nonexistent. Garrison, too canny for possible hoaxers, stayed quiet. But it was the social reformer and journalist Theodore Tilton who came closest to capturing the odd quality of the pamphlet when he wrote in a thorough critique that while he was convinced that it was a "burlesque," this did not diminish the pamphlet's impact. "The American people is . . . a stock of many grafts," he concluded. "To be frank, we agree with a large portion of these pages."[17]

The pamphlet smoked Americans out into the open on the subject of race-mixing. Some newspapers cried that "the Black is a Beast," while the influential New York *Tribune* stood up for inclusiveness: "Caucasians, Ethiopians, Mongolians, Americans or Malays . . . our business is to accommodate them all . . . [through an] honest and unlimited recognition of our common nature." The *Tribune* called for a "thorough revision" of science textbooks to delete the false theories of race that filled them. In Washington, the pamphlet was debated in Congress; Samuel Sullivan Cox, the Democratic floor manager, read long passages aloud to laughter and then quoted the flattering reviews that the book had received from abolitionist leaders. He also maligned the book: "The physiologist will tell the Gentleman that the mulatto does not live; he does not recreate his kind; he is a monster."[18] In London, the great biologist Thomas Henry Huxley caused a stir when he stated that the booklet was damaging to the enemies of race-mixing, as it pointed out their "preposterous ignorance, exaggeration, and misstatement."[19] The ripples reached even to the obscure western mining town of Virginia City, Nevada, where a young (and quite drunk) Mark Twain sat at his desk and penned a farcical editorial saying that the money from a ladies' fancy-dress ball in rival Carson City was to be sent to aid a Miscegenation Society "somewhere in the East." When the piece was mistakenly published, a mortified Twain was challenged to several duels, went around carrying a gun, and eventually had to leave town for San Francisco, writing mournfully to his sister-in-law that "I shall not drink again, Molly."

Finally, months later, the authors were revealed in the London *Morning Herald:* David Goodman Croly, the nervous, brilliant city editor of the violently anti-abolitionist New York *World* (and hardcore Democrat supporter) who would go on to invent the tabloid newspaper. The person who did as much as two-thirds of the writing was George Wakeman, a talented young *World* reporter who would die young and be eulogized by Twain. Croly, however, was the driving force, bringing Wakeman to the Astor Library where they crammed on the latest race literature. He also paid the printer's bill.

As the prime mover, Croly bears close scrutiny. There is no doubt that he was a racist, especially in his later years; his work is littered with hostile references to blacks, and he once wrote that Africans should either be forced to work or be exterminated. But he was also obsessed with radically progressive ideas. Croly founded the American wing of positivism, an offshoot of social utopianism which argued that all true knowledge was derived from scientific study, and that discerning social trends could lead to a just and happy society. In essence, the positivists were the first sociologists, rejecting both superstition and metaphysics and studying behavior as a natural phenomenon that could be perfected. There are whole passages of "Miscegenation" that are positivist in outlook: "Wherever there is a poor community of Irish in the North," the pamphlet asserts, "they usually herd with the poor Negroes and as a result of the various offices of kindness which only the poor pay to one another, families become intermingled and connubial relations are formed between the black man and the white Irish women." The pamphleteer states that such marriages would be perfectly content if old prejudices didn't make some of the couples miserable. Even if meant to arouse the poor Irish, this is too accurate and too sympathetic to be inflammatory; it is phrased as a positivist fact. Nature (in the shape of residential patterns among the poor) has chosen a course, and that course ought to be respected.

Croly went further in his eccentricity. A friend recorded that "as a form of mental diversion," he liked to pontificate about "polyandry [the taking of multiple husbands], polygamy—yes and stirpiculture [the crossbreeding of plants]."[20] Croly returned to the mixing theme in his later works. When he published his deeply strange magazine *The Modern Thinker*, he asked contributors to consider certain questions. One of them stands out: "Is stirpiculture or the scientific breeding of human beings desirable, and if so, is it practicable?" Croly was a rare animal: a utopian and a bit of a freak, "eager to shock old prejudices" trapped inside an unreconstructed Irish-Catholic conservatism. But in "Miscegenation," he clearly meant what he said: race-mixing was inevitable and completely American. He never publicly admitted to his involvement with the pamphlet, but after his death his wife confessed for him: "Tho' it was written partly in the spirit of joke, it was not a hoax," Mrs. Croly wrote. "And was not palmed off upon the public as one . . . you can rely upon the absolute truth of what I say. Both Mr. Croly and Mr. Wakeman have passed away; but I remember the episode perfectly, and the half-joking, half-earnest spirit in which the pamphlet was written."

Some scholars have labeled this as a shuffling apology from an embarrassed spouse, but it rings true. The heart of the pamphlet is essentially double-chambered. It was meant to smoke out Republican leaders on the issue of miscegenation. But it also captured in ringing passages an argument for an end to racialism through the merging of black and white. If the scientific nonsense scattered throughout the pamphlet points to satire, the clarity and fairness of the social observations makes it clear that Croly was on some level a double agent: an exotic thinker writing a document designed to cause political mischief on the subject of miscegenation, and yet designing it in such a way as to entertain, if not advance, the topic it parodied. "Miscegenation" wasn't quite rational, but that only makes it all the more accurate. Nothing else until the writings of Du Bois captures the nation's feverish, twisting moods on the subject of mixed blood. The pamphlet stands today as a kind of masterpiece of the American subconscious.

Did these interracial relationships and the tension they created in the antebellum era have a cultural effect? Yes, a long-standing, negative one: they brutalized the relationship between black women and black men, who simply could not protect their loved ones in slavery times. One wonders how much of today's static between the sexes in the black community (a perennial subject in black women's magazines and private conversations) can be traced back to the scene in Harriet Jacobs's *Narrative*, when she realizes she cannot turn to her beloved black carpenter to save her. But there might be, as it were, a posthumous effect, as well. If we can turn back in history and resist treating these relationships as Marxist battles between historical forces and resuscitate the relationship between Flint and Harriet as it really was—a battle of minds and souls in which each party came to an exquisite understanding of the other—we recover a more complex idea of the antebellum world. There is no need to temper our moral outrage at Dr. Flint and others like him; in many ways, they were *more* evil than the casual rapist on the plantations, because men like Flint had been given an intimate glimpse of the slaves' humanity and they still pressed on. Images such as the lust-crazed master with the bullwhip lose their power over time if they are not deepened and refreshed. Harriet Jacobs's portrait of those moments in Dr. Flint's study, when she fought to remain human and Flint agonized between lust, rage, and a kind of awful respect for her, should rivet us to the details of the drama as few other things can.

"The True Defenders of the Constitution."
Letters sent home from Civil War battles and newspaper editorials alike talked
of the Negro soldier's courage under fire, his unexpected toughness.
This 1865 wood engraving of slain black and white Union soldiers illustrates
the theme: in violent death, the Negro had finally achieved his manhood.
Courtesy of the Photographs and Prints Division, Schomburg Center for Research in Black
Culture, The New York Public Library, Astor, Lenox and Tilden Foundations.

4

INTERREGNUM:
THE CIVIL WAR

THE CIVIL WAR and its immediate aftermath brought a psychic break in the deep relations of blacks and whites. In the decades before the war, white thinking in the North had been radicalized by the abolitionists' insistence on seeing blacks as fully human, while the Confederate mind had been repulsed by this idea and spurred to a greater demonization of the black man. In both cases, race had become a fixation.

During the war, men of both races were thrown together in unprecedented numbers, under fire, around campfires, one-on-one, sometimes as equals. Letter after letter from white Union soldiers back home to small towns where people had never seen a black man reported on their experience with Negroes, and many, though by no means all, were favorable: blacks could and would fight for themselves, an essential measure of civilization in nineteenth-century America. "I never believed in niggers before," one Wisconsin cavalry officer admitted, "but by Jasus, they are hell in fighting."[1] Negroes had long been considered the "feminine" race, obedient, patient, long-suffering, and quick in sympathy, as set off against the masculine, tetchy, moral, and empire-minded Anglo-Saxon (or in the words of some black wits, the "Angry Saxon"). But war correspondents and white officers saw the black soldier up close and were impressed. "Put a United States uniform on his back and the chattel is a man," wrote one white soldier. "You can see it in his look. Between the toiling slave and the soldier is a gulf that nothing but a god could lift him over. He feels it, his looks show it."

The black soldier earned his humanity by being steady under fire and willing to kill. As W. E. B. Du Bois pointed out, it was not until Negroes revealed their talent for mayhem on the battlefield that whites "with one voice proclaimed him a man and a brother." Only blacks seemed to appreciate the irony.

For a brief moment, Negroes did claim their place in American life as equals. Reconstruction saw the formation of the first real biracial democracy on American soil, in the governments formed in southern states by blacks, southern scalawags, and northern white Republicans. Ordinary Negroes began shucking off their old masks, and observers commented on how determined Negroes were to make whites recognize their new position. Blacks demanded courtesies, enjoyed forcing their owners to read contracts to the last letter, luxuriated in the ceremonies of equality. Freedom meant "taking no more foolishment off of white folks," a former Georgia slave said.[2] There was a tone of comeuppance, even when it was not connected to hate for the old masters. In fact, blacks on the whole did not take revenge on the white elites, and many wanted to believe that all color distinctions had ended. Organizers like Martin Delany, one of the earliest black nationalists, found ex-slaves would shout him down when he talked about racial pride: "We don't want to hear that," the crowds told him. "We are all one color now."[3]

Despite black restraint, whites were shocked by their true attitudes. Louis Manigault, a Savannah River plantation owner, returned to his home in 1886 and fell into a discussion with a group of his ex-slaves, who had gathered around him. After a few moments, Manigault found that he couldn't recognize the people standing in front of him as the same slaves he had left; something had altered in their expressions and attitudes that made them unrecognizable. "I almost imagined

The new black assertiveness, the urbanization of the South which brought poor blacks to the cities, and most of all the increasing drive for segregation, finally enshrined in the Jim Crow laws, reduced the traffic between the races even further. The new industrial towns were segregated, with whites of any means on the hills and blacks and some poor whites living in the lowest, muddiest, swampiest shantytowns. The old paternalism was abandoned in sorrow and then vindictive joy. The white elites responded to the masses of newly citified Negroes, faceless throngs that choked the roads toward Birmingham, Spartanburg, and Charlotte, by mocking their new status as individuals in charge of their own destiny—"root hog or die" was a popular bit of advice. The planter class maintained a fierce connection to the Negro, but it was to the myth of the smiling, loyal blacks of the Old South, not this new, "biggety," stone-faced urbanite. Blacks who had once hoped for a color-free democracy now retreated in exhaustion and were often glad of the separation; they had a better chance now to protect their women, to develop their business, and to live apart from a race that grew more distant and mysterious by the year. Race consciousness solidified. Before the war, a colored Boston freedman thought himself as worlds away from the southern slaves. Though northern blacks still had things better, regional distinctions meant less than before the war, and color meant more.

As Jim Crow took hold, more and more the two cultures lived separate lives and seemed destined to do so into the foreseeable future. The Supreme Court affirmed this in its 1896 *Plessy v. Ferguson* ruling, which deemed "separate but equal" facilities to be constitutional. When he looked at America's races in *Souls of Black Folk*, W. E. B. Du Bois saw a profound estrangement that had only deepened since slavery times:

> *One will see that between these two worlds, despite much physical contact and daily intermingling, there is almost no community of intellectual life or point of transference where the thoughts and feelings of one race can come into direct contact and sympathy with the thoughts and feelings of the other. . . . While the healing of this vast sore is progressing, the races are to live for many years side by side, united in economic effort, obeying a common government, sensitive to mutual thought and feeling, yet subtly and silently separate in many matters of deeper human intimacy.*

Dressed to the nines, W. E. B. Du Bois
takes the air at the Paris Exhibition
Internationale in the spring of 1900.
The brilliant scholar's years of study on
the Continent consummated the ecstatic
and troubled black dalliance with high
European culture.

5

MEMORIZING SHAKESPEARE:
THE BLACK ELITE

AS THE SOUTH institutionalized Jim Crow, as the numbers of lynchings peaked and American blacks faced the nadir of their internal exile within the United States, W. E. B. Du Bois was ecstatically absent, abroad in Europe. Sharpening his mind for the coming battles in America (whether he would make his name in science, write a great novel, or "raise a visible empire" remained to be determined), Du Bois studied sociology and economics at the University of Berlin. But it was Europe itself that absorbed him: the museums, the concert halls, the libraries, the landscape. The young student traveled, usually alone, to the great art galleries of France and Austria-Hungary and discussed German philosophy with the best young minds of Europe. Michaelangelo stunned him, Schubert's *Unfinished Symphony* reduced him to tears (some Greek wine might have contributed), Hegel vitalized and broadened his view of life. Europe in those days was still a finishing school for the rough-hewn American minds, but rarely for black American men. As the exception, Du Bois was completing the training that he felt would make him the leading race man of his era.

The young Du Bois was then a committed Europhile and conservative, but he would later in life travel across the ideological spectrum and condemn colonialism, embrace Pan-Africanism and bitterly attack Europe's role in the world. He is, in our history, an Abraham figure, the father of not two but many tribes. Du Bois deeply influenced black nationalists and separatists. He is a model for those who believe that black Americans should divorce themselves from all aspects of white society. But, on the other hand, the most fully integrated members of the black community, the Harvard-educated black surgeon with a taste for Brahms or the marketing executive in the suburbs of Atlanta, must also trace his roots back to Du Bois. It was his call for a "Talented Tenth" in the black community, educated in the classical European tradition, that helped create the black middle class and establish its special role in the community. Du Bois's complex thinking illustrates the two most extreme positions blacks have taken toward white culture: resistance to it and immersion in it.

So one way to understand how the black community came to terms with white society at the turn of the century is to look at how it regarded the great works of Western culture. And Du Bois was at the center of that difficult reckoning.

In the early 1900s, culturally speaking, Europe was the only game in town. Modern Africa was a dead ember; very little was known about its complex societies and their achievements, and among blacks and whites it was regarded as an intellectual wasteland. The single path was toward the Continent, and from an early age, Du Bois had sought out the symbols of its culture. As a child he remembered being attracted to "books *as* books" (italics mine); he searched the rooms of his mother's poverty-haunted house in snowbound Great Barrington for obscure tracts such as "Opie on Lying."[1] Curiously, the young biblomaniac didn't actually *read* these books, only stood them together in his room and named them his "library." For him, what was important was their symbolic value as carriers of a tradition he could master. The obsession peaked in 1882, when he was a brilliant but cash-poor high school student. He spied something in a shopkeeper's window that made his heart flutter—a "gorgeous edition" of Macauley's five-volume *History of England*. "I wanted it fiercely," Du Bois remembered. In his later life, the scholar was not a collector and leaned toward asceticism when it came to material goods, but he would have done anything to get that Macauley. Typically, he did; buying it in installments of 25 cents each and taking it home at Christmas. Carrying it in his arms, the heft of it must have represented for him not only the world beyond his utterly provincial hometown, but a movable feast of intellect and achievement. Such books would represent his most intimate contact with whites in the years to come: as he wrote later in *Souls of Black Folk*, "I sit with Shakespeare and he winces not."

It is hard to recapture precisely how rare a recognition that was in late nineteenth-century America.

The young and irrepressible Du Bois went further: He believed that culture was the way up and out of misery for African Americans. Literary excellence and academic effort was for him a measure of a person's seriousness as a human being. When his lone black schoolmate received average grades, Du Bois practically disowned the boy. "I was very much ashamed of him," he later remembered. But if Du Bois was enamored of white culture, he was often tetchy with whites themselves, nursing the "great bitterness" of early prejudice; *he* had enforced the color line at Harvard before any white person could. "I had not regarded white folk as human in quite the same way that I was," he wrote. But Europe changed that; saved him, he said, from hating whites forever. Once he got to Germany, it is hard to think of Du Bois "blossoming," as tightly wound as he was; but he did at least loosen up and take down the elaborate defenses he had constructed against Caucasians. When he boarded a Rhine passenger steamer in August 1892, he met a Dutch mother and her three daughters. He tried to freeze the family out, but the confined spaces did not allow total separation: "Soon the little daughter came straight across the deck and placed herself squarely before me." The veil between the races that Du Bois would name and describe so clearly a decade later disappeared on the Atlantic; by the end of the trip he and the Dutch women were fast friends, "laughing, eating, and singing together." There was even a romance with one of the daughters.

Du Bois was always a prototypical race man, almost mystically confident in the inherent greatness of the African line. He never did want to be white; but he did, perhaps, wish to be *European*—a free mind at play in a Continental landscape. In his twenties, he was confident that Europe's way was the right way—that it was more sane and more just than any other society (if only it would admit Africa and Asia into its fold and help them along to greatness). The young scholar hated to leave Germany; he delayed as long as he could before boarding the return boat. The Europe he had imagined in his books had proved to be real; it was not unlike the Christian Heaven that the slave converts saw—fair, glittering, all-powerful. And colorblind.

Other black intellectuals and writers coming of age during Jim Crow fetishized white, and particularly European, literature in the same way. James Weldon Johnson, author and executive director of the NAACP, growing up in segregated Florida, found his deepest early connection with whites in the books his mother read to him as a child. "I am between five and six years old," he wrote in his autobiography. "In the early evening the lamp in the little parlor is lit. . . . If the weather is chilly, pine logs are sputtering and blazing in the fireplace. . . . My mother takes a book and reads. . . . The book is *David Copperfield*. . . . Night after night I follow the story, always hungry for the next install-ment. . . . I laught till the tears roll down my cheeks at the mishaps of Handy Andy." Johnson carried his tattered collection of children's books, his first library, with him wherever he went, well into adulthood.

Books were more than simple texts. "The final measure of the greatness of all peoples is the amount and standard of the literature and art they have produced," Johnson wrote in a preface to a book of black poetry. "The world does not know that a people is great until that peo-ple produces great literature and art. No people that has produced great literature and art has ever been looked upon by the world as dis-tinctly inferior." What blacks inherited from Africa could not be dug up from under the floorboards when slavery ended. There was nothing to dig up; the inherited culture was mostly invisible. There were stories to tell and oral histories of courage and wit and humor, but no songs, no Talmud, no Goyas or Rembrandts, nothing equivalent to what white society had in spades: material illustrations of its talents. Master-ing white culture was a prelude to producing significant artifacts of black culture, a stepping-stone that was unusually treacherous.

As offensive as its implications were, the strategy paid dividends. An example: In 1896, producers of minstrel shows such as *The Octoroon*, which had been a smash hit at a New York burlesque houses, brought the first black musical to Broadway. For the most part, the elaborately staged *Oriental America* followed the lines of the ordinary minstrel show, except for its finale. Instead of featuring the usual cakewalks and "walk-arounds," where whites would gawp at blacks done up in their finery, the cast presented a selection of arias and choruses from *Faust, Carmen, Rigoletto,* and *Il Trovatore.* Opera was used to amend a tradition that denigrated blacks at every turn.

The test was applied in literature, as well. The eighteenth-century black poet Phyllis Wheatley met with a group of Boston Brahmins, who questioned her closely to see if she could really have written the verses attributed to her. More than satisfied, they issued a statement that was published as a preface to the volume, testifying to her capabilities. In Du Bois's era, the prime example was Paul Lawrence Dunbar, the "poet laureate of the race," who with his alcoholic, race-maddened life also became the first black tragic poet. Dunbar was supported by white benefactors, toasted by the literary elites of the United States and England, and raised from elevator boy to celebrity, all on the word of William Dean Howells, the preeminent American writer of his time. In a remarkable piece in *Harper's Weekly* that made Dunbar's national reputation, Howell told his audience that the midwestern poet had not only produced a completely original body of work, but his achievement proved that the black race had "attained civilization in him." To modern eyes, Howells statement is a backhanded compliment at best and involves Dunbar in the heartbreaking fate of so many black artists, whose talent is seen as the exception to the rule of black ignorance. But at the turn of the century, it was a daring position, and Howells allowed himself to dream on it, predicting that the "hostilities and the prejudices" would disappear in the arts. Writers like Dunbar would serve as the "final proof that God had made one blood of all nations of men." Howells sensed that people would doubt Dunbar's true merits, and he was by now exhausted with the whole business of race. "The world is too old now." Howells wrote, "and I find myself too much of its mood, to care for the work of a poet because he is black, because his father and mother were slaves."

Howells was expressing a popular pipe dream: that race mania would abate when blacks mastered the European high arts. Culture became the final test. It was an idea that would echo through the twentieth century and complicate racial life up to the present day.

As a young man, James Weldon Johnson spent many hours in the ragtime bars of New York, where slumming whites and the black showbiz demimonde mingled freely. He incorporated scenes from his tours into his 1912 novel *The Autobiography of an Ex-Colored Man*. In it, there is one club in particular where Negro minstrels come to unwind after performing in the evening shows, and Johnson gives us one unforgettable vignette clearly drawn from his real-life experiences. "There was one man, a minstrel, who, whenever he responded to a request to 'do something,' never essayed anything below a reading from Shakespeare," he wrote. "How well he read I do not know, but he greatly impressed me. . . . Here was a man who made people laugh at the size of his mouth, while he carried in his heart a burning ambition to be a tragedian; and so after all he did play a part in a tragedy."

Johnson is a minor novelist at best, and he cannot manage to bring off the scene the way, for example, Twain does with the soliloquy of his confidence man in *Huckleberry Finn*. But the minstrel who yearns to do Shakespeare is such an apt image that you instantly wish to linger on it. One imagines the actor, who earns his living day in and day out by grinning and bucking for half-soused audiences, here given a chance to do something from *Hamlet* (it can only be *Hamlet* that he recites). To this anonymous actor drinking in a Tenderloin hole in the wall, Shakespeare is *the* name in his profession: he represents the pinnacle of the legitimate theater in which the Negro actor can and will never be allowed to perform. The ban continued for many decades, all around the world: to get a sense of the inner torment this caused, listen to a letter from the Jamaican-born actor Errol John, who wrote home (in vernacular) from England in despair and rage at his inability to get any parts in Shakespeare productions. Even the movies:

> *You ever had to go for a part in a African film that you been counting the pennies on for a damn whole year and fer the casting director to look at you and say you ent black enough? And you almost as black as the ace of spades? Or when they call yer for a part . . . all yer play-*

ing is a big black nigger, or a fat greasy nigger, or a thin sooty nigger, or just any kind a nigger.[2]

The minstrel would have had it much worse. So we have to believe that in those recitations he looked to Shakespeare for all that is in Shakespeare: the full breadth of character and emotion the plays supply. One could say all that is denied the minstrel in his actual life is available to him in *Hamlet*. That is what Negroes of the Du Bois era took from Shakespeare and the other "great authors," something that perhaps the average white reader did not ask for in just the same way: an irrevokable sense of their full inclusion in the human.

Hamlet and the other pillars of high culture provided blacks like Du Bois proof that the United States was an irregular province of Europe, and that the racism they experienced was not only an aberration in Western life but a temporary one. One could say that the Negro's closest contact during this dry period was with white texts: the Bible, the Constitution, the European writers—all of which were counterarguments to the facts of American life. But Du Bois's return to the United States in 1896 would reveal a flaw in that alliance.

A quick overview of the nation he came back to:

Reconstruction had proved to be the North's last embrace of the "Negro problem" for many decades; soon after white southerners "redeemed" their politics and excluded blacks, the North largely lost interest. One could say it moved on, into moneymaking and the Progressive era. When North and South reunited, the North dictated the terms in many areas: a federal Union, tariffs, industrialization, social patterns of urbanization. What the South brought to the marriage—and ferociously insisted on keeping—was its view of the Negro. The North's abolitionists were aging and dying off, its political leaders required southern votes, and they agreed to the bargain; in fact, they sometimes outdid their former enemies in inventing the magnolia-and-moonlight view of the plantation system. So the black man entered the America of the Gilded Age dressed largely in southern clothes.

In the South, the three legs of black rehabilitation—land, the ballot, and education—had long since been whittled down to one. Land, of course, had been a mirage; the rural legend of "40 acres and a mule" that had swept across the postwar South never materialized. Blacks did retain some political power into the 1890s, but—with the exception of North Carolina, where they retained significant voting rights—it died with the new century. In 1896, 130,344 blacks had been registered voters in Louisiana; four years later, 5320 remained. In Alabama at the turn of the century, 181,471 black men were eligible to vote; 3000 were actually on the rolls.[3] Increasingly, it was education that became the last, best hope for the race.

Blacks had worshipped learning in their bondage days. Slaves tricked their masters into teaching them to read (and write, held to be an even more dangerous skill, since slaves could forge their own passes and escape). The young Frederick Douglass paid white children to repeat their lessons to him or challenged them to define a word he wanted to learn. The slave who could read was the telegraph operator of the plantation system, broadcasting news from newspapers smuggled into the South. "The fugitive, exciting word from white political sources, telling of arguments and debates over the operation of the institution of slavery, continued to seep into the life of the Southern black community," writes historian Vincent Harding, "hinting, suggesting, revealing the basic tensions which lurked deep in the larger white society."

When freedom came, black desire for book-learning came out into the open. There was a kind of craze for education: school was taught in shifts, the morning for children, the evening for "Cooks Washers + Ironers Cigar Makers Cotton pickers—Child minders, Nurses milk carriers, toters of water." This infatuation was a mix of the practical and the mystical: farmers wanted to learn arithmetic so that white plantation and mill owners would not cheat them at counting time; laborers wanted to read their notorious work contracts. There was also a belief that the English language and the laws of math held, in some ways, clues to the secret of white dominance. One contemporary journalist wrote that blacks saw book-learning as a "fetich" that could "protect its possessor from the curse of Adam, and insure a life of dignified ease and gentility."[4] Even some masters believed this. "Charles, you is a free man they say," his former owner told ex-slave Charles Whiteside. "but Ah tells you now, you is still a slave and if you lives to be a hundred, you'll STILL be a slave, cause you got no education, and education is what makes a man free!"[5]

After the war, the famous New England schoolteachers poured down from the North to educate the ex-slaves. Often female, touched with religious fanaticism, many saw their work as the next logical step in the abolition movement. Now that slavery was dead, the ex-bondsmen were in a temporary "plastic" or "elastic" state: either they would be "molded aright" into disciplined Christian citizens or they would harden into a savage immobility at the bottom of society. The motivations and effectiveness of the schoolmarms has been debated endlessly: the teachers, in the end, were profoundly conservative in most regards. But most believed that blacks had the same intellectual and cultural capabilities as whites, a new concept in the South. Many encouraged a kind of early black pride, and they broke the image of a monolithic white society, as they were themselves so bitterly hated by the ex-rebels. A common greeting for a schoolmarm was "damn Yankee bitch of a nigger teacher"—a slur almost admirable in its compression, combining as it did a triple insult against the teacher's gender, regional origin, and racial sympathies. Southerners, who had never instituted public schools even for poor whites, despised the institutions, insulted and killed their teachers, and were driven half-mad by the idea of young black children learning. While black students were singing at one Reconstruction school, a southern woman, "very finely dressed, and apparently quite lady-like," looked in the door and cried out. "Oh, I wish I could put a torch to that building! *The niggers.*"[6]

Though most of the curriculum was concerned with basic lessons in math and spelling and instruction in middle-class Victorian morals such as cleanliness and modesty, a minority taught lessons that were more radical. One observer listening to a question-and-response session caught this exchange:

TEACHER: Now children, you don't think white people are any
   better than you because they have straight hair and white
   faces?
STUDENTS: No, sir.
TEACHER: No, they are no better, but they are different, they
   possess great power, they formed this great government,
   they control this vast country. . . . Now, what makes them
   different from you?

STUDENTS: MONEY! (Unanimous shout)
TEACHER: Yes, but what enabled them to obtain it? How did
   they get money?
STUDENTS: Got it off us, stole it off we all![7]

Educators were the natural descendants of the Baptist missionaries; as the Bible gave slaves an insight into the spirit world of white Christians, so Webster's blue-black speller gave them the code to break through secular power. The two sometimes touched. A missionary magazine reported that at one funeral on Georgia's Sea Islands, black children actually recited the alphabet over a grave. It's impossible to say exactly how the community regarded the act, but the roots of Anglo-Saxon language had clear shamanistic power for blacks denied access to it.

Du Bois and the missionaries both believed that the academic performance of blacks would lead to the full granting of rights by an impressed American public. The very image of black children bent over a primer, rapt in concentration, would dissolve prejudice. "See those people, how worthy they are!" is how missionary J. Miller McKim imagined white progressives making their case. "How industrious; how loyal; how law-abiding; how fitted for citizenship! Give them their rights!"

It didn't work out, of course; most of the freed slaves and their children received a bare-bones education: some reading, some basic writing, some arithmetic, and a heavy dose of bootstrap lectures. And then they returned to a life of sharecropping. The gears of power were still operated by white hands; in many cases, education became a taunt, a view of what life offered to everyone except blacks. One could say the slaves learned early and thoroughly what Du Bois was about to find out.

When he arrived back in the United States to begin his career, the establishment of public education for all was perhaps Reconstruction's only lasting achievement. Du Bois knew that a tiny percentage of blacks had reached "heights high enough to overlook life"; most were struggling with their faces bent to the red clay of Georgia or Alabama. It was Du Bois's so-called Talented Tenth (as historians have pointed out, that "tenth" was always a highly optimistic figure), the college-educated aristocrats of the race, that would extract from their readings of Horace and Kant the necessary strategies that would bring their people into true freedom.

Du Bois himself was engaged in intellectual uplift. The path he chose was a series of sociological studies of black America, beginning with *The Philadelphia Negro* (1899). His idea was that once solid empirical studies of the reasons behind the black community's ills—the broken families, the unemployment, the crime, especially—was provided, American society would be obliged to heal those ills. The United States was not the center of "white" civilization—Europe was. And it assured Du Bois that the Negro problem was simply an oversight in the onward march of culture toward a rough perfection. "Europe stands today for a systematic and continuous union of individual effort to promote Justice and Freedom by means of Knowledge and Authority . . ." Du Bois told lecture audiences in 1900. "These ideals differ in no respect from the ideals of that European civilization of which we all today form a part." He maintained a frosty disdain for American prejudice and advocated only dignity in the face of it; "time and common sense" would solve that problem.

The German-trained scholar also, of course, entered into his famous battle with Booker T. Washington over the education of blacks. The southern-born Washington had advocated industrial training (carpentry, farming, engineering) for blacks to prepare them for a prosperous life in a segregated United States; if whites would support such colleges, Washington would sacrifice voting rights and equal access to the society. Du Bois eventually took issue with this and demanded that bright students get a classical education in Greek, higher mathematics, poetry, and philosophy. On its face, the debate presents a precise historical reversal: Du Bois's stance is 180 degrees opposed to the stance taken by many black students and academics in the culture wars of the 1990s. He and the other radicals were fighting for the right to study the dead white males, not for relief from them.

Working like a dog, Du Bois relentlessly researched and then published his work and awaited the results. Magazines and academics praised his studies and, over the years, nothing whatsoever happened. Du Bois was not the first academic to find that the impeccable monograph that he hoped would alter society's path collected dust while the world rolled on in its old ways, but increasingly his belief in the rationality of American whites was worn down. Even by 1899, he sensed that he had been naïve. After documenting the pathologies of Philadelphia's Negroes, he noted that they were rather garden-variety problems of poverty: blacks were not as poor as most Irish, or as plagued with crime as some Italian communities, or as ignorant as most of the early Puritans. But somehow, he wrote, the black man was categorically different; instead of calls to train, guide, and heal them, what was heard was "Let them die!" and "Let them stagger downwards!"[8]

This was made clear by an 1899 murder that Du Bois felt keenly. A black Georgia farmer named Sam Hose was lynched after killing his white boss (apparently in self-defense). David Levering Lewis, in his definitive biography of the scholar, records how the Atlanta University professor, after hearing the news, "gathered up his cane and gloves" and headed into town with two letters for the Atlanta *Constitution*—one an introduction to the paper's editor, Joel Chandler Harris, the other a condemnation of the lynching for the editorial page. It was the typically *comme il faut* Du Bois in action, but he never delivered his letters. On the way to Harris's office, the professor learned that Hose had not just been killed, but butchered by a white mob of 2000 men, women, and children, that his corpse had been roasted and hacked apart, that the crowd had fought over Hose's body parts and that the man's knuckles were at that very moment being displayed in a jar in a shopowner's window on the very street where the *Constitution* had its offices. Silently, Du Bois turned and walked slowly back to the university.

The lynching had finally brought home to him that America was not on its way down a lighted path toward racial enlightenment. Du Bois was presented with a Dark Ages sacrifice carried out by a broad range of white Georgians who were neither arrested nor condemned; in fact, they were celebrated. This was a deliberate, gleeful, and above all *visceral* rejection of the rules of all civilization, a breaking of Du Bois's pact with white culture. He was still a nigger, trapped in a black body that could be separated limb from limb for no particular reason. Du Bois's deepest relationship with whites had never been personal or emotion-driven; he communed not with individuals but with dead thinkers and poets. Now he had met the primal white man eye-to-eye, and he was forced, as he later wrote, to recognize "the deadening and disastrous effect of a color-prejudice that classes Phyllis Wheatley and Sam Hose in the same despised class."

Du Bois would listen to Brahms and Handel for the rest of his life, and he would always love Shakespeare as a writer, but no longer as a god. He began to turn away from European culture as a possible cure for the race problem and to look toward political action and power. It was not only race pride that drove him to help found the NAACP, to delve into African culture and piece together the Pan-Africanist opposition to the West. It was the necessity of an alternative faith. Much later, in 1940, he would write:

> *In the folds of this European civilization I was born and shall die, imprisoned, conditioned, depressed, exalted and inspired. Integrally a part of it and yet, much more significant, one of its rejected parts.*

If we look ahead in this history, the place of high culture as a troublesome meeting point between the races would persist. In one moment at the very beginning of the civil rights movement, the hardline segregationist editor of the Richmond *News Leader*, James J. Kilpatrick, watched some black college students—enrolled at those very universities that Du Bois had championed—conducting a sit-in. Their claim was symbolized by their dress and manner and by what they carried in their hands:

> *Here were the colored students, in coats, white shirts, ties, and one of them was reading Goethe and one was taking notes from a biology text. And here, on the sidewalk outside, was a gang of white boys come to heckle, a ragtail rabble, slack-jawed, black-jacketed, grinning fit to kill, and some of them, God save the mark, were waving the proud and honored flag of the Southern states in the last war fought by gentlemen. Eheu! It gives one pause.*

For those students, Goethe represented their faith in the Western tradition. But in the decades since, he and the rest of the pantheon became things to define oneself *against*. The public break occurred in the 1960s and is still with us. Malcolm X's famous question—"Do you know what they call a black man with a Ph.D.? *Nigger*"—mocked the protestors' faith in *The Sorrows of Young Werther.* James Baldwin picked up the theme in 1972 in *No Name in the Street:*

> *The cultural pretensions of history are revealed as nothing less than a mask for power, and thus it happens that, in order to be rid of Shell, Texaco, Coca-Cola, the Sixth Fleet, and the friendly American soldier whose mission it is to protect these investments, one finally throws Balzac and Shakespeare—and Faulkner and Camus—out with them.*

The culture wars of the 1990s were fought over just these names. In one of its more popular broadsides, Andrew Hacker summed up the modern complaint against the Great Writers as he imagines a black student reacting to a work from the pantheon. "Yet no matter how diligently you think about these authors and their ideas," Hacker wrote in *Two Nations,* "you find that much of your life is not reflected in European learning. You often feel that there is a part of yourself, your soul, that Europe cannot reach."

One could even look at the lingering phenomenon of black kids accusing their book-loving black classmates of "acting white" and see the disappointment of the freed slaves and Du Bois. For black anti-intellectualism differs from the run-of-the-mill kind that is prevalent in every community: there is the undercurrent not just that learning and high culture are only for geeks, but that it is un-black, almost genocidal. The black kid spitting out his contempt for things learned in school takes his position in the wake of a long debate, which is finally about the contradictory place of black people in the Western tradition.

The black coming to terms with Shakespeare eventually became settled largely along class lines. Du Bois practically invented the idea of the black aristocracy as a cultured as well as a moneyed elite. Page through Lawrence Otis Graham's 1999 portrait of that world, *Our Kind of People,* as gruesomely fascinating as any picture of American aristocrats, and you find that the inheritors of Du Bois's push for liberal black colleges (Howard, Fisk, and Atlanta Universities, as well as Morehouse College) are duly noted as "among the six or seven schools that the old-guard black elite still consider to be most appropriate for their children today." The line of descent is direct. Of course, Fisk and Morehouse are strong centers of Afrocentric study as well as classic humanities, but they began as temples of high European culture, through which blacks passed on their way to success. The sharecroppers and their descendants, especially the black youth of the northern ghettos, created a separate idea of how to affirm oneself in America: blues, hip-hop, street humor, ghetto style. But the triumph of those styles was many years in the future.

Du Bois's growing disillusionment can be felt in the single piece of fiction from his landmark *Souls of Black Folks* (1903). In "Of the Coming of John," the narrator is a college professor, a Du Bois stand-in, who tells of a young black man who came to his university for an education. John is a country bumpkin; he clowns around and neglects his studies, taking college as a goofy adventure. The pride of the country town that sent him away, he has been loved too well by blacks and patronized to perfection by whites. But when he's informed that he is being asked to leave the college because of his chronic lateness and bad grades, John is stricken. He goes away to work for his tuition, returns a changed man, and really begins to look at the world around him: he reads deeply, studies astronomy and ancient languages, begins to make connections between past and present, between power and injustice. There is no click of comprehension, but a gradual coming to terms with the workings of the world and the place of black people in the pull of history.

Du Bois was not a natural short-story writer. "John" is the old parable of "How you goin' to keep them down on the farm after they've seen Paree?" told in a black American context, freshened but hardly reinvented. Du Bois's back-country innocent takes the obligatory trip to The City, and somehow finds himself wandering into a performance of Wagner's opera *Lohengrin*. Here Du Bois obviously pulls out his notes from his Berlin years and describes the opera with the kind of distant superlatives—"the infinite beauty of the wail . . . swept through every muscle of his frame"—that studded his lectures on returning from Europe.

But there is one scene that is new, and Du Bois nails it to the page; it is John's peculiarly American homecoming to the small town that sent him away to college so many years before. The college graduate "stepped to the platform, and paused; a little dingy station, a black crowd gaudy and dirty, a half-mile of dilapidated shanties along a strag-

gling ditch of mud. An overwhelming sense of the sordidness and narrowness of it all seized him." Depressed into silence, he disappoints the
poor black folk gathered there to welcome him back:

> *" 'Peared kind o' down in the mouf," said the Methodist preacher*
> *thoughtfully. "Seemed monstus stuck up," complained a Baptist sis-*
> *ter. But the white postmaster from the edge of the crowd expressed the*
> *opinion of his folks plainly. "That damn Nigger," said he, as he*
> *shouldered the mail and arranged his tobacco, "has gone North and*
> *got plum full o' fool notions; but they won't work in Altamaha. "*

Lohengrin and all of the rest has changed John the way freedom
changed Marigault's slaves, but in this case it is John's own people who
can barely make him out. The white postmaster, however, recognizes
the new John instantly; knows the appraising, "biggety" stare of a nigger that has gotten beyond himself. Education has dropped a veil
between John and his own people, but he and the postmaster see each
other with a perfect clarity for the first time.

The story's end is preordained. Not long after his return home, John
kills himself as a lynching party comes hunting for him. He has offended
the white elite, been mistaken for a rapist, and killed a young white man,
but the individual crimes hardly matter. He died the instant the postmaster recognized him. The learning that gave Du Bois a new appreciation
for life in Europe has turned rank and poisonous. As in the Bible, forbidden knowledge is deadly; for blacks in the rural South at the turn of the
century, this was not a metaphor for avoiding the jaded values of the city
but an unwritten law that carried heavy penalties. There were countless
real-life Johns in the Jim Crow South. In opening his monumental study
of the period, historian Leon Litwack recounted the story of Willie Hol-
combe, a North Carolina sharecropper's son who graduated near the top
of his college class and returned home to the old prejudices. Embittered
and confrontational, he was murdered at the tobacco market after an
argument about prices, his head caved in by a group of white men. In
later years, his father would show his grave to other discontented youths
and tell them that Willie "had stepped outen his place when he got dat
eddycation." Both sides believed in this: One real-life planter in the postwar South echoed Du Bois's postmaster when he told an interviewer

what needed to be done with blacks like John: "When a nigger gets ideas, the best thing to do is to get him under ground as quick as possible."

In the early part of the last century, Du Bois began to explore black culture more probingly. What Sam Hose taught him was that a positive black force must confront the visceral image of blacks in white culture—beating whites at their own game, as he had done at Harvard and Berlin, was in the final measure an evasion. *Souls* was, of course, his masterpiece in this regard. As Arnold Rampersad has written, if all American literature flows out of *Huckleberry Finn*, all black American literature points back to *Souls*.

It was in the opening essay, "Of Our Spiritual Strivings," that Du Bois did something unprecedented for himself and for black culture. Almost every word of it—from the line on "How does it feel to be a problem?" to the introduction of black double consciousness—is famous now, but it emerged then, in terms of existing American culture, out of nowhere. There is in the rising and falling cadences both an attempt to describe black culture and to produce it. Here is Du Bois on the slaves' hope for freedom:

> *Away back in the days of bondage they thought to see in one divine event the end of all doubt and disappointment; few men ever worshipped Freedom with half such unquestioning faith as did the American Negro for two centuries. To him, so far as he thought and dreamed, slavery was indeed the sum of all villainies, the cause of all sorrow, the root of all prejudice; Emancipation was the key to a promised land of sweeter beauty than ever stretched before the eyes of wearied Israelites. In song and exhortation swelled one refrain—Liberty; in his tears and curses the God he implored had Freedom in his right hand. At last it came,—suddenly, fearfully, like a dream. With one wild carnival of blood and passion came the message in his own plaintive cadences:—*
>
> > *"Shout, O children!*
> > *Shout, you're free!*
> > *For God has brought your liberty!"*

One could dip into about half of the *Souls* essays and draw up language as charged as this. The work represents Du Bois's conscious move from the describer and analyst he has primarily been to a creator spinning out the black experience from the inside. Much like the early black Christians did in "fleshing out" Protestant teachings with black spirit, epitomized in their gospel songs, Du Bois began a more complicated counterpart: to conjure a secular black cultural soul out of sheer will. Du Bois saw the combination of black and white culture as producing the true, the final American. *Souls* would give America what it lacked, a supple, moral aliveness based in black experience that would redeem the republic.

Many freedom movements have a cultural wing: one thinks of the Irish literary renaissance of the 1900s, with its rediscovery of the Celtic arts and histories, its poets reciting poems over the graves of dead patriots killed in the British occupation. And many cultural nationalists in such movements quite naturally seek values and artistic forms that are in direct contrast to the forms of the oppressor: the Irish revolutionaries turned to the Gaelic past to find theirs. The American black at the turn of the century, however, had very little, in crass terms, to measure against the weight of the Italian Renaissance or the Romantic poets. And, to be honest, those artists and poets were so good, so beyond serious questioning in aesthetic terms, that one could hardly reject them as fake or mediocre. So one is struck by the extreme nature of the demands placed upon the African American reading Shakespeare—the combination of personal glorification and negation, simultaneously. It was a large, almost maddening gift.

If one imagines the turn of the century without a Du Bois, his contribution becomes clearer. Simply take one final look at Johnson's *Autobiography of an Ex-Coloured Man*, which revisits much of Du Bois's themes of double consciousness and race destiny, to see how valuable Du Bois was. A Du Bois contemporary who grew up being tutored in European novels and culture by his Bahamian mother, Johnson led an admirable life—as a writer, ragtime songwriter, editor, diplomat, and activist. Preternaturally cool and accommodationist by nature, he wrote in *Autobiography* the story of a mulatto boy (who is never given a name), a star student and budding pianist so light-skinned he can pass for white. The emotional high point of the early chapters is the boy's meeting with his rich, white father, who has come for a surprise visit.

The scene could serve as a wish fulfillment from Du Bois's own father-less childhood. At first, the boy is tongue-tied and can barely get out a word of conversation, but he does manage to communicate with the stranger in the doorway by sitting down at the piano to play some classical pieces. Surprised and delighted, his father pays him the compliment of listening seriously. The boy wants to go even further. "I showed my gratitude by playing for him a Chopin waltz with all the feeling that was in me," the boy remembers. "When I had finished, my mother's eyes were glistening with tears; my father stepped across the room, seized me in his arms, and squeezed me to his breast. I am certain that for that moment he was proud to be my father."

The narrator meets up with a mysterious white millionaire, drawn from Johnson's own friendship with a cultured white doctor, a tragic depressive who later killed himself. He takes the pianist in tow as he visits Europe. The narrator's reaction is comparable to Du Bois's: delight bordering on intoxication. Hired to play ragtime to relieve his patron of his unbearable sadness, the narrator is performing one night at a little recital when he is astonished by one of his listeners, a "big bespectacled, bushy-headed man" who jumps up, shoves him aside, and begins riffing on the keys. "Taking the theme of my ragtime, [he] played it through first in straight chords; then varied and developed it through every known musical form. I sat amazed. I had been turning classic music into ragtime, a comparatively easy task; and this man had taken ragtime and made it a classic." Turning his back on Europe, he decides to return home to the United States and create symphonies of ragtime-classic music, whatever that might be: the aghast millionaire sees him giving up Paris to become "a nigger composer." Except that he doesn't. Falling in love with a white girl, he finally crosses the color line and lives with her as a successful white poser.

Though the novel continues *The White Slave*'s theme of infiltration and looks ahead to the influential passing novels of the Harlem Renaissance, it ends on this cheerfully gutless note. And one must point back to that crucial moment where the pianist has his life work revealed to him, the synthesis of ragtime and classic, of black and white, as the point where the novel loses its way. What one wants is to hear the two traditions merging to get some sensory proof of the new music being invented on the spot. But the writing is vapor; the imagining of the synthesis remains undone. Perhaps it is wrong to beat up on Johnson, a secondary talent, but what makes *Autobiography* hollow-sounding is very close to what makes *Souls* indispensable. Johnson had produced a reasonable black facsimile of the contemporary commercial novel, dominated by white writers. Du Bois had taken upon himself the task of creating a founding document of mulatto culture that is still black to the bone.

His materials were a bizarre hodge-podge that seemingly defied assimilation: German philosophy, American transcendentalism, black suffering, the specific responses of the spiritual and black wit. Years before, in Germany, Du Bois had felt the divisions within him and asked: "How far can love for my oppressed race accord with love for the opposing country?"[9] *Souls* broke the impasse by creating out of clashing antecedents something that was both harmonious and new. David Levering Lewis writes of the book: "It's as though the voices of Schopenhauer and Sojourner Truth were blended."[10] To the question that most self-aware black people asked in relation to white culture from Du Bois's time forward—Are we with or against it?— Du Bois answered: Neither. His importance to our history was to suggest a third way. Mimicry was inadequate; simple rejection was both stupid and insincere. A true black voice would have to sound different from anything Germany or France had produced: more guttural, injured, differently rhythmed, and shot through with rage against its inspirations. Du Bois faced a different pressure than any other American writer: if his work wasn't fresh, it would be a betrayal of its subjects.

As for *Souls*, it electrified some whites and completely eluded others. An anonymous reviewer in The New York *Times* reduced Du Bois's epic mission to this: he wanted to "smoke a cigar and drink a cup of tea with the white man in the South." But the most significant response, in retrospect, came from a poor Russian-Jewish immigrant on the Lower East Side of Manhattan who wrote the writer a fan letter after reading the collection. His name was D. Tabak, and he told Du Bois that the book had made him ashamed of being white, that he had been "overpowered by a peculiar pain that was so much akin to bliss." Finally, he said that he now envied blacks, the "despised and abused" of his adopted nation. *Envied* them. It was a new verb in black-to-white relations.

It is perhaps odd to end with Tabak, an obscure nobody who was never heard from again, but his is the only response to *Souls* that truly pointed toward the future. Whites had empathized with black suffering, and men like William Garrison and John Brown had been willing to die to alleviate it. Southern aristocrats like Mary Chesnut had recognized in black culture something lacking in their own. Howells had welcomed the black race, bravely in his way, to the table of white civilization in the person of a talented Negro poet. But Tabak is one of the first voices we find who sincerely wishes to join black culture, just as Du Bois had yearned to join European culture decades before. It is one of the first signs of a tidal shift in the society that connects directly with Elvis's attraction to black gospel and the suburban white kids' adoration of Michael Jordan. The spell of European art is about to be broken. *Souls* established an alternative interpretation of what was valuable in human experience that was rigorous, different . . . and black. Soon whites would be trying to understand and emulate it.

Perhaps Tabak tried to find the "bliss" he spoke about. Certainly he was in the right place at the right time for a new era in the deep contact of black and white. Whether he made the trip or not, Tabak lived only one hundred blocks south of a neighborhood where the change would soon be clearly visible. In Harlem.

Jazz opened the codebook of black culture to serious white fans, such as these ones at a Big Jay McNeely concert. The music brought with it a new sense of what was valuable in life, and it wasn't the old list.

By Bob Willoughby. Courtesy of Bob Willoughby.

6

CRY AT THE BIRTH: JAZZ AND THE WORLD IT CREATED

IN 1923, THE 21-year-old Langston Hughes was preparing to leave Harlem and the United States and to begin, as he saw it, his actual life. Signed up as a messboy on the freighter S.S. *Malone*, he had prepared for the trip by provisioning himself with necessities and jettisoning the things he wouldn't need. The last night before embarking, Hughes gathered up his portable library, the volumes of Shakespeare and Dickens that had sustained him through early years of loneliness and rejection and that he had brought onboard as a matter of course. With one violent boost, he heaved them over the side.

> *It was like throwing a million bricks out of my heart—for it was not only the books that I wanted to throw away, but everything unpleasant and miserable out of my past: the memory of my father, the poverty and uncertainties of my mother's life, the stupidities of color-prejudice, black in a white world, the fear of not finding a job, the bewilderment of . . . being controlled by others—by parents, by employers, by some outer necessity not your own.*[1]

Even then, New York gangsters used the local waterways for disposing of corpses, and we can look at this nocturnal splash in the waters off Manhattan as a kind of cultural murder. The European culture that Du Bois and the previous generation so adored was tossed unceremoniously over the side. Hughes wanted to get away from painful inheritances; he wanted native life, not literature; fresh experience, not received wisdom; truth, not aesthetic beauty. For him that beauty was often black and American. Europe and its literature hadn't provided Hughes with what he was looking for, nor would he find it in Africa on his trip on the *Malone*. But when he returned to America, he encountered something that began to answer his requirements: the blues and its newer cousin, jazz, the music that was amusing whites in the nightclubs and setting the black working folk afire in the rent parties and the nasty all-night black-and-tans.

Hughes became jazz's original poet, the first to write about its singers and to slip jazz tones and breaks into his poems. In "Trumpet Player," he sketches out the first lines of an archetype.

> *The music*
> *From the trumpet at his lips*
> *Is honey*
> *Mixed with liquid fire.*
> *The rhythm*
> *From the trumpet at his lips*
> *Is ecstasy*
> *Distilled from old desire.*

The jazz Hughes knew was the New York version, but the city did not invent the music, of course. Manhattan hauled it in from the heartland, quickened its pulse, dressed it in elegant clothes, and offered it more money than it had ever seen. But jazz, the most American of musics, began in New Orleans, that least American of cities. Perhaps it had to begin there; the city's foreignness should be kept in mind when discussing how jazz came to be.

New Orleans had always been musical. In its precincts, the southern tendency to make music out of the stark Anglo-Saxon tongue had reached its pinnacle. People used music to communicate and to denote who they were in life. While a New York rag-and-bone merchant might wind his way down Delancey Street shouting his profession at the top of his lungs, the New Orleans version would announce his arrival by playing a particular blues on the wooden mouthpieces of Christmas horns. "Yes, sir," remembers the jazz pianist and composer Jelly Roll Morton, a New Orleans creole. "Play more low-down dirty blues on those . . . horns than the rest of the country ever thought of."[2] The phenomenon was seen high and low. Most American cities had no opera companies; pre–Civil War New Orleans had three. And no red light district had more "professors" than the Crescent City. The lowest-down whorehouse became acceptable if it had a piano player jamming in the parlor. Storyville throbbed with music that sang vice instead of trying to disguise it.

Almost everything within reach was tested for its musical properties. Musician Danny Barker once listed the typical tools used in an early "spasm" band, composed of children who went from bar to bar looking for tips: the list included "musical saws, washboards, spoons, bells, pipes, sandpaper, xylophones, sets of bottles (each with a different amount of water), harmonicas, jews harps, one string fiddles, guitars, small bass fiddles, tub basses, kazoos, ram horns, steer horns, bugles, tin flutes [and] trombones."[3] Legitimate instruments were also freely available at cheap prices; when Civil War Army bands had been discharged in New Orleans, they had hocked their cornets and trombones by the thousands in the local pawn shops.

These factors go a long way to explain why a new music came out of New Orleans, but not why that music was jazz. The profound integration of New Orleans is surely important; on one street, you might have a Sicilian immigrant family, a black clan in the same house for four generations, a mixed couple just run out of Mississippi, a Creole pensioner, Germans, Crow Indians, and Swedes. All their native musics flowed into jazz. But the important point is not that the music steals from every available source, from ragtime to Sicilian aria to German brass band struts; it is that the music is comfortable playing all these musics from the inside. The borrowings are not mocking or unsure but marked by total confidence. From the beginning, the early black jazz musicians combined these musics as if the blood of all Americans ran through their veins. Jazz emerged from a mulatto habit of mind, and this could perhaps have happened only in New Orleans.

Likewise for the music's temperament: irreverent, pleasure-struck, shambolic, regal, and touched everywhere by blues. These qualities were very much *not* the qualities of the average American town, even the black side of the average American town. At the turn of the century, New Orleans inhabitants lived for other things than did most of America, and a hedonism of a special, decayed kind was key to that difference. "New Orleans," writes jazz historian James Lincoln Collier, "had long seen pleasure-seeking as a legitimate concern of life, unlike much of the North, still dominated by residual Calvinism through much of the nineteenth century and even beyond."

This was far from the mindless hedonism of today's Mardi Gras, where flashing your breasts passes for tradition. This was an ingrained sense of how to live, encrusted by lore and epicurean philosophy inherited from France and the Caribbean and Africa. The creation of this music reflected this; it may in fact have required it. Black originators like Buddy Bolden slurred and warped the notes of the waltzes and brass band songs, turning them from straight-out nostalgic anthems into something far different. This style spoke of a contrariness of mind; not only the black Americans' mordant wit that fed the storylines of blues and worksongs, which pervaded the entire republic, but a more localized effect, a bright but narrowed glance that might, from certain angles, be taken as a wink. Perhaps the best illustration of this comes with native Jelly Roll Morton's description of one of the famous New Orleans funerals that practically birthed the music. It is best to let him speak at length.

> *Any time we heard somebody was dead we knew we had plenty good food that night. Of course, the dead man would always be laid out in the front and he'd be by himself most of the time and couldn't hear nothing we would be saying at all. He was dead and there was no reason for him to be with us living people. And very often the lady of the house would be back there with us having a good time, too, because she would be glad he was gone.*
>
> *Then we would stand up and begin—*
>
> *Nearer, my God, to thee . . .*
>
> *Very slow and with beautiful harmony, thinking about that ham—*
>
> *Nearer to thee . . .*

Plenty of whiskey in the flask and all kinds of crazy ideas in the har-
mony which made it impossible for anybody to jump in and sing.
We'd be sad, too, terribly sad.

> *Steal away, steal away,*
> *Steal away, home to Jesus . . .*

That would be the last of the dead man. He's gone and everybody
came back home, singing. In New Orleans they believed truly to stick
right close to the Scripture. That means rejoice at the death and cry
at the birth.[4]

By the time he told this story, Morton was a bitter old man, claim-
ing with at least some justification that he never received the proper
credit for his part in inventing jazz. But even if we take into account
some hardening in his view of life, and factor in Morton's own waspish
temperament, the New Orleans worldview still rings out: that scoffing
at wasted emotion, the outrageous contrarian style (crying over the
succulent ham, ignoring the corpse) which is both very French and
very black American, a toughness that goes beyond, say, New York cyn-
icism to become an ancient amusement at all human endeavor. There
is tenderness, too, not for something as mundane as death, but for the
moment—whiskey, succulent ham, friends, hot music, the erotic glow
of the freshly minted widow, all of it under cover of the tremulous
hymn "Nearer My God to Thee."

Morton savors the bitter and the sweet taste of life on the tongue,
fading even as it is imbibed. This particular view of things forms the
bedrock of 1920s and 1930s jazz attitude. "Music," writes Amiri Baraka
in his study of black music, *Blues People*, "is the result of thought . . .
perfected at its most empirical, i.e., *attitude* or *stance*." Morton's
description of the funeral gives us the stance from which jazz sprung
and never really lost. This attitude was odd in the American scene. Its
essential spirit does not fit well with the ruling ethos of the age: the
pursuit of money, respectability, personal responsibility, and the work
ethic. The worldview of the Puritan world was turned completely
upside down in New Orleans, an effect caught perfectly in a local ditty:

> *"Mama, mama, look at sis,*
> *She's out on the levee doing the double twis'."*

"Come in here, you dirty little sow,
You tryin' to be a bad girl and you don't know how."

Before jazz, this upside-down world was accessible mainly in two ways: lighting out for the frontier or becoming a criminal. In other words, running from the social order or opposing it.

Jazz shared many of its early haunts with criminals; in Storyville, jazzmen watched prostitutes through peepholes and provided the soundtrack for sex. In Chicago, gangsters would walk into a club and instruct bands to play on, as they proceeded to beat, torture, and shoot the club owner who had failed to buy their boss's whiskey. (Even Capone came to "hot" clubs to enjoy himself, and tipped heavily for sentimental numbers.) Jazz found in gangsters its most discerning and loyal early white audiences; for underneath they shared a skewed understanding of what was worthwhile in life. They were not identical visions—jazz's was much larger and life-affirming—but they were both at odds with the view expressed in sermons from Bangor to San Francisco every Sunday, or politicians' speeches.

When this new music departed from New Orleans around 1910, it encountered a nation in flux, one seeking especially in the cities a fresher sensibility than Victorianism, which was soiling itself in the trenches of World War I. The causes for the change are too many and too well known to delve into at length here: industrialization, the great black migration from north to south, the general migration from farms and villages to cities, the growing freedom of single urban women, the arrival of modernism like microbes in the clothes of sensitive war veterans, the impatience with moralizing female arbiters, and the rising of something quicker, more hard-bitten, present-tense, romantic, and fatalistic.

And there was also something far more prosaic but just as important to the jazz craze: the desire to dance. "The decade between 1910 and 1920 can be identified primarily," historian Sigmund Spaeth observed, "as the period in which America went dance mad." The sweet Victorian ballads, which were designed to be listened to sitting down, were commercial dogs. Every hit needed rhythm. Ragtime's syncopated style set the tone, and both fans and enemies of the new dance music remarked on how it seemed to bypass the conscious mind and trigger involuntary responses in the body—old, forgotten instincts or completely new instincts, no one was sure. For the first time, this seemed like something to be desired; it was really through bodies that ragtime and then jazz conquered America. "Suddenly, I discovered that my legs were in a condition of great excitement," one ragtime advocate remembered. "They twitched as though charged with electricity and betrayed a considerable and rather dangerous desire to jerk me from my seat. . . . It wasn't the feeling of ease in the joints of the feet and toes which might be caused by a Strauss waltz, no, much more energetic, material, independent as though one encountered a balking horse, which it is absolutely impossible to master."[5] Jazz, a much more complex music, worked its voodoo in the same way. Soon America reached out and grabbed this obscure regional music.

Technology helped immensely. Even middle-class whites with no interest in crossing the tracks could buy one of the new player pianos and get their jazz that way. There were more than forty different varieties available by 1904, and the top models were said to reproduce "not only the notes but also the tempo, rhythm, dynamic changes, phrasing and pedaling of the recording artist."[6] Insert one of the hot-selling piano rolls from a Harlem stride master and it would be as if the great James P. Johnson himself was sitting in your living room. (Minus, of course, the actual Negro.) Or you could buy a Victrola record player and a few discs; in 1914, 25 million records were sold; seven years later, it was 100 million.[7] Or you might simply listen to the radio. By 1934, over 9 out of 10 American homes owned a radio and listened to it on average four and a half hours a day, with jazz-inflected dance music far and away the most popular genre. The waves of the original New Orleans invention spread everywhere, hot and racially mixed at its tiny core, cool and white at its enormous edges.

At the edges, where bandleaders like the popular Paul Whiteman played a seriously watered-down, sweet version of the music, the effect on whites was nil. The music played was faster than a schottische or waltz, but its spirit, its habit of mind, was hardly that different than the one expressed in those sentimental European tunes. As one moved toward the center, however, more intimate brushes with jazz inevitably brought, at the very least, a new appreciation for the true article. Broadway in the 1920s was one place it was featured.

The black shows that stormed Broadway during the Roaring Twenties began with the revolutionary "Shuffle Along," the musical that Langston Hughes once said was the single reason he came to New York. Mayor LaGuardia caught it three times in one week. The shows changed how Broadway danced; steps became noticeably more "intricate, daring, perilous," according to the New York *American*. The dancing was simply more expressive than anything whites could have attempted at the time. "When I see a Negro child two or three years old come out and dance a little better than anybody at the New Amsterdam or the Winter Garden," wrote theater critic Heywoud Broun, "I grow fearful that there must be certain reservations in the theory of white supremacy."[8] The shows did not present a radically different Negro than the ones audiences and critics had in their heads—these were marginally more human cousins of the minstrel shows' happy, footloose Negroes. But there were flashes of something else behind the masks. The *Sun's* Richard Lockridge reviewed "Harlem," which featured a rent-party scene where up to fifteen black couples slow-dragged, and came away uneasy. "Men and women who can dance like that," he told his readers, "have the strength for violence."[9] (The scene was later cut, precisely because of comments like that.)

But the reviews for the groundbreaking black musicals were mostly positive. Critics spoke of the shaded emotions conveyed by Bill "Bojangles" Robinson; writing in *The Nation*, the white novelist Mary Austin wrote that white eyes "filmed and covered by 5,000 years of absorbed culture" were cleansed just by watching him. It was the highest kind of praise, but it was still applause from afar. When whites and blacks actually danced on the same floor together, the impact would go deeper.

When in 1963 Alex Haley was interviewing Malcolm X for his as-told-to autobiography, he was startled during one session when the coiled and often somber Muslim preacher jumped out of his seat, grabbed a metal pipe, and began swinging with it as if it was a snake-hipped young girl. Malcolm danced beautifully, "his coattail and his long legs and the big feet flying." The subject of their interview that day was, improbably, the lindy-hop. Then known as Malcolm Little (he had yet to transform himself into the superthug Detroit Red), the teenager had been one of the thousands of young Americans, black and white, who had packed the Roseland Ballroom in Boston and later the Savoy in Harlem night after night to dance the new sensation, a scene duplicated in cities across the country with equal fervor but less brilliance. Though by the time of the interview he looked back at his young self as a racial "buffoon" (zoot suit, conked hair, white girlfriends), Malcolm came alive as he related the memory: no other moment moved him to anything like the same response. "The crowd clapped and shouted in time with the blasting band," Malcolm recalled of one Roseland session. "I turned up the steam; Laura's feet were flying; I had her in the air, down, sideways, around; backwards, up again, down, whirling. . . . Even Duke Ellington half raised up from his piano stool, stood and bowed." Malcolm would later take his skills to Harlem and the world-famous Savoy, the mecca of jazz dance.

The British poet Philip Larkin, an ocean away in England, would consider his jazz memories "a nucleus of surviving youth"; so, clearly, did Malcolm. But for "youth" one can substitute the traditional romantic substitute "joy," and Americans of the 1920s generation experienced it in a far more racially poisoned and tense atmosphere than British fans like Larkin. Take 1930s Harlem. So little in the interracial scene of that time was unmarked, consciously or subconsciously, by humiliation and dread: the awkward embrace of black literati and white socialites; white men cruising Lenox Avenue for "deviant" sex; the biracial drug market; white hipsters hugging black strangers and, as Malcolm X noted, crying out, "You're just as good as I am—I want you to know that!"; the black male tour guides selling entrée to "jungle" sex; the appearance of the first wiggers (Malcolm recalls one, a jive-talking "hippy" named Braddock who lived with two black women, but whose goodwill evaporated when he asked a white girl why she was "throwing herself away on a spade"); the uneasy relationship between the white cop and the black citizen; the resentment of Harlemites at the refusal of many white shop owners to hire black help, which would ignite in the riots of 1935; the skin lighteners, the conk shops, the fake British accents of the railroad porters over on Strivers Row. Any honest feeling lay suffocated beneath layer upon layer of history, as heavy as crushed sediment.

Jazz blasted this away, at least temporarily. At the Savoy, white and black teenagers met and created formative memories together, danced alongside and sometimes with each other, studied each other's moves (the tutorials were almost always white-on-black), and screamed aloud at the attacks of Coleman Hawkin's tenor sax or Dave Tough's drums. Whites and blacks alike spoke of being *physically* struck by the sound, of that first moment of total disorientation, and then reorientation along new lines. As in battle or sex—two things with which it had more than a few things in common—words evaporated before jazz dancing.

Jazz dancing also helped invent the cultural conservative. Parents went wild, predictably; a Paterson, New Jersey, court gave a young woman fifty days for dancing the turkey trot; fifteen girls got fired from a magazine for breaking out into the same dance at lunchtime (women seem to have been targeted more often than men, as liberating their pelvises was more dangerous). Even the Vatican weighed in with a 1914 decree expressing its disapproval.[10] But the dancing did not stop.

The ingredients that went into the music were undeniably mulatto, and its practice was biracial almost from the beginning. In 1908, the early Streckfus steamboats that plied the Mississippi featured black piano legend Fate Marable and the white violinist Emil Flindt playing licks together. The white Original Dixieland Jazz Band became the first group on record, after black bandleader Freddie Keppard refused to put his songs down, thinking that others might steal them. The attitude was partly practical but it was also touched with superstition. Jazz was not the first time that what might be called the black code, the history of the race in transcribable notes, was broadcast to white people. That had begun with the spirituals of the Jubilee Singers, who had traveled the country playing to white Christians and earned enough to found Fisk University. But whites had never become interested in the spirituals the way they were in jazz: they didn't want to sing them, or copy the flatted notes, or publish them and record them. They didn't want to imbibe the life spirit expressed and use it as a spiritual resource, or as a career move. But with jazz, they did emphatically want to do all these things. The dancers were just the beginning; others coming in after them wanted to go further into the sound. They were the musicians.

Young white men started lining the muddy banks of the Mississippi to hear Louis Armstrong play on the riverboats; they began appearing at clubs on the South Side of Chicago where white faces had never been seen before ("I see you are all out here to get your music lessons tonight" was the doorman's half-amused taunt).[11] The neophytes began watching the musicians' hands as they hit the keys; they bought records and listened to them for hours, learning the solos by heart.

The early white jazz musicians came from two environments: comfortable middle-class families or struggling ghetto backgrounds. Benny Goodman grew up in a typically vicious urban neighborhood called "Bloody Maxwell," a few blocks away from the future mob boss Sam Giancana, and the two shared the same formative milieu: a place where kids cheered the thugs and booed the cops in the local cinema. "Judging from the neighborhood where I lived," Goodman said, "if it hadn't been for the clarinet, I might just as easily have been a gangster." Musicians were considered to be one small step above hoodlums, on a level with hobos, vagabonds, magic-show performers, and circus acrobats. The middle-class devotees like the great cornetist Bix Beiderbecke, on the other hand, were not escaping danger but boredom. They factored in some standard middle-class disaffection to their love of the music.

If dancers had felt the music affect them as an intensely pleasant trance, musicians spoke of the experience as something almost painful, of feeling new pathways being cut through their nervous systems. "I felt as if I had stared into the sun's eye," trumpeter Max Kaminsky wrote of first hearing Louis Armstrong. "All I could think of doing was to run away and hide till the blindness left me." Armstrong was for white musicians what even watered-down jazz was for uninitiated men and women: a noise so shocking it paralyzed. "I dropped my cigarette and gulped my drink," Hoagy Carmichael recalled of his "first time." "Bix was on his feet, his eyes popping . . . Bob Gillette slid off his chair and under the table." The blast of pleasure-pain was a sign that, for some listeners, what was being heard required much more than applause. It immediately identified a difference between the casual fan and the young man who would go out the next day, buy a horn, and practice it for six hours a day for the next five years. The two separated cleanly. The latter became what Baraka calls "a new class of white American."

Once these performers acquired some chops and went out into the clubs to play, they had very limited contact with black musicians. The after-hours jam sessions with black and white musicians happened, but they were quite rare. What the music shifted most perceptibly was the white musicians' perspective on their own neighbors and friends, beginning with the overriding issue of taste. Most white audiences liked awful music. They demanded the most sentimental, hokey, "sweet" versions of jazz available to them. This phenomena became the impetus for the influential *Esquire* magazine jazz awards. Most Top Ten lists generated by fans awarded the top prizes to ten white jazz trumpeters year after year, with Louis Armstrong not even making the list. The situation became unbearable for serious fans, and the awards—chosen by aficionados, not the public—were born.

There was almost no way to play down to most listeners. Once, a group of Chicago musicians gathered in a studio to practice some hot numbers; they spotted bandleader Tommy Dorsey and broke out into a Dixieland farce, something they wouldn't be caught dead playing except as a joke. The recording supervisor rushed out of his booth and yelled, "That's it! That's what we want, just what you're playing there!" The song, "Shirt Tail Stomp," became a hit. "You can't imagine some of the garbage we sometimes had to play, and for what idiots,"[12] said Artie Shaw, who quit the business largely because of such humiliations.

The 1920s created the first real division in American culture between the cool (the meaning was yet to be coined, but it would be a jazz word, of course) and the uncool, the initiated and the square. Dorothy Parker, H. L. Mencken, and the New York writers composed the essential texts that divided the wits from the Babbitts. Suddenly among these writers, blackness became an antidote to the depleted moral life of the West, an unexpected national resource, like discovering oil reserves in Louisiana. The trick was getting at it. "Damn it, man, if I could really get inside the niggers and write about them with some intelligence," Sherwood Anderson wrote Mencken. "I'd be willing to be hanged later and perhaps would be."[13] He never would; nor would any white writer of his generation. But what the Harlem Renaissance attempted as a top-down artistic experiment, jazz accomplished by its very nature.

When the long and raucous party of the 1920s gave way to the Depression, the literati's smart mouth was silenced by suicide, grim reality, and Bolshekivism. Many of the Jazz Age writers would repent of their frivolous attitudes and embrace sincerity; even F. Scott Fitzgerald went somber. But when hard times came in the 1930s, jazz people didn't sober up. Their reaction to world crisis was to create swing.

What was new about jazz? The music was scary; it called on each man to develop a tone—recognizable in a few notes—as individual as his fingerprint. It asked each musician to develop that tone night after night; to turn his biography into chords; to do so especially at the famous after-hours cutting sessions that served as proving grounds for young and old where "the ceaseless warfare for mastery and recognition," as Ralph Ellison called it, took place. Improvisation was personality. When one's flow of ideas ran out, it was not only a professional disaster but a personal dissolution. This was not a new phenomenon in art—blocked writers make excellent candidates for suicide—but here it was much more public and moment-to-moment. Jazz differed, of course, from all Western musics that had come before it in that improvisation was required. The soloist became the composer, reflecting his inner world in notes and phrases.

Listen to alto saxophonist Art Pepper describe a cutting duel at the Blackhawk club in which he had been challenged by a solo from Sonny Stitt. Pepper was at a low point in his life. "I was strung out. I was hooked. I was drunk," he remembered. "I was having a hassle with my wife, Diane, who'd threatened to kill herself in our hotel room next door. I had marks on my arm. I thought there were narcs in the club, and I all of a sudden realized that it was [on] me. He'd done all those things, and now I had to put up or shut up or get off or forget it or quit or kill myself or do something."[14] Pepper came through, blowing Stitt off the stage with a hot solo ("I played myself, and I knew I was right," is how he described it) and decided not to kill himself that particular night—though next week, of course, he would have to save himself all over again. Even if the story checks off the entire list of jazz musician clichés (a club, after hours, drugs, narcs, crazy woman, suicide), Pepper's account is an example of the jazz solo as survival technique, of creating in order not to die; every musician and deep fan recognizes its particular wisdom and shares in it. Its stance would eventually leak out into the mainstream and affect even those who professed to hate the music.

But such myths have their downside. Classical music thrives on permanence: Schubert's *Wintereise* remains eternally what it is: constantly renewed and flavored by interpretations, it has a core that never changes. But, created on the fly, the jazz solo carried within itself its own death. The white trumpeter Jimmy McPartland remembers once discussing the freedom of jazz with Bix Beiderbecke. People had been asking Bix to play certain solos exactly as he had recorded them. Bix tried and failed. "It's impossible," he told McPartland. "I don't feel the same way twice." That happy freedom also brings with it the knowledge of its own passing. Once you began repeating yourself without adding new inflections, you were finished as a jazz musician, frozen at the time of your last original solo. Without the permanent touchstone of a *Wintereise*, even a particularly good solo possessed its own melancholy. As Jelly Roll understood, why worry about the dead man in the parlor when every note coming out of your trumpet sang of your own mortality?

The classic case is that of Beiderbecke, the great young white cornetist who is jazz's Keats, the young genius destroyed by the world around him. Beiderbecke was only in his early twenties when he gained his reputation. Gentle, modest, a good German boy from a prosperous Davenport, Iowa, family who had succumbed to the new music, he created a tone on cornet that was bell-clear, ravishing, and cool. When guitarist Eddie Condon first heard him play, he thought Bix's sound "was like a girl saying 'yes.' "[15] Beiderbecke was an alcoholic, however, and after years in top bands his music began to falter. (His gestures on the way down—dashing off to the Manhattan morgue and paying the attendant to look at the corpses—are so in line with the image of the doomed romantic that one cannot help but wonder if he was patiently constructing his own myth.) There were relapses, periods of rest at home in Davenport where he secluded himself in the family manse, but what might be marked as the true end came during a Camel Hour broadcast that went out live on the air. Bix played along with the tune until it came his turn to rip off an eight-bar solo; instead of improvising as he used to do as naturally as breathing, Bix froze. He simply stared, "fear and incomprehension in his eyes."[16] Another musician quickly jumped into the gap and the listening audience hardly noticed. But Bix never really recovered. It wasn't stage fright in the traditional sense; it was simply that, as a soloist, his musical personality had evaporated before his eyes. There was nothing left to call on. Bix was dead within two years.

Beiderbecke and the other talented white musicians of the 1920s and 1930s respected their music and considered it as accomplished as, if less emotionally powerful than, jazz played by black musicians. They seemed not to have experienced a flicker of self-doubt; the idea that jazz was primarily black simply wasn't in the air yet (though black musicians already felt it). But white musicians did understand that they had tapped into an understanding of life as a dare with consequences that was, at its root, black. When a local newspaper reporter called on Bix, now well into his decline, for an interview, he described jazz as "musical humor." For humor, Beiderbecke meant something more than the harmless spoofs that "nut" jazz, with its costumes, its stunts and gags, worked in; he described jazz's humor as "bitter, agonized and grotesque." It was a response to pain. "Even in the hands of white composers, it involuntarily reflects the half-forgotten suffering of the negro," Beiderbecke said. "Its recent phase seems to throw the light of the white race's sophistication upon the anguish of the black."[17]

In addition, jazz created a cultural underground railroad: in most major towns, there was a club one could go to and hear the best players; there was a person who acted as a booker for musicians looking for jobs; there were places musicians and devotees congregated; certain boardinghouses where they slept off whiskey binges; particular whores who traveled in their circles. There were certain clothes that marked one as a serious fan; in the bebop era, specific eyeglasses and black berets tilted at a certain angle. For the first time, blacks and whites had common experiences, common training, common enemies (in aesthetic terms, at least); common standards of excellence; and, importantly, a common language that could only be understood by the initiated. Terms such as "hip," "funky," "cool," and so forth, as hard-used as they are today, still describe a style of living created by the jazz world and later leaked to the mainstream. In a society as open and contentious as America's, the creation of various undergrounds was foreordained, but not their slant on American life. The one created by jazz musicians would prove an inexhaustible resource for those angling away from boredom.

For black musicians, one of the most surprising things about jazz was that white people got it. Jim Crow had seriously depleted the information that each race had on the other. By the 1910s, the black nanny and maid was the last spy in the white household, and the minstrel shows were the one major cultural link left between the cultures. The minstrel shows, as Gary Giddins points out, used many of the same gags and songs and characters from coast to coast, so that for the first time the American people, black and white, had a cultural form in common. But blacks could hardly be enthusiastic about that form, because the childlike Negroes on display showed colored audiences that white people were deeply in the dark about their actual lives. So jazz became a test for black artists, of whether "those people" were connected to them in any significant way, or had ever been. Many musicians doubted they were. Ethel Waters was reluctant to perform for whites, convinced that they simply wouldn't get her style; instead, she was quickly embraced and became one of the top-paid female singers of her time. It was a completely unexpected development.

For the first time, blacks experienced a sometimes pleasant, sometimes terrifying fear that whites would break the code. When the soulful white trombonist Jack Teagarden arrived in New York and played before the top black Fletcher Henderson band, the leader himself came up to him after a performance. "I have been listening to you," he told Teagarden. "I don't see how any white man can play like you do." Lowering his voice, he asked the crucial question. "Tell me—and you have my strictest confidence—are you coloured?" Teagarden only smiled and shook his head. It was a compliment.[18] "They played not in the zany, tongue-in-cheek spirit of the white bands," wrote jazz chronicler Ralph Berton about an influential white group, the New Orleans Rhythm Kings, "but seriously—mean and low down, pretty or funky, driving or lyrical, but always for real. As we said in those days—there was no higher praise—*they played like niggers.*"

Black musicians borrowed licks from white composers; black composers listened to Tin Pan Alley pop and European songs, stole from them, and reworked their styles—if they were any good. But they felt they owned the center of the music, the hot style that denoted true individual expression. The question Henderson was asking, without asking it, was: Can black feeling be passed on, outside the race? Like those slave owners who hid their Bibles, some blacks feared giving whites access to this sourcebook of black life. Teagarden and the most talented white musicians were cultural cousins of the white slaves: they caused black artists and fans to suddenly see themselves in white people.

This doubt caused the occasional 1920s and 1930s showdowns between white and black bands to become tense with something more than professional competition. When the white Jean Goldkette Recording Orchestra out of Detroit made its first appearance in New York in the late 1920s, the band's reputation for tearing up anyone that came in its path preceded it. The musicians faced off against the brilliant Fletcher Henderson orchestra, then *the* band in Manhattan. Before the show, as the crowd milled around and a swell of anticipation grew, Henderson trumpeter Rex Stewart could take it no longer; he leaned forward and tapped the great saxophonist Coleman Hawkins on the shoulder and asked the dreaded question. What if those "Johnny come latelies from out there in the sticks" (Stewart's phrase), these "lil' ol' white boys from out there where all that corn grows" (Hawkins's phrase, pun intended) came into *their* town and kicked *their* black asses in *their* own club? It would not only be a personal humiliation for the Henderson players but, somehow, a setback for the race. Hawkins only laughed. Henderson's arrangements were cut in glass, the band was hungry and sharp, and, besides, it was impossible—genetically impossible was what Hawkins implied—for white boys to surpass a serious black band in hot dance music. "Ain't got nothin' to say to me" was his final statement.

Of course, Goldkette all but demolished Henderson's band that night, playing encore after encore to an enraptured crowd. The black musicians crawled onstage afterwards, knowing that they had lost. It was a fairly rare event; black bands most often outplayed their white competitors. But Henderson's musicians were uncertain how to feel about the night, beyond being struck by a kind of vertigo. "[The Goldkette band] wasn't just great," said black musician Benny Carter. "It was *frightening*."[19]

It's right to be literal-minded, just for a moment, and ask: But what did jazz do for race relations *really*? Crudely stated, isn't it possible that among the crowds at various lynchings in the 1920s were numbers of people fresh from a Paul Whiteman concert the night before? Certainly, a generation later, some of the teenagers who shouted "Niggers, go home" at blacks trying to enroll at Little Rock high schools must have been hard-core Little Richard fans. To be true to both eras, the answer has to be yes. Was the Jazz Age's greatest writer, F. Scott Fitzgerald, capable of rasping at his black servant "Nigger," as Hemingway recalls him doing during one drunken dinner at home? He was. But in looking at *The Great Gatsby*, his masterpiece of the 1920s, one remembers that Fitzgerald places in Tom Buchanan's hands a white supremacy manifesto called *The Rise of the Colored Empires* as a token of his villain's backwardness and emotional coarseness. Was it placed there, in a sense, by jazz, which represented the spirit of the age that Buchanan despised? It is the likeliest suspect. Extending the search to a worldwide audience, was Philip Larkin capable of writing to (writing *to*, intimately, not about) the New Orleans saxophonist Sidney Bechet, these lines:

> On me your voice falls as they say love should
> Like an enormous yes.

and yet to sprinkle his diaries with diatribes against "niggers" and "darkies"? He was. All of which is to say: Jazz completely transformed a small number of whites and created an emotional infrastructure for future conversions. Elsewhere, its effects were mercurial, fractal, and incomplete. It acted as an undertow pulling fans and musicians toward a realization of a complex black humanity, while only barely rippling the surface of 1920s and 1930s race relations.

Jazz's effect on American society was essentially psychological and covert, but there were some legitimate social "firsts." Benny Goodman hired vibraphonist Lionel Hampton and pianist Teddy Wilson to play in his special between-sets combo (not in the full orchestra) and took them on tours through the South; this required courage, and Goodman, Hampton, and Wilson provided it. They occasionally encountered resistance, but the iron-willed Goodman countered it by refusing to play if the black musicians did not get fair treatment. Goodman's swing band was so rabidly popular that he could publicly blackmail racist sheriffs and promoters. Black groups had it harder. The entertainer Tom Fletcher remembered performing with musicians in little towns scattered throughout the South. The sight of well-dressed, unfamiliar blacks on local byways would trigger such atavistic hostility in white townspeople that the performers devised a musical strategy to cope. Traveling in their own private Pullman car, they would park at a railroad siding near the club where they were playing, dress in their costumes, and tune their instruments. Once they were ready, they'd step off the Pullman; as their feet hit the ground, the musicians would launch into "Dixie."[20] The music instantly cloaked these strange blacks in convincing good-nigger disguise; whites would smile and cheer them on, and the troupe would invariably march to the theater without incident. There, they could play jazz. But after the show and on the way back to the siding, the troupe would fall back into the Confederate anthem. Jazz had power, but not limitless power; on Alabama back roads, it was "Dixie" or nothing.

It was as if that area of the American mind that controlled racial under-standing in the white mind, where images of dumb or monstrous Negroes ran free, was spurred to a kind of freakish growth; the con-nections grew more complex; the images of the black American grew brighter and truer; synapses shot out to connect these new capabilities with pleasure, spirit, intelligence. For blacks, jazz was evidence that they were not only master Americans but that some of their life force had seeped across the color line, and more was being stolen nightly by young white men at Chicago clubs, who were listening their way into another life. And yet it was all done with hardly a whisper of the actual words "black" or "white," done with a kind of nonchalance that spoke of an elaborate ruse that animated those rare late-night sessions when black and white musicians gathered in after-hours spots to play as they felt. We will pretend that meeting up late at night in empty clubs is perfectly natural. We will not state the reason for the late hour or the locked door, the sharp look of the cop at a white on a Harlem street at three in the morning. We will play as if we were away in some other land, as we all the while play its history until dawn.

Dorothy Dandridge and Stuart Whitman in
The Decks Ran Red, 1958. The actress's final ambition
was to be a living symbol of the connection between the
races. Curiously idealistic and doomed, she is the most
intense of the black "firsts" who infiltrated white society.
*Courtesy of the Photographs and Prints Division, Schomburg Center
for Research in Black Culture, The New York Public Library,
Astor, Lenox and Tilden Foundations.*

7

VICARIOUS LIVES:
THE BLACK FIRSTS

THE MODERN ERA of the black "first" began in 1908, peaked at mid-century, and rolls on to the present day, diminished but not yet dead. In one hundred years, the entries have added up: first Negro heavyweight champion (Jack Johnson, 1908), Negro Othello on Broadway (Paul Robeson, 1943), colored man in major league baseball (Jackie Robinson, 1947), colored man with his own TV show (Nat King Cole, 1956), black mayor of Chicago (Harold Washington, 1983), African-American president of an Ivy League university (Ruth Simmons, Brown, 2000). In its heyday, new additions were once triumphantly announced in *Jet* and *Ebony* and respectfully noted in the back pages of the New York *Times*; now they are most often checked off sub rosa, mentioned in passing, if at all, a vestigial rite left over from the last century. The final entry will presumably be marked down the day Americans elect their first black president, and then, perhaps, the ledger will be closed.

How do these pioneers fit into the story of cultural integration? For historians, they play a small role. The firsts advanced hesitantly across a landscape that was being remade beneath their feet by tectonic forces: by continued migration to the North and to southern cities; by the Cold War's heightening of the race issue and the court battles to end Jim Crow; by international opinion, economic necessity, and, of course, war. Transient symbols, these "first" figures get little respect. And yet, they remain rather persistent in the national memory. Jesse Owens and Lena Horne are resurrected, rather sadly, every black history month, on Burger King placemats and in Chevrolet commercials with James Earl Jones voice-overs. They also live on in more vivid ways: 1950s actress Dorothy Dandridge was the latest to get the heroine treatment in a movie starring and produced by Halle Berry (who beat out other actresses clamoring to film the actress's life, and who later became a pioneer in her own right by becoming the first black woman to win the Academy Award as a lead actress). In interviews, Berry spoke of how she saw her own dilemma clearly in Dandridge's troubled life.

In many respects, these figures were the main public players in American racial life before the civil rights era began, and we should attempt to understand what they meant to the times, especially to black Americans, whose stand-ins and explorers they were. Here we look briefly at seven of the most interesting (Jack Johnson, Marian Anderson, Joe Louis, Paul Robeson, Jackie Robinson, Lena Horne, and Dorothy Dandridge) and regard them not as pure historical figures, but as mythological ones. If jazz centered on a black stance communicated through notes, the phenomenon of the racial pioneer centered on individuals as portents and models: their bodies, their "attitudes," and their talents— both human and superhuman. They were extravagantly loved and attacked and studied, their every movement analyzed as the Greeks did the rages of Zeus or Aphrodite.

Because they originated from the lowest strata of American society, invisible if not inexplicable to white Americans, the sudden appearance of these figures connoted more than just ordinary bootstrapping and good luck; they were often described as touched by the divine. "You have been the voice of man," wrote the poet Pablo Neruda about Paul Robeson. "The song of the germinating earth, and the movement of nature." When Universal Pictures signed black actor James B. Lowe to a contract in 1927, the press release noted:

Lowe has made history. A history that reflects only credit to the Negro race, not only because he has given the "Uncle Tom" character a new slant, but because of his exemplary conduct with the Universal company. They look upon Lowe at the studio as a living black god. . . . Those who are religious say that a heavenly power brought him to Universal.[1]

Louise Beavers, who played the cook in the 1934 tearjerker "Imitation of Life," got the same treatment: her studio called her a "black angel." And in movies ranging from *To Kill a Mockingbird* to *Men of Honor*, black actors have been given roles that displayed what film historian Donald Bogle referred to as "a superhuman humaneness," as being above such things as greed, envy, and normal emotions. The compliment cut two ways: these stars were regarded as touched by the divine, but only because they had breathed life into a race whose humanity was in question.

Blacks often referred to their geniuses in similar terms, but with a difference. At Marian Anderson's memorial service in Philadelphia, the preacher Reverend Gregory L. Wallace spoke: "Back in the first decades of this century, the members of this church saw in Marian Anderson the gifts of God. They saw in her what others had seen in Beethoven and Shakespeare and perhaps even Michelangelo." The boxer Joe Louis had an even more explicit power; the famous story of the death-row convict who, when the gas chamber jets were turned on during his execution, whispered, "Save me, Joe Louis," is hardly an exaggeration of his status. For blacks, Louis and the others displayed the divine in all black people. For many whites, it was the *contrast* that startled.

Before the pioneers, prominent Negroes—such as Du Bois and Booker T. Washington and Frederick Douglass—had mostly been heads of black organizations, but in the white American imagination they represented a separate subcolony. They spoke for black people, wrote for black newspapers, headed black organizations, and remained safely apart. But the pioneers were entering mainstream America: Jack Johnson and Joe Louis not only became heavyweight champions, they waded through white opponents to do it and mixed in white society afterward. They were seen as test cases arranged not only to showcase black talent and character (two things the majority of white Americans doubted blacks possessed), but to introduce white America to people of color who were un-alien. An early showbiz trick was to introduce the firsts as the darker equivalent of an established star: Lena Horne was "the café au-lait Hedy Lamarr"; Negro cinema's leading man Lorenzo Tucker was "the black Valentino" and later, in the sound era, "the colored William Powell"; the razor-tongued Bee Freeman was "the sepia Mae West." It wasn't just marketing; it was a sleight-of-hand way of making black performers seem familiar. In marketing this new thing, one had to begin somewhere.

The original first requires a look back to the prejazz era, when the country's attitudes were still dominated by Darwinian notions of natural science and black inferiority. Those ideas faced a real-world test when the black heavyweight Jack Johnson (who had won the title in a widely ignored Australian match two years before) faced off against the white ex-champion Jim Jeffries on July 4, 1910. The match had obsessed the country for months: most whites believed that their supremacy would be confirmed, while blacks hoped for the first great racial upset. Some Negroes bet their life savings (at 10-to-6 odds against Johnson) that their man would prevail: one employee of the Santa Fe Railroad even wagered ten years of his labor against $500, in effect selling himself as chattel if Johnson lost.[2] Newspapers trotted out freshly minted nightmare scenarios. The San Francisco *Examiner* predicted the "spirit of Caesar in Jeff ought to whip the Barbarian": the Chicago *Daily News* said white civilization would crumble if he didn't, while the *Independent* magazine warned the state of Nevada, which was hosting the fight, that it "served the devil" by allowing the contest. But despite misgivings in mainstream America (especially the South) about giving blacks a shot at a victory, a certain insatiable curiosity drove the fight. The country simply *wanted to know*, to have the confrontation between black and white take place in the most basic and primal way. Commercially, it was too lucrative to ban; psychologically, it was too inevitable.

Twenty thousand spectators showed up at ringside and, given that the fight took place before radio, blacks and whites massed anywhere there was a wire service reporting the results. Thirty thousand people swarmed outside the offices of the New York *Times*, and more heard the results in ballparks, auditoriums, and public halls. Some crowds were segregated: blacks gathered in an assembly room at Tuskegee, while the Vanderbilts and their all-white guests rented out a private club in Long Island. For all of them, life was temporarily transferred to a hot canvas in Reno.

When Johnson knocked out an overmatched Jeffries in the fifteenth round, the country promptly went berserk. Imagine Super Bowl riots in every major American city, except that they were not about a team that had either won or been completely humiliated, but one's ancestry and social position. Blacks who had held church prayer sessions throughout the fight broke into shouts. Others marched through the streets of American cities and towns taunting whites, chugging liquor, and whooping it up. "Blacks found more reasons to celebrate," wrote Al-Tony Gilmore in his study of Johnson, "than at any other time since the issuing of the Emancipation Proclamation." Whites reacted predictably. Violence soon followed in "virtually every city and town in the U.S.," leaving eight people dead and thousands injured. It was as if individual blacks and whites were reenacting the fight for themselves, over and over again from coast to coast, with knives, bats, or bare fists—and with blacks paying the cost more often than not.

The win placed Johnson in the middle of American society; most blacks adored him, most whites feared and were disturbed by him. Bold and extravagant by nature, Johnson was not about to be anyone's role model, however: in modern parlance, he was gangsta, and proudly gangsta (Gilmore's biography is entitled *Bad Nigger!*). Johnson drove and crashed a succession of high-performance cars, studded his shirtfronts with diamonds, dated and married white women, flashed fist-sized wads of thousand-dollar bills, and disdained white authority to its face. During workouts, he began wrapping his penis in a gauze bandage underneath his boxing trunks, to intimidate his white opponents. Far from seeking to ameliorate black male stereotypes, the fighter wanted to *heighten* them.

This was the essence of Johnson. When he brutalized Jeffries, it was not a metaphor: blacks felt the sting of his leather on the white man's face, felt Johnson's right whipping across Jeffries's eyes. They lived intensely through him, both in the ring and out. The boxer recalled seeing one Negro spectator in the audience at one of his fights imitate his every hook and jab to his white opponent's face; so engrossed was the man that, after Johnson threw one roundhouse, his imitator threw the same punch, lost his balance, and fell off his perch. Johnson was the first Negro gladiator, his body a place of a million black dreams. And he is the first to make clear the essential role of the black pioneer: to do for the ordinary black man or woman what that person could never dream of doing himself.

The fighter and the great white hopes that he regularly KO'd with disdain channeled the nascent American taste for celebrity into something larger: a tradition of representative men and women who would improvise racial dramas. One observer, Rev. Reverdy Ransom, saw Johnson-Jeffries as the first of many contests:

> *The black singer is coming with his song, the poet with his dreams, the sculptor with his conception of some form of beauty and of awe . . . and the scholar with his truth. . . . The greatest marathon race of the ages is about to begin between the white race and the darker races of mankind.*[3]

It was the singer and actor Paul Robeson and the contralto Marian Anderson who were called on to redeem the pioneer role. Johnson had entered the society through a brutal sport populated by the most economically desperate groups in America—Irish, Jews, Italians, Negroes. This time Broadway and concert halls would be the proving ground. Robeson and Anderson were Du Bois's Talented Tenth strategy in action.

Anderson began her career in earnest in the 1920s and by the time the Daughters of the American Revolution denied her permission to play Washington's Constitution Hall in 1939, she was well known in the best circles. Anderson took her concert to the Lincoln Memorial, an event that would make her a household name. The confrontation was heavily symbolic: the DAR held the line for conservative purity, while the white liberal establishment, led by Eleanor Roosevelt, was appalled by the racial affront to fair play and so engineered the concert at the Lincoln Memorial, the premier symbol of black suffering and white nobility. Roosevelt cabinet member Harold Ickes spoke for those liberal elites, and in his speech struck the note that would be so familiar to all the pioneers. They were idols who were paragons of the race, but they were somehow not really *of* the race. "Genius, like justice, is blind," Ickes said. "She has endowed Marian Anderson with such voice as lifts any individual above his fellows, as is a matter of exultant pride to any race." But then Ickes went further and cast Anderson as a kind of love-child fathered by Thomas Jefferson and Abraham Lincoln:

> *For genius has touched with the top of her wing this woman, who, if it had not been for the great mind of Jefferson, if it had not been for the great heart of Lincoln, would not be able to stand among us a free individual today in a free land. . . . And so it is fitting that Marian Anderson should raise her voice in tribute to the noble Lincoln, whom mankind will ever honor.[4]*

Walter White must have winced at that. A tough and brilliant NAACP leader, he had worked behind the scenes to turn the concert into a protest against segregation. White saw the concert as the strategic maneuver it was; but he also knew the significance for the masses Anderson had just been told she had risen above. For White, the response of the common man was illustrated by one "slender black girl" he spotted in the audience:

> *[She was] dressed in somewhat too garishly hued Easter finery. Hers was not the face of one who had been the beneficiary of much education or opportunity. Her hands were particularly noticeable as she thrust them forward and upward, trying desperately, though she was some distance away from Miss Anderson, to touch the singer. . . . Tears stream down the girl's dark face. Her hat was askew, but in her eyes flamed hope bordering on ecstasy.[5]*

This was not just pride or a hysterical reaction to celebrity. Women like Anderson with her deep black skin tone, her ramrod-straight posture and impeccable clothing, must have been somewhat familiar to the girl. There were many such women in the segregated black neighborhoods of D.C., and the local churches had their own remarkable singers who could approximate Anderson's power. But had the girl seen Anderson sing in some raggedy storefront church, her reaction would probably have been much different. For here the singer's rightful place had been fully recognized, and that, along with her talent, was a cause for wonder. Anderson was great not only in her own right but because she had elicited the appropriate response—*respect*—from the hard world around her.

In her journey from Philadelphia to the world stage, Anderson had help from both whites and blacks interested in racial progress. She was nurtured and promoted by a circle of prominent black Philadelphians, who took up collections for her education, gave her career advice, fought for access to concert halls, and steered her toward the proper repertoire. The tradition would continue with other singers, such as Lena Horne. The great care taken in their management shows how these high-toned singers were the carefully chosen representatives of the race. No one ever took up a collection for, say, Billie Holiday; nor did Holiday ever have her mother invited to the White House, as Anderson's was. Both the NAACP and the Roosevelts were interested in, as Horne puts it, those who "represented quality."[6] Her success was a carefully plotted biracial project.

The singer conquered a worldwide audience, and in some foreign places she was able to see what so few blacks, mired in ghettos or on farms, were able to realize: people the world over felt intimately connected to the sensibility of black Americans. With her Negro spirituals, Anderson became a kind of symbol for the despised and dispossessed everywhere. In the Soviet Union, the poorer members of the audience would abandon their seats near the rafters, rush to the stage, pound their fists on the wooden planks, and beg her to sing the Negro songs, whose language they did not understand but whose message they clearly did. "Deep voices were roaring in Russian accents, 'Deep River,' and 'Heaven, Heaven,'" Anderson remembered. "It was disconcerting for a few moments, but how could one resist such enthusiasm?"[7] What she didn't know was that Stalin's purges had just commenced.

Anderson was one of the first public explorers blacks sent out into the larger world, and her experience as a racial representative was largely positive. Protected by powerful Americans of both races, she brought the American black to the world stage, and there she received some startling information from people from east to west: Your people are not unique in the world; your suffering is deep but rather commonplace. But your response—the toughness and the almost irrational hopefulness embedded in the black spiritual—is something new. This was the exact reversal of what Anderson and her entourage expected. It was not her German and French repertoire that made her an international figure; it was the slave songs.

The singer also fulfilled the second role of the firsts: exploration. White racial sentiment was mercurial. Nobody could predict what the particular combination of elements (besides black interest in a white woman, which in the South was an automatic riot-starter) would send Caucasians into a rage. Some things seemed surefire triggers but failed to elicit a murmur, while others, such as Emmett Till's alleged whistle at a white woman, resulted in murder. When Anderson decided to bring a white European pianist, Kosti Vehanen, to accompany her on an American tour, insiders predicted disaster. A black woman and a white man together onstage? "You won't be able to give her away," one concert promoter told Anderson's manager. In fact, the move caused "hardly a ripple of comment" in both black and white newspapers: no one demanded a refund, and the reviews were glowing. What had allowed this to happen? The fact that Vehanen replaced a black man, not the reverse? Vehanen's courtly manner, his graying hair? Nobody knew. But each tiny foray mapped out a new piece of American territory: people began to see where the treacherous areas lay.

Paul Robeson would follow Anderson to Moscow and elsewhere. But first he took America. Robeson arrived on the scene in the early 1920s, seemingly handmade for the task. His list of talents grew until it bordered on the embarrassing: star athlete in high school and college; the highest ever score in the Rutgers scholarship competition; world-acclaimed singer; the first black man to play *Othello* on Broadway; a linguist of casual brilliance. Born into a preacher's family, he was simply never indoctrinated into black self-doubt, as his biographer Martin Duberman wrote:

> *He had never learned as a youngster, as had almost all black Americans, to deal in limited expectations; treated in his own family like a god, he had met in the outside world far fewer institutional humiliations than afflict most blacks attempting to make their way.[8]*

The young Robeson acted naturally with whites; he had little self-doubt or any of Du Bois's almost maniacal need to crush his fairer-skinned competitors. It was as if he had been born and raised on another planet and then set down in Princeton, New Jersey, where he grew up. Robeson carried himself like someone who expected to be respected and admired and, eventually, he was—to a remarkable degree. This happened early: In 1916, when he was a junior at Rutgers, white players on the West Virginia football team that faced off against Robeson's side were determined to punish him for daring to take the field against them. One player whispered, "Don't you so much as touch me, you black dog, or I'll cut your heart out." In a preview of the physical hazing that Jackie Robinson would face, Robeson stoically played and scored touchdowns through the pile-ons, the vicious tackles, the spikes raking his legs and, without saying a word in retaliation, led Rutgers to a win. After the game, every West Virginia player lined up to shake his hand. Their coach exclaimed: "Guts! He had nothing else but! Why that colored boy's legs were so gashed and bruised that his skin peeled off when he removed his stockings."[9]

After college, Robeson turned to the stage. Of his 1943 *Othello*, *Variety*'s critic wrote that "no white man should ever dare presume" to play the part again.[10] But it wasn't his acting that made him stand out; other Negro actors such as the brilliant Charles Gilpin were better interpreters of the role (Robeson tended toward stiff declamation). It was, for lack of a better word, Robeson's *aura* that struck people: his cut-from-obsidian physique, first of all, that thrilled white women and more than a few white men (in theatrical circles especially); his deep bass voice, his serene confidence untouched by the desire to please; his regal bearing. At a time when the black individual was regarded, as one writer said in 1939, as "a clown, a buffoon, a gangling idiot or a superstitious fool,"[11] Robeson was psychologically whole, undeformed, magnificent, and black.

Those early stage performances were not put down on film and are lost to us, but the productions' stills are startling in themselves, mostly because Robeson isn't smiling. This alone separates him from the black showbiz tradition up to that point: black male personalities from minstrely onward strained to show their teeth in a display of harmlessness. Even Louis Armstrong flashed a minstrel smile, and Duke Ellington curled his lips suggestively. In his pictures, Robeson has let the mask fall completely and looked the viewer in the eye without anger or fear. He has leapt ahead two full generations.

Robeson's triumphs on Broadway and in the concert halls, where he combined folk songs with Negro spirituals, made his name in cultural circles, but it was his left-leaning political stance that made him known around the world and infamous at home. The singer exhausted himself singing for crowds in Moscow; he learned smatterings of Slavic languages so that he could sing local folk songs to those audiences. Robeson was the super-Negro; when progressives needed a black man to speak for the race, they called him. Duberman captures the "whirlwind" that Robeson lived in during the 1930s and 1940s. "Would Robeson sit for a portrait, read a script, listen to a song, contribute an essay, issue a statement, sign a petition, meet a delegation, join a rally, support a strike, protest an outrage, declare, decry, affirm, affiliate?"[12] He almost never said no.

Robeson's mistake was that he believed his notices. He felt he belonged to the world and would be instrumental in its improvement. In reality, he was an odd character: a selfless man who was enchanted with his own power to effect change, a man whose closest relationship was to his beloved father. He barely noticed his own son, who starved for his attention all his life; Robeson left the boy in others' care for years at a time. "The people" were vitally important to him, but individuals such as peers, lovers, and his long-suffering wife Essie often felt ignored, as if Robeson considered himself above mere friendship or marriage. Robeson permitted himself this because he truly believed that his talents had marked him as an epitome. One more trip, one more speech, one more concert, one more marshaling of his clearly God-given talents, one more conversation would break the illusion of black inferiority once and for all, would tip the world into a realization of what was a maddeningly simple truth: race is a fiction.

The singer was loved extravagantly. Monarchs called him friend; white women threw themselves at him and he gathered them in. One actress playing Desdemona to Robeson's Othello recalls waiting in the wings for their cues. Just before they were to go onstage, Robeson reached over and grabbed her private parts with his massive hand. It was the gesture of sexual ownership, an emperor's privilege—Robeson *was* Othello! This bit of sexual harassment is important because Robeson did it, as he did everything, not only for himself but, in a way, for the race. He was one of the few black males alive who could treat a white woman like that and not get lynched. (The actress was startled, but happily relented and began an affair with her co-star.) And that was the point, not some fetish for the forbidden white women, though that surely played a part. Robeson dared to do it because his brother could not even think of doing it. The boldness and the deliberate crossing of boundaries is what counted; Robeson dared the white fates to punish him. But he would respect no boundary, and that tendency, which he displayed his whole life, created small freedoms for the black imagination.

And so it was right that Robeson became famous through the Shakespearean roles that minstrel performers dreamed, in their cups, of playing: He had grown into the playwright's towering characters and saw nothing he couldn't conquer. "The country is really mine," Robeson wrote his wife in 1932 after returning to the United States, and the statement is doubly meaningful: he belongs to America, and America belongs to him. "And strange I like it again and deeply."[13]

In the end, Robeson naively thought that his personal success around the world had proved that barriers could be overcome by force of will. Racism was only a component in the worldwide oppression of the poor and weak, and socialism was the only way out. But he had misread things: Stalin turned out to be a killer (a fact Robeson shamefully ignored for far too long); in the mid-1950s Robeson was savagely attacked at home as a red; and the burgeoning civil rights movement avoided him. When he saw that he had misjudged the country and its ability to transform itself, he collapsed into mental illness. Robeson wrote to a friend in 1964 that he had failed; he had been "unable to bring forth the victory."[14]

Paranoia and psychotic trances blurred the last years of his life; he spent most of them insensible to the world. And how his delusions traced his broken dreams! Once famously gregarious, he became a recluse, terrified of meeting people because he thought they would "expect" something of him. He convinced himself there was an underlying structure to all of the world's languages, a code that indicated common ways of thinking, and for years sought to unlock their secret unities. Whatever the underlying chemical and genetic susceptibilities to mental illness, Robeson's collapse followed the pattern of his life. When the code failed to turn up, he attempted suicide.

No major figure of the time invested more in his race, in psychic terms, than Paul Robeson. He was the story of the black first writ large: the awesomely gifted man who finds that his gifts are inadequate. The story is straight out of a Greek parable, of course, with Robeson as the demigod who was granted everything in life except what he most wanted: the ability to share his rewards with the people he had been raised above. He was a colossus who was cut up and hobbled by the times, but the very dimensions of his daring and of his personal disaster changed what both races imagined was possible for the Negro. Under Robeson's image in the pantheon of firsts, one word should be written: Hubris.

Before and just after World War II, sports became the central forum for the drama of the firsts. Olympic stars who captured the headlines and then faded away—such as Althea Gibson and Jesse Owens—were paired with epic figures such as Joe Louis and Jackie Robinson. Louis followed Robeson into the society: his big fights, his every word and expression, were studied like the tea leaves of Chinese emperors. Like Anderson, he was backed by prominent blacks, especially his manager John Roxborough, who molded the fighter into the anti–Jack Johnson by setting out a strict set of rules: no taunting his white opponents, no going to nightclubs alone, no white girlfriends. Roxborough was hewing to the silent pact between the black middle class and the white ruling class; there would be chances given only to those who were beyond reproach in matters of racial etiquette.

At first, Louis was portrayed as most aggressive black fighters were: as a jungle-bred killer. Before Louis's 1935 bout with Max Baer, one sportswriter for the New York *Daily News* summed him up this way:

> *Louis, the magnificent animal. He lives like an animal, untouched by externals. He eats. He sleeps. He fights. He is as tawny as an animal and he has an animal's concentration on his prey. Eyes, nostrils, mouth, all just forward to the prey. . . . He enters the arena with his keepers, and they soothe and fondle him and stroke him and whisper to him and then unleash him.*

This was standard description, if heightened by the writer's Poe-like imagery. Louis began his professional life as a man-animal, but over the course of two decades, he became a beloved figure. His modesty in the ring (head down after every thrashing of an opponent), his service in World War II, and his quiet dignity worked on white America. Beating Hitler's favorite fighter, Max Schmeling, was a national event. But the moment when he peaked as a transformative black hero was on the night of his 1951 defeat to Rocky Marciano, who knocked him through the ropes with a vicious right hand. After the fight, Marciano rushed to Louis's dressing room in tears, saying over and over, "I'm sorry, Joe, I'm sorry." It was one of the few times that a white person publicly acknowledged that a black individual had become somehow more intrinsic to the life of the nation than he was.

Louis proved that the firsts could not only map the American landscape, but alter it. Louis gave whites who were perhaps not brave enough to make friends with ordinary blacks the illusion of knowing one; and after observing him under the most grueling physical and psychological stresses, that illusion had become mostly real. That was the gift of the boxing ring, which does not tolerate fakes for long. The last stop in Louis's long career, as a greeter in the Las Vegas casinos, gives an estimate of his final position in the culture. Gangsters do not extend their affection to the untested; Joe Louis had converted the hard-core.

During World War II, blacks grew more active and their cause grew in resonance. The war was to bring major changes in the relations of blacks and whites in the workplace and in housing. Short on labor, factory owners hired black workers by the thousands and put them on the assembly line next to whites, while a tiny minority of interracial military units were actually formed during the war. White soldiers initially opposed the experiment: a 1942 Air Force survey found that 65 percent of white servicemen thought blacks should be allowed to serve; the overwhelming majority, however (75 percent of northerners, 86 percent of southerners), demanded they serve in segregated units. Postwar surveys found those numbers had hardly budged. Such sentiment was at least one of the key stated reasons for resistance to integration. But the results for those units to which Negro platoons *were* attached are startling: over 80 percent of white soldiers who had served with Negroes thought those units had fought very well in combat (only

1 percent gave them an unfavorable review); 73 percent of the officers thought that black and white GIs had got along very well; and over 70 percent of officers and NCOs came away from the experiment favoring integrated units. The most positive responses were among those white soldiers who had the closest contact with their black peers. As historian Neil Wynn writes, the numbers proved that "experience of integration in wartime could bring radical changes in men's feelings." The situation was duplicated at home: Before the war 47.8 percent of workers at a West Coast airplane factory opposed the hiring of blacks. But after necessity forced management's hand, the black workers were integrated into the factory, and by 1944, protests were "weak and infrequent." White workers went on strike elsewhere to protest the hiring of black laborers, but when dealt with firmly, they returned to the job and friction often gave way to harmony.

Still, sharing a factory floor rarely led to significant relationships between workers of different colors. For that, there were only the firsts.

In terms of the pioneers, the case of Jackie Robinson bisects the century into before and after. He became the archetypal first: whenever a black first followed him in another area of society, he or she became "the Jackie Robinson" of that world. Jack Johnson's value was to make black rage visible; Robinson's, in another era, was to remake it.

His entry into the major leagues was explicitly mythic. Robinson was a lowly but talented man chosen for a test that would strain his body and mind to the breaking point: alone, he was sent out against enemies, in full public view, where his humiliation and failure would be clear. Robeson and Anderson had been allowed into polite musical and theatrical circles, and Louis had thrived in a sport, boxing, that was seen as the escape hatch for semisavage lower classes. But Robinson entered the cool, intellectual game that was at the center of American sports life. That was an altogether different matter. And as in all worthwhile myths, Robinson carried within him both the chrysalis of possible greatness and a secret flaw: not his baseball skills, which were formidable, but his anger. Throughout his life, Robinson had struck back at anybody who crossed him—white athletes, black athletes, white cops, even the Army, where he was nearly court-martialed for disobeying a driver's order to sit in the back of the bus. Even in old newsreels, his bursts of temper on the ball field are still impressive.

The facts of his time in baseball are so well known that they do not need repeating here: Subject to intense pressure on and off the field, Robinson won the first Rookie of the Year award, changed the way players ran the bases, and generally proved himself out. He was the first pioneer to be almost as important to decent-hearted whites as he was to blacks. But one feels at a loss to say anything new about Robinson's achievement. There have been so many heartfelt tributes to him that another is unnecessary, and an edgy, contrarian reappraisal is hardly warranted. The "secret" Jackie Robinson probably does not exist; neither does his dark side. But his experience in baseball did shape the national psyche, for there is something about sports that even most male bigots consider sacred. Many American men, especially, regard violations of the National Baseball League rulebook with more alarm than they would breaches of the Constitution. Jack Johnson and Joe Louis were often caricatured and attacked outside the ring, but sportswriters most often gave them their due as athletes and mocked the skills of their white opponents. Nor were there any accusations of referees or judges throwing a fight because of the boxer's color. Robinson often felt the only place he could relax was on the diamond, where geometry and physics ruled and fair play was enforced. In a sense, it was the only place he was free.

The exception of sports often leads Americans to regard it sentimentally; it is the Olympian arena, where, at least ideally, politics and history are forgotten, and talent rules. It allows things that could not happen off the field: the famous moment when Pee Wee Reese put his arm around Jackie Robinson's shoulder in front of a hostile crowd, for instance. But one cannot ignore the feeling that the sports world is also really a peaceful simulacrum of true violence. The slashing of Robeson's legs, the brutality Louis took and delivered, the spiking of Jackie Robinson, were references to events outside the arena, mock lynchings, if you will, or ritual woundings that satisfied a certain need in the audience. Especially for men, only in this kind of heightened atmosphere can the appropriate emotional pitch, for either violence or reconciliation, be reached.

This filters throughout the culture. The union of black and white men in situations involving danger or simulated danger is a recurring image in American culture, from war movies to convict flicks such as *The Defiant Ones* to football elegies such as *Brian's Song*, in which a white-athlete-dying-young passes his spirit to the young Gale Sayers. (It remains one of the only movies at which it is permissible for men to cry.) It is no accident that the leading interracial genre in Hollywood is the cop drama that joins black and white actors as buddies; Sidney Poitier and Rod Steiger kicked it off in 1967 in the masterpiece of the genre, *In the Heat of the Night,* which centers around a murder investigation and the brooding violence of a small southern town.

The black hand grasping the white hand after the enemy has been shot and killed, or as one of them is dying, remind us of the atavistic roots of racial feeling that lie just beneath the surface of the games the pioneers played. Robinson, alone on the field with half the crowd baying for his blood, certainly would have understood that. His every move was a small-scale alternative to larger events. The crowd understood that the famous temper that Robinson contained on the field was not only personal: in those silenced outbursts were also contained riots that never occurred, cities that never burned, when perhaps they ought to have.

Robinson and the other pioneers were uncannily successful in drawing out hidden emotion; they experienced bewildering amounts of both anger and love, rushing in at them from odd vectors at unpredictable times. Take an example from showbiz, concerning Nat King Cole. Cole was the epitome of postwar black cool. With his famous conked hairdo, sleepy-time eyes, and that voice, he exuded a strong, if buttoned-down, sex appeal. Studiously avoiding the whisper of confrontation on the segregation issue, Cole still decided to play an interracial concert in Birmingham in 1956. It was a relatively small, but courageous, first: the singer and his band were performing onstage with an eighteen-piece white orchestra, separated by a thin curtain. The event had brought out Birmingham's progressive elites; even the mayor was there. But so were people unhappy with the breakthrough the concert represented. Midway into the show—during a treacly number called "Little Girl"—at the prearranged signal (a wolf howl) five white men burst from the crowd and rushed the stage.

Fans? Assassins? Not quite. They were members of the racist

White Citizen Council who were planning to *kidnap* Cole and hold him for undisclosed, nefarious purposes in the forests outside Birmingham. One of the gang tackled Cole by the leg and attempted to drag him off while the others battled cops who had rushed to protect the singer. There was Cole, dressed in a $3000 suit, playing ultrasophisticated pop for a respectable audience, and suddenly he had a mountain man reeking of whiskey attempting to drag him off to a cabin. It was an utterly American tableau and the crowd looked on, rapt with horror. When policemen pulled the men away and rescued Cole, taking him backstage, the mayor came and expressed his embarrassment and the crowd shouted for a chance to apologize to him. (Cole's frantic wife in L.A., on hearing about the attack, even called Frank Sinatra, who told her, "Don't worry, baby. We'll get him out of there." The Mob was now involved in battling the mob.) Nevertheless, Cole spent a sleepless night first at the theater (outside, a silent black crowd watched over him) and then at a local hotel. He and the band rushed to the airport at first light.

But they had not escaped the white faces yet. Birmingham came to the airport, not to attack, but to repent. "That morning was really scary," remembered black band member Lee Young. "It was real foggy. And now the plane couldn't get out. And so many people came there, all white, came there to the airport in the fog, apologizing." Cole just wanted out of the city, but the whites kept arriving, and they wouldn't let the plane leave until he had recognized their grief. "They kept coming, a mob of them, more than fifty all around the plane, shouting that they didn't agree with the hoodlums, and apologizing, apologizing. . . ."

Young's recollections sound like nothing more than a scene from a zombie movie, and the experience for the musicians must have been not far off: these pale, inexplicable creatures arriving out of a fog, pressing forward, forward, hands outstretched. *What the hell did they want?* The color of one's skin, so unmysterious to Cole and the other black musicians, worked these people into frenzies. Despite Cole's many white friends and his mansion in a white L.A. neighborhood, there were times when the white heart must have been simply terrifying to him; Cole and the others provoked in it extremes of devotion and hate, sometimes in the same hour. Like figures in the Greek dramas where gods lusted and died, they provided relief from emotions too intense for civil society.

When it came to the female pioneers, Cole's subterranean glamour was abandoned: the women were there to be ogled. The tradition began with Lena Horne. Inventing a role for Dorothy Dandridge and Diahann Carroll after her, Horne was the first socially acceptable black sex object—one that it was permissible for white men to lust after, not only in private but in public. When she first got bookings into swanky white clubs, Horne was advertised as the first black "sex symbol" outside of the all-black stage shows. And she resented it. Performing in nightclubs to largely white audiences, propositioned at every turn, Horne threw up a wall around herself with her cold affect and death-ray stares. She was present, but not available. In that stance we see the first appearance of the black showbiz diva. The stage hauteur, the regal distance, the talent and loneliness, the strength through tragedy, have been adopted by divas from Tina Turner to Whitney Houston to Patti LaBelle (all of whom followed Horne into crossover success). The word "diva," of course, is Latin for "female god" and was originally given to opera singers, but its American pop origins reach back to Horne's desperate attempt to maintain some dignity while being marketed as a chocolate bonbon. She created the type that even white singers, or secretaries, can now inhabit.

Horne didn't want the job of racial hero. After she first went to Hollywood to break into films, she returned to New York in a manic state. After a night of drinking, she ended up crying on the shoulder of the great Kansas City bandleader Count Basie.

> *"I'm not going back there. I can't go back. I'm lonely; I can't see my own people. I don't want to be a movie star . . ." I kept saying.*
>
> *"You've got to go back," [Basie said.] "Nobody's ever had this chance before."*
>
> *"But I don't want it," I sniffled.*
>
> *"No, you've got to go back. They've never had anyone like you." They. The white people.*
>
> *"They have never been given the chance to see a Negro woman as a woman. You've got to give them that chance."*

It was an archetypal moment in any pioneer's life: the moment of doubt just before stepping into the unknown. Horne's dilemma was compounded by the fact that, as the daughter of an aristocratic Brooklyn family, she didn't feel particularly black. "It's almost satire to hear you sing the blues," said Barney Josephson, owner of the interracial Café Society. Horne admitted it was true. She was a freak, but that's what the times demanded.

Horne's situation makes clear another side of the firsts' role: they were often the objects of blacks' secret hatred and not-so-secret envy. A famous bandleader once told Horne that her own people would never accept her. "Only the white people are stupid enough to think there's something to you," he told her. Dandridge would get the same treatment; Robinson was attacked by Amiri Baraka and other black nationalists for being an integrationist poster boy; Nat King Cole was criticized viciously during his career. After the Birmingham attack, he refused to demand integrated audiences wherever he performed, and black anger was visceral. In Harlem, bar owners removed his records from their jukeboxes; his fans smashed their copies on the sidewalks or sent them flying down 125th Street. James Baldwin, who would suffer similar attacks when he was the toast of white literary New York, looked on with guarded sympathy. "Those who do [cross the color line], do so at the grave expense of a double alienation," he wrote. They play-acted for the society, and so lost the respect of their own people, "whose fabled attributes they must either deny or, worse, cheapen and bring to market."

The black community knew it had made a devil's pact with whites. One chosen person was let in to the mainstream. The black masses were then allowed to watch Nat and Jackie in the society pages, in the newsreels, on the screen, as they laughed and triumphed and were feted. It was Lena up there on the screen, but it was the phantom life of the black shopgirl in Cleveland that she was living, at least in the eyes of the Cleveland shopgirl. It wasn't that the shopgirl craved white acceptance, so much as she wanted the potential of full mobility and self-creation that Lena's grand life so clearly demonstrated (never really imagining the torments that came with it). And so when the firsts gave the slightest hint that they had made it to the screen or the society page on their own, and not as stand-ins for those waiting impatiently outside, blacks could respond as if personally betrayed.

If you are looking for deep contact, the films of Dorothy Dandridge are not the place to go. Dandridge was a natural beauty, but, like Robeson, not a natural actor. James Baldwin's cool one-liner about Dandridge in *Carmen Jones* still holds up. "One feels—perhaps one is meant to feel," wrote Baldwin, "that here is a very nice girl making her way in movies by means of a bad-girl part." But Dandridge's rather disastrous life is a different story. For insights into midcentury America, and for moments of vicarious horror, it is unmatched among the biographies of black stars.

Much of Dandridge's unhappiness had to do with being a very beautiful and ambitious woman in the 1940s and 1950s, a woman who had a rotten childhood trying to find a meaningful life in Hollywood, a place that is built for other things. Her dilemma transcended race. You could lift whole passages from the life of Marilyn Monroe or Rita Hayworth, slot them into Dandridge's autobiography, and they would blend seamlessly: missing or cruel fathers, the driving need to be a star, unquenchable emotional needs, relationships with powerful and emotionally clueless men, deep confusion, suicidal thoughts. All three of them—black, Anglo, and Latina, respectively—were sisters underneath the skin. But Dandridge dealt with another factor in her life, a recurring presence that shifted her stars out of their course. "Some people kill themselves with drink, others with overdoses, some with a gun," Dandridge wrote. "A few hurl themselves in front of trains or autos. I hurled myself in front of another white man."

Dandridge's early years were rough. She traveled the Baptist Church chicken circuit, worked relentlessly, didn't know a true home, and was treated with little warmth or understanding. Her racial consciousness, which consisted, really, of a racial fantasy of escape, began early, in an odd vision.

One soft memory returns to me out of that grinding, blurry, abnormal childhood. . . . After I performed, a white man in the audience picked me up and carried me on his shoulders through the crowd and out of the church. . . . I was happy with him, for he was a kind, nice man. He wandered around outside the church, carrying me in some emotion of tenderness.

In later years, Dandridge could not swear whether this event actually happened or whether she had dreamed it. But in any case, whiteness figured prominently in her thinking. It represented the diametric opposite of her own rather tawdry upbringing: power, money, security, normalcy, glamour. Dandridge did not want to become white, but by the time she was a young woman, she began to see herself as "an integrated product": not only physically (her light skin spoke of white ancestors), but emotionally and spiritually. "Contradictory currents flow inside me," she wrote. "They often go in opposite directions at the same time. . . . You have a part of white America in your soul, and a part of black America in your spirit, and they are pulling against each other." She was fascinated by her genetic mix and thought that everything that had happened in her life was connected, "in mystical ways," to this mulatto composition of skin and blood vessel.

If this sounds like ordinary self-hatred (and one can imagine many African-American readers nodding, yes, that's *exactly* what it sounds like), the facts are really more complex and saddening than that. Dandridge was aware of her importance to the black community and wanted badly to make black people proud; she agonized over whether the roles offered her degraded black women (in fact, she came very close to turning down the breakthrough role of Carmen Jones and wrecking her career for just such reasons). She was devastated by gossip intimating that she would only date white men and wrote a letter to a black magazine denying it.

Remarkably self-aware, Dandridge knew she was in the same situation as Horne. There was little in her act that spoke of black style. "It was a style closer to the mood of upper-class Caucasian life," she said. She was halfway between white and black, perfectly poised to act as a conduit for what she called "the transfer of human emotion." Dandridge saw her intimate life as an experiment in breaking down prejudice. But her nightclub act and Hollywood films could only take her project so far; she was not even allowed to kiss a white man onscreen. On the Spanish set of *Malaga*, she and British actor Trevor Howard were filming a steamy love scene on the tree-lined banks of a river. During their closeups, Howard brought his face closer and closer to Dandridge's and as her fingers dug into his back, she awaited the first interracial on-screen kiss in Hollywood history. When Howard's lips nearly brushed hers, however, the director called "Cut!" The kiss would never be consummated: Howard's lips hovered just above the forbidden fruit, forever. An apt image, and it drove Dandridge manic with unfulfilled possibilities.

To break the spell, the actress turned to her real life. Husband-hunting became her obsession; she was "hellbent on marrying a white man." She jetted from coast to coast, to Vegas and Brazil and Europe and back, and dated a dazzling array of entertainers, bankers, mobsters, directors, and executives; even the ultimate midcentury bachelor, Peter Lawford, squired her around Hollywood. They all loved to look at her: one casino owner even offered her $1500 a week just to hang around, light his cigars, and look exquisite. But none offered to marry her; it is the lament that echoes through her autobiography. Her most heart-breaking affair was with a Brazilian aristocrat who treated her as a twentieth-century princess. "Am I really Negro, Earl?" Dandridge wrote to her manager. "He never mentions it. Takes me everywhere, introduces me to everyone, and proudly. It's a beautiful dream and I hope I never awake." At the end, he offered her a castle (literally a castle, with footmen and tapestries) in the hills of Rio; but with it came only the position of mistress. When offered it, Dandridge went back to her hotel and attempted suicide, not for the last time.

When the actress finally married, he was a poor specimen of American prince: a gregarious and shady club owner named Jack Dennison, nicknamed "The Silver Fox." Even Otto Preminger noticed something odd about Dennison: "He had long white hands and fingers," the director recalled. "He had *white* hair, and *white, white* skin." It was almost funny: Dandridge had married the most Caucasian person Preminger had ever met, and Preminger was Austrian. But at least Dennison had agreed to a wedding. The quest, at least in name, was over, and she could hold up her marriage as a "human transfer" of the first order. But on their wedding night, as soon as they arrived at the honeymoon suite, Dennison began talking about money: how much he owed, how much he needed (thousands of dollars), how Dandridge could bring customers into his bar. It was clear that he had married her as a business proposal.

The actress's decline into despair shares one vital aspect with her fellow pioneers. She became agoraphobic; she chattered for hours over the phone (always about herself) but rarely appeared in public. It was a malady that, in various ways, also struck Paul Robeson, Lena Horne, and the brilliant pop-jazz singer Ethel Waters, who inserted into her contracts several rules: Number one was "I don't mix with white people"; number four: "I am an isolationist." In her later career, Horne avoided contact with people as much as possible and carried her ice-queen style offstage. Robeson was terrified, as we have seen, of meeting people who might expect something from him. No doubt being displayed as wonders of the race had affected them each deeply. Because they symbolized the dream of equality that never seemed to arrive, their own physical selves must have on some level become repellant to them.

Dandridge risked more than any of the firsts, more than anyone should have risked in such a difficult cause. Her story is bizarrely patriotic: she devoted her life to the idea that the cultural mulatto was the only true American. Eventually, of course, this belief destroyed her. Her life was a kind of dream that depended for its drama on the goal staying just out of reach. One might compare her to Aphrodite, goddess of love, but there is nothing in the Greek myths quite as strange as her life. She is closer to a human sacrifice than to a goddess.

The era of the firsts sets the stage, in mostly negative ways, for the revolutions of the late 1950s and 1960s, both the cultural shock of rock and R & B, where jazz's mongrel audiences would multiply, and the civil rights movement, the "black is beautiful" movement, the Great Society and the rest—the world, essentially, that we live in today. In the coming era, black stars would not be honorary whites; they would be *black.* With the arrival of protests focused on access for all black people, the "firsts" era was brought to an abrupt close. After it was over, Horne's evaluation of her own part was harsh. "We were not symbols of the approaching rapprochement between the races," she wrote. "We were sops, tokens, buy-offs for the white race's conscience."

Perhaps. But the firsts were essential to the civil rights movement that made them irrelevant. One could argue convincingly that without a Joe Louis there would have been no Jackie Robinson, and without Jackie Robinson there would have been no *Brown v. Board of Education.* And psychologically, the pioneers did make their mark, if only by proving that whites were capable of something that few really believed they were capable of: sustained affinities for black figures. It turns out that the theory of the Other—the idea that societies cast certain populations as representing all that is alien and unworthy—has an unexamined flip side: The chosen few who rise from the oppressed population can be almost terrible in their power. They have potency no whites possess, because their skin speaks of authority gained in unique conditions. That power was real, effective at certain turning points, dangerous to the narrow-minded and to themselves.

The flaw in the pioneer strategy is easy enough to locate: the dazzling entrance of one man or woman into previously restricted areas and the attachment formed by whites for those individuals was no substitute for the needed structural changes in economic life, voting, and a dozen other areas. They were dream relationships, often used to divert the nation's attentions from the reality of Jim Crow, of huge inequities in education, income, and social place. Certainly the pageant holds little weight compared to the hard, dangerous work of opening up schools, of daily protest in obscure towns, of what Medgar Evers and a few thousand men and women did without a flashbulb going off. But life without the pioneers would have been duller and trickier. They added dimensions to the black imagination; like Tiger Woods striding through the crisp Scottish air of St. Andrews, they were spacemen sent to alien worlds, while the masses back home watched on television or listened on radio.

Sam Cooke was Elvis's partner in the mid-century raids across the
color line that transformed American culture. Ridiculously gifted,
he wanted all the society had to offer—and took it.

Courtesy of the photographs and Prints Division, Schomburg Center for Research in
Black Culture, The New York Public Library, Astor, Lenox and Tilden Foundations.

8

LOST AND LOOKING:
SAM COOKE AND
THE MIRACLE OF BLACK POP

IN 1964, SAM COOKE was shot to death in the manager's office of a
cheap L.A. motel. In a time when pop stars died clean martyr deaths in
plane or car crashes, the circumstances were sordid: The married
Cooke, naked except for a shoe and an overcoat when he was shot, had
been at the motel with a Eurasian woman, and she later claimed he
tried to rape her. The shock was palpable, if you cared. The New York
Times had the grace not to pretend to, and carried the news in a small
item on page 34. But for Cooke's fans, the effect was immediate; his
wake and two funerals (one in Chicago, one in Los Angeles) drew over
80,000 people. Ray Charles sang "Angels Watching Over Me" at the
latter service, after the gospel belter Bessie Griffen was overcome with
grief and unable to perform.

Cooke was not the first star of the rock and roll era to die: that
title belongs to Buddy Holly, Ritchie Valens, and the Big Bopper,
whose plane crashed in an Iowa field five years earlier. But he was the
first *black* star to die violently, and he did so years before the assassinations of civil rights martyrs such as Martin Luther King and Malcolm

X. Black Americans especially felt this loss keenly. There were sponta-neous protests; private eyes were hired; rumors of foul play linger to this day—the Mob killed him, a jealous boyfriend, "the establish-ment." A five-part series in Cooke's hometown black newspaper inves-tigated the claims and found no clear answers. If Cooke had died of natural causes, the grief would still have been present, but not the out-rage, which was caused not so much by Cooke's death itself but by its manner. Sam Cooke was Mr. Elegance, his voice communicating a world full of ease newly available to everyone. "Sam was clean—a per-fect role model," said Bobby Schiffman of the Apollo Theater.[1] He was the first black singer to own his own record company (paving the way for later moguls like Berry Gordy and Puff Daddy). He had come up through gospel music and had risked everything by going pop, but had turned his betrayal into a coup. He cleared territory for others, from Otis Redding to Michael Jackson, to settle. He was on his way to Vegas, Broadway, and places beyond. So how could that beautiful man with that beautiful voice have died like a pimp in some south L.A. dive?

The truth was that Cooke had always been a split personality, an enigma who pumped out hits that are pivotal moments in the creation of American pop culture. In fact, it wouldn't be irresponsible to call him a partner to Elvis Presley. Elvis's importance in American life begins with his trips to black churches and juke joints, where he had the common sense to fall in love with the music he heard there. When he went into Sun Records to record his first songs in 1954, Elvis took that black sound and all it represented and fused it to his hillbilly roots, the fervor and sentimentality of white gospel, and his own deep idiosyn-crasies. The moment when the young Elvis, out of nowhere, started singing "Blue Moon of Kentucky" in his half-breed style is the pivot on which much of modern culture turns. Rock and roll, youth culture, and all that followed was born that day in Memphis.

Meanwhile, Sam Cooke has been forgotten, or worse. Members of the hip-hop generation cite Curtis Mayfield, James Brown, and Al Green as living influences. They relegate Cooke to the oldies station, where he becomes less relevant with every spin of "Cupid" and "Won-derful World." But it is impossible truly to understand the 1950s with-out understanding Sam Cooke.

He was born in Clarksdale in 1931, the son of a Mississippi preacher. A clean-cut prodigy, he led various teen gospel quartets before receiving, in 1951, the proverbial tap on the shoulder: At only 19, Cooke was chosen to take over the lead of the legendary Soul Stirrers, the greatest and most famous gospel group of the time. Gospel had passed through several stages by then, from spirituals to jubilee, but the Baptist groups still carried a message of deliverance that had its roots in bondage. "They had a beat, a rhythm we held on to from slavery days," said Mahalia Jackson. "Their music was so strong and expressive."[2] Cooke began to play with the tradition almost immediately. His voice was a hypnotically clean and thrilling instrument, endlessly changeable and yet controlled, its tone grounded in Mississippi soul. But it had been made urbane, self-regarding, swinging, cool.

Even at the beginning there was something new and disturbing in Cooke's voice. In the singing of almost every other gospel singer, you can hear their relationship with their God. Sometimes it is so reverential it is as if the singer can't really address the Lord directly; it is half turned away (R. H. Harris, Cooke's predecessor in the Soul Stirrers). Sometimes it is a reverential, almost jazzy, appreciation (the Golden Gate Quartet) or a vessel breaking as God's power flows through it (Mahalia Jackson). With Cooke you heard something else. He was curiously secular. His voice soared and dived, played with the words, impudently stretching and remaking them in his own mouth. There is a great joy in Sam Cooke's singing, but little or no reverence; it is pop music disguised as gospel.

When he trades off the lead with Harris in the Soul Stirrers classic "Come, Let Us Go Back to God," the difference is clear. Harris's rich but guarded, grimly experienced singing is in the tradition of the slave hymns. His voice is full of black history and means to be. When Cooke takes over, he's *swinging*, vamping up and down the notes like a child released. He never beseeches God; on record, at least, he sings as though free from all of Harris's dread. This new attitude carried over to Cooke's original gospel songs. In "That's Heaven to Me," Cooke wrote:

A little flower that blooms in May
A lovely sunset at the end of the day . . .

Even the leaves growing out, growing out, growing out on the tree
That's heaven to me.

This is a gospel song without God—just kids and birds and tangible happiness. It is not so much a vision of heaven as of black suburbia.

As Daniel Wolff points out in his Cooke biography, *You Send Me*, the gap was at least partly generational. If Harris is praying to God, he's also praying for protection from the realities of Jim Crow America. Cooke was an optimistic postwar kid and he wasn't about to beg anyone for anything. In his voice you can hear not only self-assurance but also defiance. "In my generation," the Soul Stirrers' Founder, S. R. Crain, said, "we didn't demand nothing. We prayed for it."[3] Cooke's peers were different; they were perhaps the first to expect that things were going to be significantly better for them than for any black generation that had come before.

There is a parallel here to another young black man who was growing up at the same time with much the same attitude. Muhammad Ali and Cooke would become fast friends as they both rose in the world. After winning his epochal first fight against Sonny Liston, Ali embraced Cooke, grabbed an interviewer's microphone, and introduced Cooke as "the world's greatest rock and roll singer." (The hell with Elvis.) Cooke returned the compliment, calling Ali "a great example for our youth." This was just after Ali had shocked America to its Christian core by proclaiming himself a Black Muslim. (The hell with Ali's critics, Cooke was saying, white *and* black.)

Ali and Cooke began by filling the old role of miracle blacks left vacant by the "firsts" like Paul Robeson. Ali's most clear-eyed observer, boxing doctor Ferdie Pacheco, believed that the boxer was a "divine" man, literally molded by God. "He was the most perfect physical specimen I had ever seen, from an artistic and anatomical standpoint, even healthwise," Pacheco said. It was a theme that ran through much of the writing on Ali, and Cooke was often regarded in similar terms. Cooke's touched-by-God reputation was widespread on the gospel circuit. He was a pop arranger of genius. And voicewise, Atlantic exec and master producer Jerry Wexler, who gave "rhythm and blues" its name, called Cooke "a perfect case." "[He] was the best singer who ever lived, no contest," Wexler said. "When I listen to him, I still can't believe the things he did. It's always fresh and amazing to me; he has control, he could play with his voice like an instrument, his melisma, which was his personal brand—I mean, nobody else could do it—everything about him was perfection."

The suspicion of divine touch stands the test of time. There was something unearthly in the gifts both men possessed and in the way they used them. But if both possessed the air of black gods, Ali and Cooke went further, publicly leaving the God that blacks were almost obliged to worship. Ali's rejection of the white Jesus in favor of Islam was a huge event, a satchel charge tossed into the placid cultural camp of early 1960s American life. But Cooke made a far more dangerous and lonely switch; he left Jesus for more traditional alternatives: money and women. "This is my God now!" Cooke is said to have told gospel singer Clarence Fountain after he went pop, holding in his hand a fat wad of cash. He wasn't kidding. The singer was obsessed with material goods; he gave away furs and automobiles like candy and toured relentlessly to earn more cash. He reveled in the high suburban lifestyle and took Hugh Hefner's de luxe swinger credo as his own.

Having conquered the gospel audience, in 1957 Cooke decided to go pop. Black music fanatics often think of this moment as a disaster. Certainly, Jerry Wexler thought so; he refuses to this day even to listen to Cooke's pop records. Art Rupe, the white owner of the Soul Stirrers' label, agreed. When Cooke wanted to record a piece of fluff called "You Send Me," Rupe reacted with disgust. He couldn't believe Cooke would trade the Soul Stirrers' ecstatic, deeply meaningful harmonies for white backup singers, strings, and pop crap. It was more than a commercial decision; Rupe genuinely loved gospel, its "fervor, raw intensity and sincerity."[4] Cooke was demanding to sound light, carefree, even empty—emotional terrain that was reserved for whites. (In fact, the crooning style that he aspired to was perfected by Bing Crosby and others during the days when singers used megaphones; the device produced "a curious deadpan and emotionless manner of expression," as music historian Charlie Gillett writes.[5]) Cooke stood up to Rupe. "If that's how you see me . . ." he shot back at the label owner, "I quit your label." The singer took "You Send Me" to another record company, where it vindicated his instincts and shifted black culture further into the mainstream.

And if we pause at this moment, in 1957, when "You Send Me" is about to be released, we can get a sense of the era it would summarize so well.

If you paid a visit to Harlem or southside Chicago or downtown Detroit in 1957, the year that "You Send Me" went to number one, what would you encounter? Divide the picture into sight and sound: Sight told different stories. People were better dressed than they had been ten or even five years earlier; there were more Cadillacs on the street, a better selection of food in the markets (often owned by blacks, especially West Indians). There was more snap in the air; people looked more prosperous, because they were more prosperous. Black neighborhoods were connected to the economic miracle that was transforming 1950s America. During World War II, black workers holding manufacturing jobs jumped from 500,000 to 1.2 million, much of them in northern industrial cities.[6] Black women could get work as something other than domestics: the numbers of employed black women working as maids dropped from 72 to 48 percent.[7] Blacks were spending $3 billion on consumer goods in 940; $11 billion by 1950; $20 billion by 1961. As historian James Patterson has noted, American business in the 1950s was introducing a string of new products: freezers, dishwashers, detergents, hi-fis, tape recorders, long-playing records, Polaroid cameras, and air-conditioning in private homes. And some of them were making their way into black homes. Mary Wilson, later of the Supremes, was growing up in a Detroit household where her father worked the assembly line at the local Chrysler plant and moonlighted odd jobs at night. Her mother was employed at a local dry cleaner's. They lived well.

> *Our house was full of wondrous things: a new Eureka vacuum cleaner, freezer chests, a beautiful radio that was as big as a refrigerator. We were the first family on the block to own a television, and every year Daddy bought a shiny new Chrysler for himself and a stylish Chevrolet for Mom.*[8]

Socially, the streets were tense. Blacks were still penned in the inner city, kept out of middle-class neighborhoods by housing covenants, and kept out of working-class areas by mobs with bricks and torches. One study called the methods used in such areas "chronic urban guerilla warfare." [9] With no place for residents to go, the tenements were bursting. Drug use was commonplace; cops were scarce, indifferent, or brutal. Street gangs swept down the avenues at dusk. Education was a scandal: in one year, Harlem's only high school had a senior class of 2000 but handed out only 38 academic degrees.[10] As a teenager, future rock pioneer Bo Diddley had moved from the South to the same neighborhood where Sam Cooke grew up, and it had not been a pleasant experience. "I've had my money taken, man, I've been robbed," Diddley remembered. "I've been hit upside the head with a *hatchet!*"[11] But if, in any of these neighborhoods, you closed your eyes and listened, you would have imagined yourself somewhere far away from the dirty avenues. California, perhaps? Shangri-La? Wherever it was, it was full of teenagers, they were all in love, and they sang about it in exquisite harmonies.

A music called doo-wop was everywhere. In places like Harlem, quartets and quintets such as the Five Crowns, the Harptones, and the Clovers sang for hours on streetcorners, their harmonies filtering down airshafts and through alleyways. "It would have been possible to walk down 115th Street in 1955," writes doo-wop historian Philip Groia, "and pass groups singing on the corners of Fifth, Lenox, Seventh, St. Nicholas and Eighth Avenues."[12] Often they would be singing the same song. You could transverse almost the breadth of upper Manhattan in 1957 and hear a hit like The Silhouettes' "Get a Job" in six or seven different renditions.

Doo-wop became *the* sound of the 1950s inner city, very much as hip-hop is the dominant sound there today. It began in northern black neighborhoods in the early 1950s, and soon became a juggernaut. By the end of the decade, 15,000 black vocal groups had recorded songs.[13] And that number represents only the elite few; for every group that recorded, there was a handful that never made it off the corner. Being in one of those successful groups earned young black men and women respect on the streets, as Groia attests: "The Vocaleers rivalled Jackie Robinson and Willie Mays as Harlem folk heroes."[14]

Certainly doo-wop and its first cousin, smooth R & B vocal music (The Drifters, the later Motown supergroups) was an odd music to come from the ghetto. Down through hip-hop, R & B, and electrified blues, the black American inner city has usually produced a certain sound: slick and wised-up. The city artist and his music must be able to meet the stare of his or her most hardened critic and pass without challenge, because it is often the toughest person on the block who sets the tone. If that artist fails inspection even once, he is finished. If there is one thing that is forbidden, above all, especially for male singers, it is naiveté, because naiveté is dangerous in the inner city, and no one wants to be accused of it. Innocence in music, which has always been associated with pop, is strictly for the country or the suburbs.

Prior to doo-wop and the black vocal movement, most black artists were shunted directly into the "race record" market, where white record companies' ideas about black taste dictated the style. As Brian Ward writes in his brilliant history of 1950s and 1960s black music, *Just My Soul Responding*, those executives practically decreed that black R & B "should never be anything other than raw, relentlessly up-tempo, sexually risqué or riotously funny." But doo-wop classics like "Crying in the Chapel" were a revolt against expectation; they showed the black audience was eager to have a dreaming music of its own.

The times certainly played a part in forming this desire. Before Malcolm X and black power, white middle-class society set the aspirational model for blacks and whites alike. One look at the 1956–1963 *Billboard* R & B charts, which measured those records popular on black radio and among black consumers, turns up some startling names: Paul Anka with six hits, the Beach Boys, four; Elvis, twenty-four; Ricky Nelson, nine; the Everly Brothers, eight. In all, 175 of the Top Ten hits on the R & B charts in those years belonged to white artists; black fans were buying millions of records by artists who have completely disappeared from communal black memory today.

Was black consumers' love for blue-eyed pop an example of cultural brainwashing? When a 1950s black teenager passed over the latest Ray Charles single and instead bought a 45 of "Surfer Girl" or "Heartbreak Hotel," was he revealing a strain of internalized racism? Certainly, after 1963, black audiences would reject most white artists in favor of black soul performers. But there was more going on than an abject surrender to mainstream taste.

Doo-wop was a speculative bubble in ghetto optimism. It had essentially only one theme: unrequited love. But, as with Romantic poets, love in doo-wop was really only a vehicle to allow for the expression of a feeling about the singer's world. The lyrics were designed to be throwaway, bordering on nonsense. For the first and last time in the history of black urban music, young black men competed to see how unworldly they could sound. And they strove to look, if not innocent, at least collegiate. Clothes were a deadly serious matter: pant creases were knife-sharp and each doo-wop group had its own signature look. The glamorous Hollywood Flames wore tuxes with thin bowties and scalloped satin collars; the elegant Blue Notes wore homburgs and three-button dark suits; the wild Nolan Strong and the Diablos sported purple satin jackets with yellow ties, yellow shirts, and yellow pants. Singing with hands behind their backs, they were part of what Gerald Early called "a fierce black bourgeois ambition that sought to consolidate, not rebel."[15] Optimism was a given; these groups shared with white teens basic assumptions of what life could be.

Yet for anyone growing up in Harlem or Detroit, the street was close at hand, and if the singers were not directly acquainted with it, they at least got their news of darker experience firsthand; friends or cousins or brothers who ended up dead, or in jail, or criminal legends. As a kid, Sam Cooke barely scraped along, sang for nickels, broke wooden fences apart and sold the slats as firewood, and was arrested for possession of a porn magazine. Many of the doo-wop groups were affiliated with gangs; the singers often were either trying to stay out of serious criminal activity or dabbling in it on the side. The great doo-wop group The Dells produced ecstatic teenage symphonies like "Oh, What a Night" and "Open Up My Heart," but bass singer Chuck Barksdale remembered there was a certain dissonance between the songs and their everyday lives. "Man, we were stone hooligans," Barksdale recalled, though even their lawbreaking was minor. "We were bad, man, but we were always singing."[16] Frankie Lymon of The Teenagers was a heroin addict, and Jackie "Higher and Higher" Wilson was a member of Detroit's infamous Shaker Gang, which freelanced in everything from grand theft auto to murder. A member of The Romancers, a smooth Philadelphia group, was shot five times at a party and later died, all for talking to another man's woman. These young men had day lives and night lives.

Doo-wop described their ambitions, not their circumstances. Charles "Kenrod" Johnson of The Chips composed the lyrics for the first of the great nonsense doo-wop songs—(1956's "Rubber Biscuit," revived by John Belushi in *The Blues Brothers*)—while walking the yards of Warwick School for Boys in upstate New York. The lyrics were just phrases such as "a-blubba lubba," "chicky hubba lubba," and "ricky ticky" strung together for their internal rhymes and ability to carry the beat. It was hip baby talk for hip babies. The song was really an ode to goofiness, but Warwick was an unlikely place to compose it. The Dickensian home was rife with various terrors: violence of every description, sexual abuse, and robbery. In his classic memoir of Harlem in the 1950s, *Manchild in the Promised Land*, the young Claude Brown recounted his feelings on learning he was being sent upstate after being shot in the stomach during one of his countless street dramas. He knew the kind of boys who ended up at Warwick.

> *Bumpy from 144th Street was up there. I had shot him in the leg with a zip gun in a rumble only a few months earlier. There were many guys up there I used to bully on the street. . . . There were rival gang members . . . who just hated my name. . . . I knew that if I went up to Warwick in my condition, I'd never live to get out.*

The 1950s black generation certainly possessed a double consciousness: a direct acquaintance with ghetto life, and yet, rather outrageous hopes for their future as Americans. "If you will permit me to say so," said playwright Lorraine Hansberry in *To Be Young, Gifted and Black*. "I believe that we can *impose* beauty on our future." It is as good a description of the doo-wop worldview as any.

Doo-wop and R & B vocal music followed in the tradition of ultra-smooth black outfits like the Mills Brothers and the Ink Spots, but the music's temperament was very much in keeping with lighthearted white pop. This is hardly surprising: 1950s and 1960s R & B superstars often had—to modern eyes—unlikely white heroes. Jackie Wilson was a hardcore fan of light opera star Mario Lanza, and his favorite song was the unofficial Irish national anthem, "Danny Boy." (Of course, Wilson took the ballad and altered it almost beyond recognition, bending twenty-three separate notes across the single word "for" in the climactic verse, for example.) Berry Gordy was so enamored of America's girl next door Doris Day that he named his label Tamla after her 1957 country-bumpkin comedy *Tammy and the Bachelor* and wrote his first song for her. "I knew when she heard it she would feel about it the same as I did and would die to record it," said Gordy,[17] his eyes already on the prize of mainstream success.

Most southern black artists grew up listening to country music; R & B shouter Ruth Brown listed Hank Williams as an early influence. The Grand Ole Opry was de rigueur on Saturday mornings in thousands of black homes, including 1960s hitmaker Carla Thomas (whose "Gee Whiz" would practically launch Motown rival Stax Records). Those influences went deep; musicians are formed partly by what they hear and love as children, and this generation heard songs across the racial spectrum. Isaac Hayes was a brilliant Stax songwriter who pumped out high-energy hits for Sam and Dave: "Hold On, I'm Coming" and "Soul Man" were his. In 1969, he went out on his own with *Hot Buttered Soul*, an album that completely redirected black music toward funk and deep masculine soul, not to mention creating a permanent piece of black male iconography with the superbad cover art showing his bald head and thick rope chain. But few remember that half the tracks on the album were pop or country remakes: from Burt Bacharach's light-as-air "Walk On By" to the smash country tune "By the Time I Get to Phoenix." "I first heard 'Phoenix' on the radio," Hayes recalled. "Glen Campbell was singing it. I stopped and said, 'Damn, that's great.' "[18] The singer took those songs and remade them into hypnotizing soul workouts, but the album's biracial inspirations became a personal statement. "What it was, was the real me," Hayes said. "I mean, okay, the real me had written those other songs ["Soul Man," etc.], but they were being written for other people. As for me wanting to express myself as an artist, that's what *Hot Buttered Soul* was."[19] It is ironic that the album that, along with James Brown's *Live at the Apollo* and Marvin Gaye's *What's Going On*, pointed a new way for black music and served as the soundtrack for the black power revolution, was, at its core, deeply mulatto.

Hayes's black power fans could at least be grateful that he stayed away from the Perry Como material. For Hayes, the 1970s soul brother number two, had grown up singing Como's songs in grammar school contests, earning the nickname the "Swoon Crooner." And strangely enough, it is Como, the whitest of all the 1940s balladeers, who runs like a crazy thread through the early lives of many black stars. Even Marvin Gaye fell under the man's spell, as he told biographer David Ritz.

> *Now this is going to surprise you, but I also dug Dean Martin and especially Perry Como. They weren't monster singers, but I liked their relaxed presentation. Perry had a great attitude. When I finally got some money together over at Motown in the sixties, I used to sport Perry Como sweaters. I always felt like my personality and Perry's had a lot in common.*[20]

Gaye's taste in *black* singers was irreproachable: Ray Charles and the Drifters' Clyde McPhatter, two artists whose reputations are large and secure, and Little Willie John, a criminally underappreciated R & B torch singer. But Perry Como and Dean Martin? You almost have to suspect he was joking, that Gaye and the others were involved in a conspiracy to mock white music by promoting the stiffs in the cardigan sweaters as lost geniuses. But they were serious; they heard something in that music that white hipsters were deaf to. Gaye knew Como was a mediocre singer at best, but he liked the breezy way he walked through his blue-skied world. And there were other things in the crooners' style that you could find attractive: the lack of drama, emotional nonchalance, a facility for illusion, freedom from worry, a hint of erotic control (in Dean Martin's Lothario act, especially), and an easy confidence that things were going to be all right. These were attitudes not readily found in the blues or gospel. Perry Como was the voice of an optimistic midcentury America, and Gaye and the others wanted their fair share of what he had.

In its music and in its ambitions, this black northern generation wanted, even expected, it all. They wanted good jobs and a measure of respect as black Americans; they wanted to move into the white suburbs and to remain self-respecting Negroes; and they wanted to sound black and also to sound white, to do Perry Como better than Perry Como did, and to still sell out the Apollo. Their music was a signal that they considered all of America to be rightfully theirs. They were the A students of cultural integration.

Which is not to say that Gaye or Hayes or any of their peers were entranced with white society. Gaye hated what was there to be hated. Growing up in Washington, D.C., he experienced segregation in theaters and restaurants and looked at the Lincoln Memorial and the other hometown monuments with a jaundiced eye. "How's the average black kid supposed to buy the Bill of Rights," Gaye said, "when he sees on the street that his own rights aren't worth shit?"[21] Gaye boycotted Motown's "charm school," where musicians learned diction and table manners. He thought the idea was insulting, teaching people how to "not act like niggers." The singer emulated Frank Sinatra ("the king I longed to be"), but he looked out at the world through the eyes of a black man.

There were other reasons for black artists in the 1950s to look beyond their given music for fresh styles: some of them were, in a word, freaks. Black people didn't get, or didn't want to get, vital aspects of their personalities. Chuck Berry loved country music and had his first hit with a country-and-western parody called "Maybelline." He recalled once playing a favorite hillbilly tune . . . in a soul club: "I got booed by a belligerent crowd for the audacity."[22] Elvis would occasionally face some of the same hostility when he sang his blues-flecked songs; his gospel hero, the great Ira Louvin, once called him a "white nigger" for abandoning his Pentecostal roots. Berry felt similar pressure, but he never changed his style. His songs were sketches of both black and white American life as finely observed and as precise with language as John Cheever's short stories, and he paid special attention to phrasing them correctly. Singing them, he inhabited a range of American selves:

> *Listening to my idol Nat King Cole prompted me to sing sentimental songs with distinct diction. The songs of Muddy Waters impelled me to deliver the down-home blues in the language they came from, Negro dialect. When I played hillbilly songs, I stressed my diction so that it was harder and whiter. All in all it was my intention to hold both the black and the white clientele by voicing the different kinds of songs in their customary tongues.[23]*

Little Richard was, for obvious reasons, an even more extreme case. Makeup, bouffant hairstyles, eyeliner, lipstick, jackhammer rhythms, songs about anal sex ("Tutti Frutti," before its lyrics were cleaned up): he was far too flaming for most 1950s black listeners. Whites would fill up most of his shows. Richard even failed in the last refuge of black America, the church: when he answered God's call, his tales of bisexual orgies so horrified church audiences that he couldn't earn a decent living. At the same time, whites of every sort and description gravitated to his outrageous image; a young Bob Dylan, exiled in rural Minnesota, wrote in his high school yearbook that his ambition was "to join Little Richard." The Beatles worshipped him. Literally. They showed up backstage during his British concert tour and were happy just to gaze upon their idol or touch his sleeve. But few blacks felt the same way. "When I came to town, you would get ten thousand whites, and about ten blacks," admitted Richard. "I was always supported by white people, but I was never antiblack or antiwhite or anti-anything."

There were refugees from strict Baptist households. Hank Ballard of the Midnighters (who later recorded the classic sex romp "Work with Me, Annie") ran away from home at 14 because his devout family would beat him if they caught him singing anything but gospel. "They couldn't understand," he recalled. "I had to get out of that."[24] But mostly it was not escape from one territory—no one steeped in black gospel ever really leaves it—as it was annexation of another. Gaye heard the siren call of pop when he was around 13. "I still felt the call," he remembered. "I still believed in Jesus." But pop claimed him nevertheless. As a young man, Sam Moore was singing for a struggling group called the Melionaires when he was chosen to replace Sam Cooke in the Soul Stirrers, which in the gospel world was the equivalent of being picked out of a crowd to become the Prince of Wales. But the night before he was to join the group, Moore made the mistake of going to see a Jackie Wilson show. Wilson was a killer on stage, a singer with four octaves to play with and a knee-dropping act that caused decent women to tear their clothes and physically assault him. "I saw the electrification, the excitement," Moore remembered. "Oh God, he was a hell of a showman. I said, 'That's what I want to do.'" The Soul Stirrers left town without him, and Moore became the Sam in the R & B houseburners Sam and Dave.[25] It was a reverse conversion.

And then there were those northerners who had not been as profoundly touched by black gospel as their southern cousins. When The Supremes traveled to England, writers chided them to "Get back to the church, baby!" Mary Wilson reared back.

> *What was this church business? None of us had ever sung in church. This segment of the press completely disregarded the fact that our roots were in American music—everything from rock to show tunes—and always had been. We weren't recording standards because they were foisted upon us by Motown; we loved doing them and had since we were fourteen years old.*[26]

Some singers, such as Little Richard and Al Green, did feel pop life took them away from God, but that was something that afflicted almost every early rock singer raised in a Christian community. Before his death, Buddy Holly talked of returning to his small-town fundamentalist roots. The notion that singers such as Little Richard were less black because of an attraction to sounds across the color line didn't ring true to them. When Aretha Franklin began trying out show tunes in the early 1960s and in later years devoted entire albums to (sometimes hideous) pop tunes, her fans reacted as if she had been kidnapped by aliens. As Gerri Hirshey recounts, reviews of one series of her concerts were topped by the headline "ARETHA, PLEASE COME HOME," and black audience members would shout at her, "Be your bad self." Franklin was hurt and confused by the reactions. "I'm being myself," said the singer. "Maybe the public just doesn't know me."

Of course, Franklin's version of "That's Entertainment" does not compare to "Natural Woman." Aesthetically, her fans were most often right and Aretha was wrong. But the mistake comes in seeing Franklin's love of material that is not representative of the black tradition as being somehow a betrayal of her inner self. It was, to the contrary, an affirmation of it. Nor was it a commercial sellout. Franklin's pop albums sold far less than her classic R & B sides. If anything, the singer was penalized not for singing black; she suffered, instead, for loving Burt Bacharach.

For all the singers listed above, black music was their primary influence; they couldn't have escaped it if they wanted to. The 1950s generation was probably the last to have a wide experience in all kinds of American music; young blacks today are scorned for listening to

Elvis or, say, Nirvana: if they dare to express a love for country music, they might be drummed out of the race.

Cooke stood at the center of the black pop movement; he was its pioneer and its perfect example. Other rock and rollers had preceded Elvis, just as doo-wop and other smooth black vocalists preceded Cooke, but none of them summed up the era the way he did, and it all began with "You Send Me."

The song is an almost bizarre departure in the history of American music. If the fierce "That's All Right, Mama" was a midnight raid across the color line to steal some deep blues feeling and emotional freedom, "Send Me" is a counterattack on the storehouse of white American style. Like the best doo-wop songs, it is a masterpiece of nothingness, so airy it's barely even there. There were no verses, no story, no content. For much of the song's two minutes, Cooke just repeats "You send me" over and over. It was a trick he would repeat again and again, in "Just for You," "Soothe Me," "That's Where It's At," and others. He wanted to showcase his voice's modulations and the purity of his gift.

But, in doing so, he also created a musical world apart from the deep-feeling blues and gospel that had mirrored and influenced black life. Cooke was not abandoning that feeling, but he wanted to unchain blacks from their sense of racial obligation to certain views of the world, to allow them to fantasize in new ways. The fanatical perfection of the song influenced everyone from Otis Redding to Rod Stewart, but it anticipates nothing so much as the Carpenters, the true poets of masked white emotion. It was as if Cooke was stealing back the right of black Americans to feel innocence.

"You Send Me" hit first in black neighborhoods, selling 80,000 copies in Los Angeles alone before ever being played on a white radio station. "The kids were going apeshit," Cooke's manager Bumps Blackwell remembered.[27] Commercially, the song took up where black vocal groups and doo-wop left off, going number one pop *and* R & B. Cooke had conquered new territory but had brought his black fans with him. His incredible string of hits throughout the late 1950s—"Only Sixteen," "Wonderful World"—were pop fantasies in the same mode. But Cooke's ultimate reversal of what was expected of a black singer (even by blacks themselves) was epitomized in his 1960 smash, "Chain Gang."

The song was written after an experience Cooke and some band mates had while touring the South. Driving through deepest Georgia, they saw a strange vision ahead of them. "There against the endless red-dust field," Wolff writes in *You Send Me*, "they'd seen a dozen coal-black men dressed in eye-stunning pure white uniforms." It was a gorgeous sight, until they pulled closer and saw the chains around the convicts' ankles and the shotguns in the hands of the white guards. Who else but Cooke could see this tableau, the prisoners chanting in a call-and-response pattern as old as slavery itself, and think "Top Forty hit?" Another black artist might have turned his dread into money through a single, but the shock of recognition wouldn't have been lost in the music. Imagine Ray Charles or James Brown doing "Chain Gang." There would have been some gesture toward the scene before them, a note to say, "There but for the grace of God and RCA, go I." But not Cooke.

The song starts with the echoing, grooving bass line and the chant of the chain gang: "Huuh," "Ha." The rhythm and moaning go on for almost a full minute, an eternity in a 1960s pop song, before Cooke cuts in on the first verse. Clearly this is what attracted him to the idea of the chain gang: the sound. Cooke's voice floats in: "I hear something saying." Cooke's unsentimentally is striking; he hears "something" not even "someone." A basso profundo voice has to intervene and tell him: "Don't you know / that's the sound of the men / working on the chain gang." Cooke places himself in the role of startled onlooker; he has to be told what this beautiful noise disturbing his peace is, as if he were a society matron out for a Sunday drive.

His lyrics are typically light; he imagines the convicts dreaming of the day they'll return home and see their women, but until then "they've got to work right here." He's matter-of-fact about it. Clearly Cooke doesn't see himself in that chain gang. He feels the emotion a good reporter might—in fact, he credited his songwriting abilities to "observation," an unusually cool term for a soul singer. And yet that is not to say the song is cold and unfeeling. It swings hard, and like all Cooke's songs, it is supremely in the moment, not a convict's moment in the hot sun but Cooke's transformation of it into a pop artifact. Listening to "Chain Gang" is like watching a Rodgers and Hammerstein musical about prison life: it's not quite real, but it's intoxicatingly artful.

Could it be that perhaps his coolness is one thing his black, and even his white, audience loved about Cooke? In the brief integrationist moment of the late 1950s, Cooke represented, or at least he sounded as if he represented, a release from all the drama, toil, and horror of black American history. He sang as if elegance could transform not only his own troubles but the past itself. If Elvis channeled gospel depths (and thus black history) through the voice of a southern white boy, Cooke claimed the other half of the bargain.

The singer did not cross over without costs. There was the emasculating disaster at the Copa lounge in New York, where he was taught some "elegant" dance moves, dressed up like a butler, and sang drivel to a bored audience. There was the story (still disputed) that when he tried to return to the black gospel circuit, and was shouted down with cries of "Get that blues singer off the stage!" Cooke, barred from going home again, left in tears. But Cooke crossed the color line mostly on his terms, and that took a special, and perhaps cursed kind of man. In the stories about him, Cooke comes across as strong-willed, nobody's fool, full of deep surface charm. He had the looks and cockiness of a high-school quarterback who never loses but is always searching for something beyond the applause.

Cooke was emotionally opaque; one comes away from Wolff's biography feeling that no one in it got a fix on the singer's inner self. He was not mysterious; it's just that he had the super-controlled inner toughness of the suburban 1950s businessmen in *The Man in the Gray Flannel Suit*. He slips through his times like a ghost, with his swellegant patter and his bursts of rage, so that we never get a real sense of him. Nobody did. One could see in the singer a figure not from Toni Morrison but from William Inge.

One indication of his true self was his bleak romantic life. Cooke had his pick of black American women in the late 1950s, from debutantes to starlets. But he chose women one could only describe as "hardened", marrying twice, both times unhappily. He cheated ferociously on his first wife, sired a handful of illegitimate children, and tolerated his second wife's open affairs. "I often said Sam would walk past a good girl to get a whore," said his manager Bumps Blackwell after the singer's death. His widow showed up at the funeral with Sam's replacement, Bobby Womack—dressed in *his* clothes. A cold gesture, but appropriate to Cooke's whole romantic life.

It was like some kind of biblical parable: the greatest soul singer of all time seemed to be as inwardly bereft as a game show host. Perhaps that is why he could inhabit his pop fantasies so brilliantly and sell millions to suburban whites; he knew about their searching for things that the suburbs did not provide. Songs such as "Cupid" not only made him rich (as his critics point out), they satisfied the part of his soul not appeased by gospel.

Cooke's life is now told as an American morality tale: the brilliant young black singer who rose to the top of the gospel world, forsook his God and his people for white money, began to despair, attempted to return to the fold, but was killed before he could truly return to his roots. Even soul's Boswell, Peter Guralnick, now accuses Cooke of passing most of his musical life. In his liner notes for Cooke's 1963 album, *Live at the Harlem Square Club*, Guralnick writes: "This is not the same Sam Cooke who appeared on *The Tonight Show*, who presented himself as a kind of urbane 'swinger.' The Sam Cooke who sang to this club audience made up of working men and women is a harder, grittier version of the Sam Cooke that we have known from his records, a singer closer to the ecstatic gospel music with which he started out. . . . He is home free."

In other words, this is the black Sam Cooke. (The "black" is there, in the euphemism "working men and women.") The album was recorded on the chitlin' circuit, where Cooke spent large swaths of his life earning his living and wearing his voice to an exquisite edge. In trying to bring Cooke home and restore his blackness, Guralnick ignores one thing: *Live at the Harlem Square Club* is not Cooke's most authentic album; it is by far his worst record, his phoniest, his biggest sham. Here Cooke misuses his gifts, vulgarizes his art instead of authenticating it. Every note is forced and roughened. "You Send Me" is made raw, which is a mistake. The performance might have been the gutbucket version the crowd wanted, but delivering it Cooke seems uncomfortable and robotic—a puppet as surely as he was at the Copa.

Before his death, Cooke did finally bring his two impulses together. Near the end of his life, he had announced plans to do all of these things: act on Broadway, promote the songs of early black geniuses like Fats Waller through his publishing company, play Vegas, and spark a gospel revival on his SAR record label. To the emerging question of "Integration or black nationalism?" Cooke said: Both, thanks. In his songs, he claimed the full citizenship in American life that was, in the real world, denied him.

In the early 1960s, his music got moodier, funkier, with songs like "That's Where It's At," "Another Saturday Night," and "Sad Mood." Whether Cooke was following his heart or only the pop market (which was drifting away from 1950s ethereal pop) is hard to say, but his music changed. "Bring It On Home to Me" his raucously felt single from 1962 (recorded late one night after Cooke had been drinking) is the signal song in this final act, and perhaps the high point of his entire career.

With Lou Rawls shouting behind him, Cooke cries after a departed lover and here, for once, his coolness is gone. He begins in a convincingly self-centered way:

> *I know I laughed when you left,*
> *But now I know I only hurt myself.*

That sounds like an authentic moment from Cooke's messed-up romantic life. And he follows it up with some playboy bullshit, now made urgent by how Cooke is practically screaming the words:

> *I'll give you jewelry—and money too*
> *That's not all, all I'll do for you. Whooaaa.*

His voice cracking and hot, he is singing like he has never sung before on his pop records. In the next verse, his lyrics match the voice:

> *You know that I'll always be your slave,*
> *Till I'm buried, buried in my grave*
> *Oh bring it to me.*
> *Bring it on home to me.*

For a black man to call himself a slave, for *Sam Cooke* to call himself a slave on a pop record, when his whole career has been a rejection of the necessity of hitting the slave note, is a devastating moment. Cooke reaches back to a haunted past the only way he can understand, through his own personal desolation. But the line also touches on his own gospel lineage, for it is a reversal of a lyric from an old spiritual called "Oh, Freedom." The original goes this way:

Before I'll be a slave
I'll be buried in my grave
And go home to my Father
And be saved. . . .

"Oh, Freedom" would come to be one of the great civil rights anthems; young protestors broke into it during a protest march following Medgar Evers's funeral in 1963, and Martin Luther King sang it a year later in St. Augustine, after some deadly riots there.[28] For Cooke, quoting the line was a quick wave of the hand to his Soul Stirrer days— but, a couple of decades down the road, life has ground into him an understanding of the gospel pleas he sang so blithely all those years before. In the song, he hasn't found God, nor is he protesting Jim Crow; he's just calling after some woman, and probably not a good woman either. But he's desperate now, out there alone in the world, and he's pleading for redemption in the only way he knows how.

Cooke was killed in 1964; his death coincided with the end of the era he helped create. After 1964, the country began to diverge and splinter, not in the least musically: the Beatles conquered rock, while black audiences increasingly turned away from white acts toward Motown and, later, soul. Cooke even recorded his first protest song, the supernally beautiful "A Change Is Gonna Come," which was one of the last singles released before his death. And he completed his spectacular exit from this world by leaving us one final tableau to consider. As his body was carried off to the morgue (where it would lay unclaimed for many hours), police found the singer's beloved red Ferrari in the motel parking lot, bizarrely out of place in the low-life surroundings, its engine still humming. On the seat lay an open whiskey bottle and a book: *Muhammad Speaks*, the handbook of the Black Muslims, whose pro-black message intrigued Cooke. The Ferrari, the bottle of liquor, and the prayer book: the image captures Cooke's dilemma with a bluntness he might have laughed at. Certainly, he would never have been so crass in summing up himself, or America. Cooke's synthesis of the forces that were reshaping the national character in the 1950s was as pure and shimmering as light off a lake. Perhaps only a ghost could have pulled it off.

Norman Rockwell's "The New Kids in the Neighborhood" turned on the idea that individuals could exorcise centuries of mistrust and hate through millions of one-on-one encounters. It was never going to be that easy.

By Norman Rockwell. Courtesy of Norman Rockwell Family Agency.

9

EVERYWHERE:
THE '60s

THE 1960S ARE enough to unnerve anyone interested in the fugitive relationship between the races. Americans no longer intimated questions of color in a jazz riff or the line of an obscure Stax single; instead, they poured into the streets, held signs aloft, met with the president, or committed public murder. Art was cast aside in favor of direct action. In the summer of 1963 alone, civil rights campaigns hit 900 cities, and 1 million people across the nation took part in demonstrations.[1] Race relations invaded most sectors of the national life: TV, Broadway, labor relations, everyday conversation, fashion, politics, even meteorology (around 1967, the phrase "long, hot summer" ceased to describe weather). You no longer had to go to a certain part of town or buy the record of a certain musician to contemplate race's role in American life. Accounts of protests filled your morning newspaper and by the time of the evening news, the situation might have taken a new and even more unpredictable form. The masque was over; the revolution was on.

The writer stands back, speechless. Revolutions this complete change character by the week. Where can one direct one's gaze? How do you leave anything out, when most features of the landscape were radiated by race? Forty years later, the anger of the 1960s has begun to cool and it is possible to cut a few modest shapes into the forms of our memories. But only a few. Perhaps one can begin to understand what passed between the races in the civil rights era—the most incendiary in American history—by listening again to the words that were spoken and asking what lay behind them.

One should begin by attacking the official history, which has frozen many Americans' view of the era into a neat chronology. The fact that blacks could not vote, serve on juries, or live where they chose just four decades earlier is so bizarre and clearly wrong that most Americans, both black and white, want to believe that the nation quickly realized its mistake and corrected it. In the minds of many Americans, the movement was a quick 10-year march from the 1955 Birmingham bus protests to the 1965 Voting Rights Act, a procession that gained momentum by the month, hewed to a logical calendar, and was always destined to arrive successfully at its destination. But nothing could be further from the truth. A moment in illustration: on one of the first Freedom Rides into the heart of the South, the protestors were seen writing their names on small pieces of paper and then pinning them to the insides of their coats. Like soldiers in the Civil War, who used the same technique a hundred years earlier, they were providing a quick means of identification should they be killed. By doing this, the Freedom Riders were simply being practical since, should they be killed, their bodies stood a good chance of being burned or disfigured. But they were also demonstrating that they held two opposed realities within their grasp: they had an unshakable conviction that their cause was right, so much so that they were willing to give their lives for it. But they also knew the society they were about to confront had no idea that they were right, could not even conceive that they were anything but zealots of the worst kind. The truth of their crusade was felt inwardly, only: they had no army behind them, no government sanction, little press coverage (in the very beginning), and few vocal constituents. The world was oblivious, at best, and soon to turn hostile. "I begin to realize that it is a war that I will enter," one volunteer wrote home. "And that the enemy is even lunatic, even driven into frenzy by his fear."[2] In this atmosphere, the idea of quick and certain success was ludicrous. "It was not a rational movement," observed Chuck Morgan,[3] a white Birmingham lawyer who witnessed the protests firsthand.

The early protests, in Birmingham, and the sit-ins that began in Greensboro, North Carolina, were aimed at Jim Crow restrictions on whites and blacks eating and traveling together. To our eyes, striking out at a segregated lunch counter seems like an underwhelming idea (as it soon would to many blacks in the South as well), but the protestors' targets were strategic, in psychological terms. The southern white attitude toward eating with blacks was comparable to the modern American's view toward, say, cannibalism. It was a social custom that, through a long and intimate acquaintance, had become felt on a visceral level. The unspoken ban on eating with blacks had a long history. During the 1930s, southern progressives told the true story of the young white woman from rural Georgia who came to visit her mixed-race child at the colored orphanage. Just by showing up and acknowledging the 4-year-old, the woman showed a rare open-mindedness; but when caretakers invited her to sit down to lunch with her child, she flinched. "Well, I couldn't do it," the mother replied. "Eat with niggers?"[4]

That "couldn't" wasn't meant to indicate the presence of a minor social custom that should be honored; this was a country girl, with few pretensions. One imagines that the girl was expressing a horror so deep that, physically, she *couldn't* have eaten with her own kin and kept the food down. One southern man recalled walking into a northern restaurant during the 1950s and seeing blacks and whites eating together for the first time in his life; he rushed outside and vomited in the street. It was not an unusual reaction.

Perhaps the best articulation of how racism had pierced into the physical being of the southerner came from a progressive Atlanta high school teacher who had gone north to New York to do graduate work. Living in a college dormitory, she shared a bathroom with several students. One morning, she took a shower as usual and stepped out of the stall to find another graduate student, a black woman, drying herself a few yards away. The southern woman froze: "I didn't know what to do," she remembered.

It was as if I'd seen the Devil himself, or I was about to face Judgment Day. I felt sick all over, and frightened . . . I thought of run-

ning out of the room and screaming, or screaming at the woman to
get out, or running back into the shower. . . . I felt like fainting, and
vomiting, too; it was shock, like seasickness; it took hold of me all over
and I wondered whether I was about to die.[5]

The woman later "recovered" enough to jump back into the shower and wait for the woman to leave, but the shame of the moment stayed with her for years. That these racial attitudes, which had rooted themselves in the very nervous system of many white Americans, extended up to infiltrate every level of government hardly needs to be mentioned. Those matters would be addressed later in the movement. But the protestors began with the lunch counters and the buses, out of a sense that here lay the first, the fundamental, denial of their dignity.

The blacks and whites involved in those protests shared a common philosophy, but they waded into the battle with very different pictures in their minds. Again and again, the black protestors remember thinking of a particular moment of humiliation or a memory that had been passed down one or two generations. One of the first black students to integrate Atlanta's high schools left the police car on his first day saying a prayer, but when he approached the school door, just at the moment of truth, "he looked quickly at the building and thought of words he had heard from his grandparents as a boy: 'It's going to get better for us, don't you ever forget that.'"[6] When he had to decide whether to accept a ministry in Georgia or pursue his original dream of becoming a scholar in the North, Martin Luther King reviewed his personal list of southern humiliations: the time a white bus driver called him "a black son of a bitch," the experience of having a curtain drawn around his table—to protect other diners from the sight of him—in a railroad dining car heading south, the white boys in his childhood who were forbidden to play with him. Many times, the memories involved a family member who had been publicly humiliated. It was the image of his father saying "Yessir" to a young white boy that spurred 17-year-old Robert McClain to join the famous Birmingham children's crusade.[7] Angeline Butler, one of the Fisk University students who spearheaded the movement in Nashville, flashed on the day she left for college from the small town of Eastover, South Carolina. Having decided that obeying Jim Crow would mar this fresh chapter in her life, she sat in the seat directly behind the driver, who told her to get to the back. Seeing the confrontation, her minister father ran onto the bus and ordered her to obey the driver. Humiliated, Butler did as she was told, but cried bitterly the entire trip.[8] Like her, many blacks were driven not only by abstract principles, but by stinging memories of scenes that crystallized for them the evil they faced. There was no such thing as "black history" in 1955. There were few objective books on slavery or Reconstruction or discrimination, and even black colleges copied the melanin-free curriculums of the Ivy League. Blacks relied on family oral histories and their own eyes and ears for a sense of what they were fighting for.

For blacks, the movement remade them, and remade the white man in their imaginations. After Freedom Rider John Lewis was arrested for the first time, he emerged from the jail underwhelmed by the mythical power of the white man. "Is this all there is?" he remembered thinking. "Is this all they can do to us?" It *wasn't* all they could do—Lewis himself was nearly killed later in the movement—but the spell was broken. Again and again, the activists felt a feeling of personal power akin to that gained by the early black Christians who emerged from the conversion experience able to see whites in human scale for the first time. Protestors spoke of "cleansing," of gaining new respect for themselves. In David Halberstam's wonderful account of the movement, *The Children*, he records a shift that occurred when the Reverend C. T. Vivian responded to a Nashville driver who had demanded he walk to the back.

> *Suddenly, a revolutionary concept became quite clear to the driver: C. T. Vivian wanted the confrontation even more than the driver did. In the past black men had run from any showdown with even so marginal a figure of authority as a bus driver. Not, apparently, anymore.*

When the Ku Klux Klan marched through Montgomery's black neighborhoods, the residents—who had once hidden in their darkened houses during such processions—stood on their porches, house lights blazing, and applauded the marchers. Unable to "comprehend the new thing," they left and never returned. The physical boldness Jack Johnson had vicariously provided the race sixty years ago now came into play in individual lives.

White civil rights workers, of course, had no "lynching stories": their outrage was most often constitutional and moral, only to be fleshed out later by such mythical figures as Bull Connor and the white citizens who torched their headquarters or spat on them in the street. But the white sit-in protestors, Freedom Riders, SNCC, and CORE members did, however, symbolize the purest effort to venture near the core of black experience. White protestors were the vanguard of this effort, and had been for some time. In the 1940s, Cy Record, a young southern white activist, traveled with CORE founder James Farmer through the South to test Jim Crow. The abuse he witnessed, the abuse he suffered himself, left him gasping. "How could I possibly have grown up and lived in the South all these years without seeing, without knowing, the hell that we put you through every day of your lives?" he asked Farmer and his companion. "How do you live with it? . . . Why don't you commit suicide?" Farmer, a veteran of many integration efforts, couldn't help but be amused by Record's questions; the treatment they had experienced was old news to him. His companion deadpanned that they were so busy fending off murder attempts by whites that they had no time to think of killing themselves.[9]

Still, the particular kind of heroism that the protestors showed, as impressive as it was, was useless if it earned no converts; to have meaningful results, it had to be duplicated, in thought and action, millions of times over. How did the average citizen, who was not heroic or willing to die, absorb the protestors' demand?

The 1960s—and the 1970s, for that matter—were mostly "about" blackness: black rights, black culture, black identity. Blacks studied blackness; whites studied blackness. In the South, the attempts were often personal. Whites tended actually to know someone who was being desegregated: a nephew whose school was now admitting black students or a store owner whose lunch counter had just served its first black customers. This was an intimate process.

The child psychiatrist Robert Coles studied young people involved in the civil rights movement, particularly the desegregation of southern schools. Perhaps his most fascinating case study was that of George, a decent, middle-class white Atlanta boy with all the prejudices whose high school had been marked for desegregation. George's class was assigned two black girls, one of whom, Lois, he took special interest in. In the beginning, his curiosity was purely malign: he slipped threatening notes into Lois's locker (though he originally denied it) and directed heated glances her way in class. But, slowly, impressed by her courage and her faultless good manners, he began to study Lois in earnest. "She's as tense as can be; I can tell," he reported to his family and to Coles early in the school year. "She sits around with no one to talk with, and you can see her worrying about what's going to come next."[10] This was the decade's first contribution to the culture: directness. Whites were no longer encountering blacks as metaphors or as musical heroes, but as individuals.

By turns generous and self-righteous, intensely conscious of social rules, mannerly and prone to mob thinking, George was about as spectacularly average a specimen of middle-class southern youth in the early 1960s as you could find. And what soon became clear was the intensity with which he was studying Lois. George found that when she was supposed to be reading her schoolbooks, she spent too long on each page, "like you do when you're wanting to read or fill up an empty piece of paper but can't, because your mind just won't concentrate." Lois was trying to find a reason to smile, but couldn't. Lois wanted to know what students were doing behind her (including George), but she was "afraid to move her head and look." Lois was whip-smart, but she tried not to show it, because she was afraid of riling her white peers. It sometimes seems miraculous that George kept up with his own work, so engrossed was he on deciphering the motivations and nuances of mood that passed through this black sphinx. The southern white obsession with black psychology that stretched back to slavery had, at last, fully emerged from underground.

As time went on, southern whites were forced to choose sides. The small hill town of Clinton in eastern Tennessee was a case study: the local high school was integrated by court order, and soon after residents began receiving calls during the night, in which a voice told them that "the niggers got to be pulled out of the high school." The anonymous caller told them a meeting had been called, and they had better come. Things soon degenerated into a pitched battle between the segregationists and a group of white "volunteers" who were determined to obey the law. One memorable night the volunteers assembled, armed themselves with a motley assortment of weapons, and headed out for the town square, where the "segs" had gathered. (A light moment before the confrontation: one man tapped a neighbor, a man "with whom he had been feuding for years," to clarify that he was only putting aside their differences for the moment; as soon as this mess was over, they would be feuding again. The other man agreed wholeheartedly.) A skirmish line was formed—military service in the South being almost de rigueur, old skills quickly returned—and the line advanced into a hostile crowd, where their fellow townspeople waited for them, screaming, "Let's get the nigger lovers." "It was friend against friend, neighbor against neighbor," the New York *Times* reported.[11] It was also a microcosmic scene of the South in the mid-1960s, dramatized by weaponry but essentially accurate. The whole drama and cast of characters, from the black protestors to their enemies, emerged from the local scenery.

To understand how the early civil rights movement functioned, and how it was understood by the northern audience before the demands for black power emerged, it is important to remember that blacks were asking to be integrated into a very different society. The United States in the late 1950s and early 1960s was a place where respectable middle-class ideals had something approaching the force of religious law. The Cold War had intensified the power of the status quo. Youth culture had not yet won out; it was expected that one would dress, speak, comport oneself, and believe in certain ways, and that expectation was grimly enforced.

The early movement obeyed the rules scrupulously; the protestors were students not only of American constitutional law but of Emily Post. The sit-in participants especially were the cream of young black America, college students dressed in suits and pleated dresses, their posture *comme il faut*, their striving families solid as rocks, their English crisp and bookish. They represented a widespread hope. "I thought all we had to do was march . . . and put on nice clothes and let them know we bathed and everything," said Joseph Lattimore, a black insurance broker who supported the early protests. "And they would accept this."

It was the culmination of a social idea that had animated Du Bois in Germany and Dandridge in Hollywood: blacks who could meet white norms of behavior would be admitted into the society. The 1960s destroyed that model forever; blacks no longer wanted entry on those terms. In fact, they began to wonder if they wanted entry on any terms. The decade did not so much upset the racial balance as erode confidence in its foundations. The idea that cultural integration was a positive good itself became suspect.

But the early civil rights heroes still believed in it, and they needed a foil. Their most serious opponents, the racist businessmen, politicians, and judges who had more than emotional investments in keeping blacks down were most often too canny to provide one. So it was left to the faceless redneck, the linthead, the cracker—that is, the working-class and poor white male youth—to star in the role of villain. Every respectable southerner claimed to know these folk. Down in Mississippi, future *Harper's* editor and writer Willie Morris sat in math class.

> *They were as distinct a group as any in the school. They wore faded khakis or rough blue denim and heavy torn shoes; their teeth were bad and their hair was never combed. . . . Their habits ran to violence of a general kind, and they performed unique acts on an instant's whim.*[12]

In his classic *Lanterns on the Levee*, Walker Percy, scion of a powerful Delta family, was more vivid.

> *They were the sort of people that lynch Negroes, that mistake hoodlumism for wit and cunning for intelligence, that attend revivals and fight and fornicate in the bushes afterwards. They were undiluted Anglo-Saxon. They were the sovereign voter. It was so horrible it seemed unreal.*

Southern elites had always been united, at least nominally, with their poor down-home cousins in the bonds of white supremacy and the southern way of life. The civil rights protestors slowly, inexorably, began to drive a wedge between them. The wedge was economic and political: the elite saw that black protests were going to make the South unfit for business, a political pariah once again, and they dreaded that possibility. The contrast between the clean-cut protestors and the malnourished, raw-boned, hate-spewing poor whites—and their chieftain, the local sheriff—became *the* visual metaphor of the early movement. It was so glaring that even segregationists recognized it immediately.

During Little Rock's school integration crisis, the New York *Times* identified the "troublemakers" who were attacking black students as "a group of perhaps one hundred to one hundred and fifty students who came from 'disturbed' homes. They had absorbed the racial hatred of segregationist parents who felt that their whole way of life was being threatened by 'race mixing.'" Mainstream commentators began to see racism as a social aberration, separate from the healthy functioning of the American town—the *Times* also noted that "not one of the student leaders, not one of Central's championship football team joined" the troublemakers.

What one is watching here is the transformation of moral heroism into something more digestible by the average American: snobbery. Racism in the mid-1960s became associated with greasers and dropouts. The 1960s punished the southern redneck for his honesty and rewarded the gentry for their discretion.

The cliché remark about northern versus southern whites—that the former liked blacks in the abstract without actually knowing any, but discriminated against individuals, while the latter knew and liked individual blacks but waged war against the group—proved serviceably accurate. Middle-class northern whites were given a simple choice by the violence at places like Selma: see yourselves in the black protestor, or see yourself in the sheriff's deputy with the cattle prod. It was the brilliance of King, Shuttlesworth, and others to make the choice absolute. One could not have it both ways, as Americans had for so long. "If I have learned anything from my six days in Alabama," wrote Robert Gutwillig, a book editor who had flown to Birmingham on business and had been swept up in the protests. "It is . . . that there can be no neutrals in this war. To be neutral is to side with the enemy, to side, I see at last, with Evil. It is a wonderful thing to be able once again to recognize Good and Evil, and to be free to choose between them."[13]

That euphoria lasted awhile. "I think I was slightly in love with every black person I came into contact with," said one Birmingham doctor of the early civil rights era. There is a glow to memories of the Birmingham days, burnished of course by what came after. Detectives monitoring the church meetings during the bus boycott were seen to break down in tears and place dollars in the collection baskets. There was a sense that the veil had finally dropped and whites were seeing blacks for the first time in their true dimensions. "They are just like we are," said Diane Romano, a devout Catholic mother who had invited blacks to her home, holding out hope even in 1968. "They talk and they have manners and they eat like we eat, and they think and they have feelings."[14]

The brunt of the civil rights protests were not aimed at the southern white man and woman. The protestors knew that, left alone, the old Confederacy would break heads in perfect contentment for decades to come without changing a single "Whites Only" sign. The activists were looking north. The objective was to force the federal government to intervene, and the only way to achieve that would be through the medium of white, northern middle-class opinion: they were the real audience for Selma and Freedom Summer. Robert Moses, the architect of the 1964 Freedom Summer, laid out the logic behind inviting white students from the best colleges in the country, from families with a median income 50 percent higher than the national average. "These students bring the rest of the country with them," he said. "They're from good schools and their parents are influential. The interest of the country is awakened, and when that happens, the government responds to that interest."[15] The sacrificial theater of the movement—the on-camera beatings, lashings, and verbal abuse—was performed with this audience in mind, the citizens in their living rooms in Cleveland and Westchester, rustling their papers in disgust or sitting, slack-jawed with disbelief, as Walter Cronkite narrated the latest outrage. For in the North, of course, the medium which passed news to these people was not the dinner conversation or the local meeting; it was the newspaper, the television news, and magazines.

In the North, few whites knew any blacks in intimate ways and, not until the busing fights of the late 1960s and early 1970s did they feel they had much at stake personally. They "met" blacks through the media. The influential news magazines were enjoying their last glow of preeminence; television news would replace them as the nation's leading source of news in 1963. Early on in the civil rights movement, magazine editors saw the writing on the wall and set to work. The mission was to introduce the perfectly nice, respectable black person to their readers, or the *idea* of nice, respectable black people, and they were not subtle about it. *Ebony*—showing the way for less adventurous white magazines—detailed "How to Meet Negroes" in August 1962. "A Negro couple we know were invited to a party at the opposite side of town," the article began. "They had so much in common with the other guests that after the first few awkward minutes, their color was forgotten. . . . The hostess was approached by her friends. 'What charming people,' they remarked. 'Where can we meet Negroes like that?'"

The revelation that whites were denying themselves perfectly wonderful dinner guests *for no good reason* wasn't meant as parody; there was not yet any social situation to parody. This was a straightforward service piece about social contacts between better-off members of both races. There was so little generalized folk knowledge of black life in the North that it had to be supplied artificially. "The desire is there," says Chicago Urban League president Edwin C. Berry. "But it's the mechanics that puzzle them." *Ebony's* helpful how-to list provided some basic rules:

> *2. Don't talk about the "race problem" or your colored maid . . .*
> *4. Don't expect them to come at your every beck and call. They, too, have social obligations.*
> *5. Don't be surprised if you meet with rebuff. They have been rebuffed by white people for years.*

Corporate America stepped in to support the drive. Right in the middle of the *Ebony* piece was a full-page ad for "Apex Beauty Products" of Baltimore, which showed two young women, one white, one black, both slim and fashionable, having a leisurely lunch and discussing . . . the right private schools? Curtains? Certainly, judging by their relaxed expressions, which implied they were old girlfriends, the pair was strictly obeying rule number 2: "We at Apex are proud to publish [this picture]," the ad read, going on to reveal that the space was originally going to be used for a garden-variety shot promoting the "Apex Natural-Perm" until "a different, and better, path" had presented itself. "We'd like you to see it as we do: two attractive American girls enjoying a quiet moment of friendship." The ad, like a WPA mural extolling an American virtue, had a rather grand title: "Progress."

The *Ebony* piece was unexceptional; the get-to-know-the-good-

Negro primer was common in early 1960s America. There were inter-racial coffee-klatsches, panels, family get-together programs, Interracial Home Visit Day in one hundred cities, vigorously biracial cocktail parties, and even the occasional wedding. The lifestyle magazines took up the genteel tasks: the now-defunct *America* lectured on "Interracial Etiquette" in May 1965, and *Redbook* featured a story from a white mother who asked a local pastor to find her a black family to make friends with (which he did). Even *Seventeen*, which was more attuned to acne outbreaks than civil unrest, broke out the mid-decade piece "What You Can Do for Human Rights in Your Own Home Town" and followed it up two years later with the racist-dad piece, "My Parents Are So Narrow-Minded!"

Television's role was grittier. Programs such as 1963's CBS Special Report "The Harlem Temper" (double entendre on "temper") profiled integrationists and nationalists, featuring some scary remarks by Elijah Muhammed and badly lit scenes of decrepit Harlem tenements from the inside. Another program, 1961's "Walk in My Shoes," sponsored commercial-free by technology giant Bell & Howell, was a minor classic of the genre. "We're difficult to know, harder to understand," said the narrator at the beginning. "I know because I'm a Negro. The only way the white man can know me . . . is to walk in my shoes." On the screen flashed blurred shots of a pair of feet, shot from above, as they hurry down a city sidewalk. In a flash, the viewer has been slotted behind the eyes of a black man. It is soon clear that the camera had been handed to an unseen black narrator, who points it at Harlem taxi drivers ("It's like hell to live up here"), middle-class Negro executives talking about miscegenation (hilarity when a very light-skinned woman remarks that it is far too late to raise "the bedroom issue"), and a young black man waking up in his Harlem tenement who soon heads downtown to his job as a serf in the garment district. "A hundred blocks or so, you're in the brighter world of the whites," the voice-over says.

And yet this fairly radical piece of cinema verité was financed by a large and powerful corporation, which sponsored a series of such documentaries in the 1960s. How confident Americans were that they could incorporate the civil rights movement into the whole tone of middle-class life can be witnessed in the first of them, broadcast in 1961, called "Cast the First Stone." Its subject was prejudice; its style

unadorned, covering topics from Elijah Muhammed to racial turf battles in Chicago. But its opening is the most intriguing. After a bravura
attack of violins, suitable for a high-toned gangster picture, we cut to a
male announcer, who introduces the series in the vaguely British-
inflected voice that newsmen used until the mid-1960s. Dour, almost
solemn, he speaks in dramatic bursts.

> *You will see [the program] in the only form that can give it meaning:*
> *totally frank . . . sometimes controversial . . . often terrifying . . .*
> *always truthful. Such a candid picture of life today would not be pos-*
> *sible without the support . . . including the moral support . . . of Bell*
> *& Howell.*

Now we encounter one of the more remarkable segues in 1960s
television. The screen cuts to a backyard scene in suburban America,
where young boys on bicycles are playing, of all things, an American-
ized version of polo, with mallets and miniature goals and a dog chasing
after the ball. Dad is filming it all. In fact, we are watching the footage
through his Bell & Howell camera, zooming expertly from wide-angle
to close-up. An excited male voice (not the newsman's) cuts in:

> *He got it! Every fast furious second of it! Power-zoomed at the touch*
> *of a button, shot in slow motion—with this great new Bell & Howell*
> *"Duo-Power Zoomatic."*

Bell & Howell and Consolidated Electrodynamics Corporation, makers of cameras, projectors, and space-age technology, can move seamlessly from depictions of backyards where helmeted boys play the
favorite game of European royalty to scenes of hard-core ghetto life
and Elijah Muhammad, serene in his hatred of all things white. There
is no break in the logic, no humility in the face of worlds that are so far
apart as to be unrecognizable to each other. Bell & Howell proposes
itself here as a representative of American civic life, flexible enough to
speak of Harlem and of the white suburban pastoral. The company's
mission is stated at the end of the voice-over: "To record and control
the mysterious things we cannot see and to photographically picture
the things we can." One could hardly say it better.

Such series were important for their time, forerunners of the 1977
blockbuster *Roots*. And the corporations who sponsored them showed a

small amount of courage that shouldn't be gainsaid. But it is the daz-zling confidence of that voice, a tone everywhere in the North in those years, that is breathtaking. Here in Bell & Howell's vision, we are at the furthest possible remove from the Freedom Riders pinning their names to their coats, ready to die. The heroism of the civil rights movement has been fully digested and distributed to consumers. All, despite what you may have heard, is well.

The society sought in the beginning to deal with discrimination as a kind of public nuisance that was no different than the measles epidemic or rural electrification. It was a problem that could be managed within the existing tone of American life. White prejudice had no destructive implications for the culture; caused by ignorance and mismanagement, it would soon be cleared up. But after centuries of rising pressures, race could no longer be contained in the words of a Chamber of Commerce brochure. Martin Luther King's sermons were changing the tenor of the nightly news, and Malcolm X's icy bon mots were intimating race war. The racial question was shredding the polite talk of the best people.

The naiveté about the depth of the racial problem manifested itself in numerous ways, large and small. The most serious was a political maladroitness bordering on the delusional. When Selma mayor Joseph Smitherman received word that Martin Luther King was planning to march on his violently segregated town to demand the full range of constitutional rights, he held a meeting with local Negro leaders. Smitherman desperately wanted to avoid King coming in and pointing out the relevant facts—the terrorizing of black citizens by police, the housing discrimination, the ban on black voting, etc.—and he had come up with a plan to neutralize the threat. He suggested that Selma's blacks come to his office, demanding—and this is where his listeners must have shook their heads in helpless amazement—that *he pave the streets in the Negro part of town.* Smitherman was just getting started, however. The mayor would actually refuse their outrageous request, pleasing his white constituency and giving blacks something to rally around. The conspirators would then wait it out; in Smitherman's mind, editorials would be written, northerners would call for some kind of compromise to be worked out; the tension would build to the breaking point. Finally Smitherman, the reluctant statesman, would give his opponents their victory and send the Sanitation Department trucks rolling into the black community, King would find another town to march in, and Selma would be saved.[16] This, in the face of the greatest freedom movement in modern American history, was the mayor's plan: fresh blacktop.

The depressing thing was that, as Southern politicians went, Smitherman was a moderate; he imagined that he knew blacks and liked them. In fact, it was the disconnect between what blacks were asking for and what moderates and liberals thought they needed that caused Dr. King to call the white liberal the greatest impediment to black progress, far more dangerous than the KKK bomber or the southern sheriff. The chasm was symbolized by Robert Kennedy's meeting with black intellectuals and activists at the White House. RFK expected something of a Lincoln moment: shiny-eyed Negroes taking his hand and thanking him from the bottom of their hearts for standing up against the lintheads. In the spirit of the thing, he gave a little speech about the administration's efforts and the wonderful fact that a black man might be president in thirty years. Then he sat back and waited. Instead of getting a slap on the back, of course, Kennedy spent what may have been the longest three hours of his life up to that point, as the black attendees pointed their fingers at him, shouted, screamed with rage, did everything but throttle him for his requests for "patience." Even Lorraine Hansberry, sweet, moderate, upper-middle-class Lorraine Hansberry—married to a white man!—talked about getting a gun and shooting the next white person she saw. It wasn't that Kennedy was a racist; it was that he imagined he knew what black people were going through in this country when he knew, from the black perspective, nothing at all. The meeting ended with Kennedy smoldering in anger, but it marked the beginning of the end of his naiveté about black realities.

The politically debonair John Kennedy, far too smart to open himself up for such abuse, did manage to articulate the best side of the new white attitude during the standoff with George Wallace at the University of Alabama. He went on national television to ask white Americans to visualize their lives if they had been born black. One imagines that some of Robert Kennedy's humiliation went into the language, whose theme was accurate empathy.

If an American, because his skin is dark, cannot eat lunch in a restaurant open to the public; if he cannot send his children to the best public school available; if he cannot vote for the public officials who represent him; if, in short, he cannot enjoy the full and free life which all of us want, then who among us would be content to have the color of his skin changed and stand in his place?

The address hearkens back unconsciously to William Garrison's call for "imaginative substitution." But just a few years later, the approach would have been outmoded. By then, the idea that black and white experience of America was essentially the same was out the window.

The ironic thing is that the civil rights movement helped to dissolve the society that everyone from Du Bois on was clamoring to join. Some of the black protestors who in 1960 read Goethe at Woolworth's while waiting to be served were, eight years later, reading Frantz Fanon and contemplating armed struggle. The civil rights movement had helped usher in a world where the middle-class tone was disappearing, its values were in question, its heroes dead, and its children in revolt.

As the decade progressed, the races increasingly saw each other as alien. National polls taken in 1963–1966 showed downward trends in prejudice and the races converging on key points from voting rights to the Negro character, but by 1968, as riots hit city after city, the numbers were going the other way: whites and blacks were increasingly more hostile toward each other. A desire for law and order replaced empathy: In 1968, 27 percent of blacks thought rioters should be shot on sight, while 67 percent of whites were for the use of live ammunition.

Whites began to handle a new idea, or an old idea enforced from the other side: that the black experience was unknowable. When interviewers quizzed Americans in 1968 about race relations, a theme emerged: A white printing pressman in his fifties: "The biggest thing it has brought to me is a realization that it is probably impossible—if not impossible, very close to impossible—for the average white person . . . to fully understand what the period of slavery and ever since . . . has had on the personality, character, makeup . . . of the average black."[17] A white officeworker: "*Nobody*, nobody can put themselves in the place of a black man and say, 'Yeah, I know how you feel.' Because you're not black, you don't know how they feel."[18] A black secretary: "A white can't feel what a black person feels because he hasn't gone through the experience we had."[19] The theory that leaders of both races from Douglass to Garrison to Kennedy to King had espoused—that whites needed to put themselves in the shoes of blacks to begin to overcome prejudice—was now in disfavor. New philosophies and curriculums and canons would have to be created for African Americans. The reason put forth was not just of pride, but the fact that the races were psychologically incompatible. Dorothy Dandridge's dream was now truly dead and gone.

The commonly accepted moment when the movement's mood changed course is Stokely Carmichael's cry of "Black Power" on a march through the South, instantly taken up as the new motto by the youngest and angriest protestors. Martin Luther King Jr. and the more moderate leaders were shocked by the new tone. When, soon afterward, marchers continuing James Meredith's March Against Fear suggested that the words to "We Shall Overcome" should be changed to "We Shall Overrun," King felt the times passing him by. "The words fell on my ears like strange music from a foreign land," he remembered.[20] What was at stake here? Integration versus nationalism, nonviolence versus violence? Yes, but more than that. Carmichael had smashed the not-so-secret pact that had controlled the movement. He declared that he and millions like him were not going to obey the rules of respectable society any longer.

Black intellectuals and activists, especially, began to compete in exorcising the white culture they had absorbed all their lives, shedding it like clothes from a leper colony. Blackness became almost purely contrarian: whatever was furthest away from whiteness was the true article. Students at Howard University announced the change with protests to its Uncle Tom administration: "Howard University is desperately trying to remain an imitation white school turning out imitation white people," read the undergraduates' open letter. "It is time for the HU administration to recognize that the days of the movement based on bleaching, straightening, brainwashing and otherwise molding the black student into a strange and pathetic hybrid acceptable to whites are gone forever."[21] Radical celebrities rose on how outrageous their rhetoric was: Stokely Carmichael, H. Rap Brown, and others became almost purely theatrical figures. "Instead of taking racial insults, blacks were calling the names—'whitey,' 'honky,' 'racist,'" writes historian Bob Blauner about the period. "Whites were learning how it felt to be the object of racial hatred, to be viewed categorically rather than as individuals. To many, it seemed as if the customary relationship between the races was being turned on its head."

What lay beneath this turn was complex but clear: centuries of suppressed rage; deep feelings of emasculation among black men; continuing block-by-block resistance to black equality on the ground; assassinations; social chaos; and hard-core black poverty about which the freedom movement could do little. In 1965, the violent crime rate in one poor black Chicago neighborhood was thirty-five times the rate in the safest white neighborhood.[22] The national black infant mortality rate was 66 percent higher than the white rate in 1950; by 1964, the gap had reached 90 percent.[23]

Where expectations were the highest, the fall-off was often drastic: the hippies of Haight-Ashbury, for instance, were startled by the new ethos. Shoeless by choice, they were taken aback when black kids from the local ghettoes pointedly smashed glass bottles on Haight Street. They were sending a clear message: Your barefoot Eden isn't real. Whites in the district got attacked, hoodwinked, spit at, and lectured incessantly. The Diggers, a Haight-Ashbury band of activists, found out about the new thing (which was really a very old thing) when they opened a clothing store supported by donations.

> *These people from the neighborhood, these older black women, came into the free store and said, "How much do these clothes cost in here?" We said, "Oh, it's all free. You just take what you need, and then if you have extra, you give." . . . They said, "Really?"*

The women started coming in with bags and loading up on the clothes. When the hippies protested, the women replied that they needed to take the clothes and sell them to buy groceries.[24] Faced with reality, the project collapsed.

In retrospect, what white Americans received in the 1960s was a partial education in the black experience—first through the great drama and rhetoric of the civil rights movement, and then through the mock-violence, actual violence, and the overall scariness of the black power era. It was an initiation, really. Blacks wanted their fellow citizens to taste the ashes that had been their diet for the last few hundred years. And they largely succeeded, for a brief moment.

Since music had been the prime point of contact between the races until the 1960s, when the whole society turned into one huge encounter session, it's worthwhile taking a look at how the era played out sonically. One could posit four discernible stages in civil rights music. The first, as we have seen, occurred when singers like Sam Cooke glided into the mainstream and firmly integrated it *from the black side*. Black pop announced a precondition necessary for action: namely, that the waiting game for full participation in American life was over. (One high school student who was the first black admitted to an Atlanta high school reflected on the difference between his parents and himself with regard to equal rights: "They said, maybe *my* children," he remembered, "and I said *me*."[25]) Expectations were high and rising.

Gospel, sung in a new way, was stage two. Its ancient lyrics were now put to a fresh purpose: they animated the movement in the late 1950s and early 1960s, when it was largely southern, black, and church-driven. The Birmingham protests proceeded to a soundtrack of songs such as "Swing Low, Sweet Chariot" and "Over My Head I See Trouble in the Air" (with "freedom" now substituted for "trouble") and, many participants believe, would not have been possible without the spiritual sustenance provided by that music. The words to the hymns were the same, but the feeling behind them had changed. "When I listened to the older Negroes sing, I knew that it was the idea of heaven that kept them going," wrote activist Anne Moody in her memoir *Coming of Age in Mississippi*. "But listening to the teenagers . . . they felt that the power to change things was in themselves."

The third, and most emblematic, stage is represented by "We Shall Overcome." For all the good done under its mantle, the song is ruined now by overuse: these days, Belgian office workers seeking better dental care launch into it at the drop of a hat. But it represented an important shift in the movement: though it borrows heavily from a turn-of-the-century gospel number, it was a folk song, and black Americans are not, and never have been, and probably never will be, folk fans. "Shall" was an anthem geared toward the arrival of the northern college student into the movement, an individual who was, in the mid-1960s, mad for Pete Seeger and Joan Baez. It represented the shift to a national, biracial movement—an awkward mix of old-time religion and folkie pacifism.

The final stage? In fact, American music never really managed to match, pitch for pitch, what happened in the society in the late 1960s and early 1970s. Greil Marcus makes a case for the great Sly Stone's later and very bitter albums as one sign of the times, but one might as well say the final stage never could have its music, except for Sonia Sanchez or the other black nationalist poets reading a hate-whitey poem or the whine of a fire eating through a tenement. Even something as blasted as Marvin Gaye's *What's Going On* or as incendiary as James Brown's *The Payback*, which come as close to the mood of late 1960s America as anything, did not go all the way to riot. There is no American music that can capture void and breakdown on that large a scale.

Studio 54. In the '70s, street life came out of the shadows and deeply influenced sports, fashion, and social life. At the center of it all: the discos.
By Christopher Makos. Courtesy of Christopher Makos.

STREET LEGAL:
THE '70S

IMAGINE FOR A moment the life of a young working-class white male growing up in a major northeastern city during the mid-1970s, a situation with which this writer is deeply familiar. Like many of his peers in Pittsburgh and Cleveland and Boston, our subject lives in a neighborhood that is as white as driven snow, where dark-skinned Latinos, let alone blacks, don't even bother to inquire about houses for sale. A place where using the word "black" instead of "nigger" or the more liberal "jigaboo" can, at certain times, among certain people, seem a suspicious choice, indicating the speaker might bear watching for foreign sympathies. And where the sight of an African American in the neighborhood, a place defined by invisible beams only a native can sense, is enough to cause his heart to stitch with fear. (Fear not for himself, but for the black guy.) It is safe to say he is reacting in such cases not to the actual person but to the dark cloak of potential mayhem, the limitless possibilities for scenes and confrontations of one sort or another, all of them ugly and each of them liable to expose things better left undisturbed, that the man seems wrapped in, and about which, judging by the strained look on the man's face and the quickness of his stride, he is more than a little aware.

Needless to say, the young man's contact with actual black life is limited. There are three or four black kids in his high school class, imported from the inner city to play basketball. (And treated well, as far as he's heard, though he's spoken only a handful of words to them.) He's heard stories about the lives of blacks in his city. His uncles and neighbors and father's friends are cops and firemen and utility workers and are required by their union jobs occasionally to work the precincts downtown. And they report back on what they see. Some of these reports are positive, though most of them are not. (For example, when he rides the city bus downtown, our subject knows to move to the left row of seats as the bus passs a notorious all-black housing project on the right where it is rumored that sharpshooters like to take target practice on white faces in the bus windows.) But blacks are a distant population, living another life; to a fairly average northern white teenager in fairly average American circumstances, black citizens in the same city are strangers. What contact the white has with them comes streaming in over his head, in radio and television signals from New York and Los Angeles: *Good Times*, The Spinners, *What's Happenin'*.

All of this makes our subject's neighborhood a cultural laboratory with sterling credentials: any strand of black culture that made itself felt on his street has cleared many defenses. The fact that the neighborhood feels no guilt whatsoever toward black Americans at large, in fact quite the opposite (except when confronted with crimes or even discourtesies against worthy individuals) makes it an even more rigorous environment to begin a study of the decade.

One needs a clean beginning, because crosscurrents rip across the surface and the depths of the 1970s, the most chaotic and contradictory decade in terms of racial style this century. The legal changes begun in the 1960s were beginning to work their way through the systems of real estate, academia, business, and popular culture. The old forms of prejudice among whites were dying off rapidly. By the late 1970s, up to 95 percent of white Americans opposed segregation (or *said* they did), a shocking improvement, although the botched policy of busing often disguised the progress.[1] In 1958, nearly two-thirds of white voters told pollsters that they would not vote for a "generally well-qualified" black candidate for president; by the time the 1970s were over, 80 percent said they would.[2] But there was still resentment over demands for black political power, resistance to black residence in many neighborhoods, and a doubting of black skills and ability in the workplace.

For their part, black Americans were just beginning to feel their way into their increasing affluence. "A church-going, home-owning, child-rearing, back-yard barbecuing and traffic jam–cursing black middle class" grew, and yet they felt betrayed by the continued presence of racism in their lives. Encouraged by black nationalists and lingering prejudice, they grew more distant from whites and closer to ideas of the homeland: in the early 1970s, pollsters found that the question "Would you want to live in an integrated neighborhood and have your children attend mixed schools?" resulted in landslide positive responses. But by decade's end, two-to-one majorities were saying that they actually felt closer to black people in Africa than to American whites.[3] For the most part, blacks were granted some breathing space and some measure of security, and they spent the 1970s getting acquainted with themselves. One could hardly blame them.

And yet the decade somehow *feels* black, if only in contrast to the Reagan years to come. In retrospect, it was where one aspect of black culture arrived and solidified its place in the culture. Approach the shift in this way: If you asked what black figure most captured the society's imagination since the beginning of the civil rights movement, the late 1950s and early 1960s clearly belonged to the preacher, and the late 1960s to the black radical. In the 1970s, the black radical was discredited and another kind of figure altogether loomed up from the boulevards to fill the void, a collective image rather than an individual. Namely, the pimp.

The pimp was not so much an actual person as the personification of what can only be collected, however awkwardly, under the term "the street." The street in the 1970s came to mean many things: sex, freedom, violence, knife-edge creases in houndstooth trousers, Blaxploitation, flamboyance, escape, solitary life, hard drugs, a certain toughness of mind, and a new adventurousness. It was not about free love in Haight-Ashbury, it was about New York sex: it was not ponchos and love beads, it was Saville Row as interpreted on 125th Street, by hustlers. It could be said that Travis Bickle cruised the street in *Taxi Driver*, and that Diane Keaton fell victim to it in *Looking for Mr. Goodbar*—but that represents only the negative side of things. The street was a fantasy of ghetto life; it embraced most things that Main Street had failed to provide the republic. And the pimp was the point of entry to this netherworld.

The sharp-eyed black activist and writer Michele Wallace watched the infatuation develop, and in 1979 bitterly admitted that the black male revolutionary had self-destructed, taking the black power movement with him. In his place, American society had embraced another type.

> *Appropriately enough the manhood America finally conceded to blacks was . . . flashy and attention-attracting like a zoot suit. Black men kicking white men's asses, fucking white women, and stringing black women along in a reappearance of the brutal Buck on the silver screen. Black men in big green hats, high-heeled shoes, and mink, with "five white bitches" around the corner turning tricks for him.[4]*

The pimp's outsized influence begins, oddly enough, with fashion. Return for a moment to the young white working-class northern dude we began with. If he looked around his immediate surroundings in the mid-1970s, he had to realize that something strange was going on. If he looked across his row of desks in high school senior English, he would see that one or two of his classmates sported what appeared to be blown-out Afros above their Polish and Irish faces. If he opened his closet, he would have found velour shirts, pants cut to emphasize the crotch and wild flares on the legs, so different from the straight-arrow collegiate clothes of the past generation and so out of keeping with his bare-knuckled neighborhood. The full contradiction of the era registered at the local bars on Saturday night: Local guys in their twenties wore hip-hugging corduroys, mustard-and-plum-colored platform shoes, polyester shirts in the colors of the rainbow, all of it quite clearly lifted, in inspirational terms, from the wardrobe of the black pimp. And yet they watched reports of the latest riots or Jesse Jackson's latest statement on the bar's TV and talked about "nigger this" and "nigger that." He and his friends were dressed in the clothes of their enemy.

It was ironic; it was the '70s.

The decade's look clearly emerged from the inner-city street. Tom Wolfe captured some black New Haven men heavy into the style:

> *All the young aces and dudes are out there lollygagging around the front of the Monterey Club, wearing their two-tone patent Pyramids with the five-inch heels that swell out at the bottom to match the Pierre Chareau Art Deco plaid bell-bottom baggies they have on with the three-inch deep elephant cuffs tapering upward toward that "spray-can fit" in the seat, as it is known, and the peg-top waistband with self-covered buttons and the beagle-collar pattern-on-pattern Walt Frazier shirt, all of it surmounted by the mid-length leather piece with the welted waist-seam and the Prince Albert pockets and the black pimpmobile hat with the four-inch turn-down brim and the six-inch pop-up crown with the golden chain-belt hatband.[5]*

No one, mind you, was crazy enough to go walking around a white ethnic neighborhood looking like *that;* the more adventurous whites wore a watered-down version bought from Sears or JCPenney or other stores at the mall. But the trend came from somewhere "downtown," and it respected no barriers. There are high school yearbooks in small, out-of-the-way towns in the middle of the country where most of the senior class has never even *seen* a black person, and yet, in their senior photos, the boy's shirt collars are three inches wide and bright purple. "The whole panoply of discowear leapt across the lines of class, race and sexual orientation to become the evening garb of Midwestern college boys," wrote David Frum in his chronicle of the decade. It was as if one was traveling through Iowa and saw a juke joint out in the middle of a cornfield, lifted from the Mississippi delta and set down in the American heartland.

What did these wardrobes convey? What did white people hope to gain by dressing this way? They were nightlife clothes, meant to show off the body and to be worn in settings where to see and be seen was the primary objective. People were dressing for a good time; they were advertising however falsely their connection with hipness, with street knowledge, with born-wise attitudes. Much of this boiled down in their

minds to their availability for sex. (The clothes accurately reflected a
shift in sexual mores: in the 1950s and 1960s, the percentage of Americans having premarital sex stayed consistent at around 46 percent for
women and 56 percent for men. By 1973, with the sexual revolution in
full swing, the numbers had climbed to 73 percent for both sexes.)[6]
The clothes invited close inspection of the bodies inside, for bodies
were both safe and beautiful back in the 1970s, a decade that saw the
simultaneous rise both in health clubs and in fine eating and drinking.
What Frum called "the sacraments of the cult of the body" took hold.
"Though the trend in clothing was towards a more relaxed silhouette,
it was imperative that the body inside be lithe and well toned," observe
the authors of *20th Century Fashion*. And much of the fashion industry
began to take its cues from young blacks. The socialite Amanda Burden
spoke for her class of trendsetters when she stated that "the sophistication of the baby blacks has made me rethink my attitudes" toward fashion.[7] Black boulevard style was not the only one available for young
Americans: in the 1970s, you could dress like a seventeenth-century
maiden, a longshoreman, a Maoist or, later, a punk. But it was the high-
living black look that, improbably, was the greatest success in commercial terms.

What the clothes expressed was a desire to know that sensual life
that, whites had been reliably informed since childhood, blacks
excelled in. Of course, hipsters and adventurers had been flirting with
such things since at least the jazz age, but now the fascination spread
across the entire culture.

If the clothes the average white man and woman wore expressed a new
and serious interest in pleasure, the place where they wore them in
hope of fulfilling those ambitions was the disco. In the 1970s, it was the
disco that is the screen between the white world and the world of the
black pimp. It was the epicenter of the new forms of cultural integration that focused on the body.

One only has to look at the making of the 1977 film that spawned
these places to get an idea of the forces at work. *Saturday Night Fever*
was based on a fantasia by Nik Cohn, an Irish-born writer who had
tried and failed to report on the emerging Brooklyn disco scene for *New
York* magazine, and so made up a story instead. It was an excellent story,

too, based on Cohn's working-class childhood in England, and the veteran Hollywood screenwriter Norman Wexler took it and turned it into a much more American product: the tale of Tony Manero, a restless, ambitious Italian kid waking up to the fact that he is trapped in a ghetto—an Italian-American cultural ghetto, not an economic one. Disco, and a Hollywood love story, provide the moments of clarity that allow him to see through the narrowness of his surroundings.

The script was given to John Badham, a Hollywood director who had been born in England, spent his childhood in the South of the late 1940s and 1950s, and then left that all behind when he went to Yale and, later, Hollywood. "I grew up in a very racist area of the country in Alabama," says Badham today, "and it had been drilled into me over the years that this was the only place [racism] was, and we were horrible people for being part of it."[8] Arriving in Brooklyn, a place he knew nothing about, the director set out to learn about the people he was making a movie about; acting "like a documentarian," he went out of his way to talk to the locals. What he found unsettled him: the Italians were every bit as hostile to other races and ethnic groups as his Alabama childhood friends; in fact, they were in a state of low-level warfare with the local Puerto Ricans. "They *hated* each other," Badham remembers. "They didn't mix at all."

This was a rather exaggerated example of the old, standard American neighborhood: clannish, tight-knit, culturally unadventurous. Things were about to change.

Even an Italian hero like Travolta, who had earned his fame playing Vinnie Barbarino on *Welcome Back, Kotter,* was treated by some in the neighborhood as a scourge. The neighborhood girls thrilled at Travolta sightings and screamed his name wherever he went, but the guys were intensely jealous and hostile. One particular *Saturday Night Fever* scene stands out in Badham's memory: a nondescript one where Travolta and his dance partner played by Karen Lynn Gorney walk down a Brooklyn street. "We've moved everybody across the street, easily a thousand people," Badham remembers. "And here we are trying to record sound and the actors are trying to concentrate on the scene and there is screaming from the girls and then there are guys yelling 'You faggot!' at John and holding up signs saying 'Travolta Sucks Dicks.' I felt so bad for him."

It was a classic method acting moment: the crowd was exhibiting exactly the same kind of atavistic hatred of outsiders, of anything not native to their turf, that Tony's friends and neighbors revel in.

In the movie, this confrontation between the clan and the open-ended world on the other side of the East River came into focus in the film's pivotal dance contest scene. Tony, the local hero, goes up against a Latino and a black couple at a Bay Ridge club. The Puerto Rican couple Badham hired were ringers, by intention. "We got this hot, hot, hot Puerto Rican dance couple, and you'll notice there is no camera work of any kind there," says Badham. "I just set the fucker down and said 'Go.' And when they got going, you were saying 'Whoa! Holy shit!'" The black couple were professionals—about equally as good as the Latino couple, but dancing in a less flashy style; Badham brought them in from the Broadway run of *A Chorus Line*. After these stars had danced for the crowd and the camera, the director asked the locals what would happen in real life if blacks and Latinos had come in and danced the Italian studs into the ground. "One guy said, 'We'd just fucking walk away,'" Badham remembers. "He said, 'We don't want to have anything to do with them.'"

In the film, Tony quickly realizes the other pairs are miles above him and his date; they dance with a passion and a fluidity that make him look like a beginner. But the local judges nevertheless award him first prize; disgusted, he thrusts the prize money and the trophy into the hands of the startled Puerto Rican couple and stalks out of the club. For him, the craft and objective excellence of disco have slowly undermined the grip of the block: "Good is good," he snaps at his friends, who refuse to give the "spics" their due. Soon Tony gives up his membership in the old gang and moves to Manhattan. One can imagine him a year later in the crowd milling outside Studio 54 waiting to be let in. And failing. But at least he had found a new tribe to travel with, the lonely, rootless freebooters of the disco era.

Disco music was beginning to be heard in black, Latino, gay, and some working-class clubs as early as 1972, but *Fever* launched it into a mass phenomenon. By 1978, *Billboard* estimated that 36 million Americans had frequented one of the country's 20,000 discos; there were disco proms and cruises and a disco wedding package—smoke machines, DJ, lighting included—advertised in Dubuque, Iowa. By 1980, there were more than 100,000 clubs open for business around the world, and their gross receipts passed the $8 billion mark.

It is a cliché to say that disco was a reaction against both the seriousness of the 1960s and the malaise of the 1970s, which attracted even during its lifetime the most despairing kind of evaluations. Nearly half the population considered the republic a "sick society." "I have begun to think that the 1970s are the very worst years since the history of life began on earth," wrote *Time* columnist Joseph Alsop, and he was expressing a common sentiment. In this era, a disco club's essential function was indicated not by the music but by the lights, those lavenders and hot yellows and pastels—colors not readily found in nature—that shot off the disco ball; they announced that this was a place of illusion. "Lighting is to disco as love is to marriage, as tonic is to gin," said *Billboard*'s disco editor at the time. Steve Rubell certainly knew this; his Studio 54 featured an $80,000 system. The unearthly colors sent a clear message to the dancers. Changing the world had been tried and it had failed; only by perceiving it differently could things be made bearable.

Disco music is not Dylanology; it doesn't need a lot of interpretation. The simplest music America has produced since World War II, it had a backbeat that anyone, literally *anyone*, could dance to, and that was the point. Discos were revolutionary in that everyone was expected to get up and move. "With disco, you were not an observer, you were a participant," said Ray Caviano, disco promoter and label owner. "You weren't going to the party, you *were* the party."[9] Carnal, initially democratic, welcoming, it excluded politics for the far more ancient concern of exaltation. The music had no rhetoric and few messages; the lyrics were not written to be contemplated, but to be subconsciously absorbed or screamed out at the right moment. And the early days of the music were far more successful in bringing together disparate elements in American life than any movement since the civil rights struggle. "There were really no barriers in the clubs," said Felipe Rose, a Puerto Rican–Native American who performed as "The Indian" in the Village People. "There were blacks and whites, gays and straights—it was really more a harmonic thing."[10]

Gay men gave disco its strongest fan base, much of its sensibility and ritual, but it was black women's voices that gave disco its warmth:

their strong, embracing voices powered the best songs. This was the first black music since gospel dominated by female performers, and they were broadcast at maximum volume. The bass was a live presence and the enormous speakers drove it into the dancers. Disco was like a sonic pimping device; it worked on the body like a great voice telling the Catholic secretary and the office worker that pursuing sexual gratification was a positive good. The scene was intensely participatory, and it paired the dancer with a dream of sweet sexuality that was derived from a hazy rumor about black life. Erotic surrender, drugs, sex without attachments, and escape: that's what the voices of disco promised. "The whole disco scene of our day," wrote journalist Albert Goldman in his 1978 book *Disco*, "is basically an extension of the old-time [Harlem] rent parties: a classic example of the ghettoing of America."

The song that launched mainstream disco—Donna Summer's 1975's "Love to Love You, Baby"—epitomized the phenomenon, and yet it was created in Munich, a product of European illusions of what America was like. "Love" was inspired by Serge Gainsbourg's 1969 smash "Je T'Aime," in which Jane Birkin moaned like a Paris schoolgirl either being stroked to a stupendous orgasm or strangled to death. Italian producer Giorgio Moroder, who had always been in love with Motown pop, thought he could do the concept one better, and he chose Summer as his vehicle. She was a young black singer who had come to Germany to break into musical theater; a "funny, clean-cut American girl" (in her own words), Summer was hardly the sexual entrancer she would become famous as. The singer grew up in a strict Baptist family and had found her way through a solitary, depressive childhood by listening to Mahalia Jackson's great gospel sides. But Moroder didn't want the overwhelming Mahalia sound; he constantly told the singer that she was "too R & B," too soulful. What he wanted was a black woman singing as if she were in an erotic trance: he was looking for an ethereal pop with only the echo of Summer's church passions. When she had grasped the mood he was looking for, Moroder improvised a riff on his Moog synthesizers, doubling the otherworldly feel, and called Summer in to a Munich studio.

But during the first moments of recording, Summer kept breaking into nervous laughter. The incantory lyrics and the moaning was just too personal, too explicit, too fantastic; it was not her. Moroder cleared the studio, asking all the musicians to leave; then he turned down the lights, until all Summer could see were the glowing reds of the console levels and all she could hear was the alternating tones of the Moog synthesizers. Privacy was required, but also darkness in which Summer could play a role. "'Love to Love You' was approached as an acting piece," said Summer, "as what I imagined it to be like for a man seeing his wife for the first time, or for a woman seeing a man for the first time."[11] Disco's first smash was a European dream of a Motown girl having sex. Even Summer was fantasizing that day; "Love" was created at a double remove from reality, and that set the tone for the decade.

The effect of the song launched Summer on a decade-long odyssey as the goddess of disco, an image so intimidating that reporters sent to interview her would literally become speechless and just gape. Summer lived to regret the song's success: She felt small and unsexy compared to the Amazon on the record. Her mail became unusually explicit, even for a celebrity, and the singer found herself involved in a thousand erotic dramas.

> *I get letters telling me about people's fantasies and dreams about me—people have sent me paintings and pictures. You can't imagine what these people say to me! One guy had this obsession with seeing Raquel Welch make it with me—oh, and Ann-Margret, too. I would have a whip or something, and they would be completely at my mercy. He went on for four or five pages, telling me how he found my album in his son's room and took it, and how he plays it when no one is home and just thinks about these things.[12]*

Summer admitted in the late 1990s that she, too, was taken in by her image; she began to "get off on my thinking what it would be like if I were really like the person that people fantasize about." This is perhaps the final statement on disco's effect: even Donna Summer dreamed about being Donna Summer.

If previous incursions of black culture had worked primarily on the American mind and spirit, the 1970s began in the physical. The working-class stalwart in Brooklyn or Boston or Pittsburgh might be deeply racist in his outlook, but in the 1970s he had to come to terms with the black body: he was probably dressed like one, he was dancing like one, he certainly worshipped ones on the gridiron or basketball court. When in 1972 Wilt "The Stilt" Chamberlain wore a sweatband onto the court, they sprouted on playground courts around the country within weeks; the same thing happened when he wore the first pair of knee-high tube socks in Philadelphia. But the effect went beyond clothing; it was most basic in the noticeable shift in posture among white Americans. If you study footage from the 1950s and 1960s, you will see that most whites walked with a very correct, straight-backed carriage, coached by the likes of Emily Post. Films from the 1970s and beyond reveal what Europeans remark on: white Americans have adopted some of the loping, bopping, street-rhythmed walk of the inner city, known in its most extreme form as "the pimp limp." One could say that the average white American with any sense of physical cool walks today like a cross between a cowboy and a black kid. It could also be seen in the fact that the handshake—a gesture that dates from the Middle Ages—was abandoned for the soul shake. Six centuries of Anglo-Saxon tradition were abandoned in a few short years.

Disco accelerated the process under way since jazz dancing: the liberation of the body, black and white, from still-powerful Puritan and Christian mores. Unlike jazz, however, that was about its *only* mission, and with its narrowed focus it succeeded more thoroughly. With "Love to Love You, Baby," a psychological barrier in the frankness with which Americans could address their physical selves had been passed. Not only because Summer simulated twenty-two orgasms during the song's sixteen-plus minutes, but because "Love" was a smash, staying in the Top Forty for fourteen weeks and eventually going to number two. Never before and never again had so many Americans embraced carnal freedom so completely.

Disco died many deaths. You can take your pick of the official ends of the era. It was when Steve Rubell made his famous remark that Studio 54 made more money than the Mafia, which epitomized the club's ugly hubris. Or the night of the "Disco Sucks!" event in Chicago, when thousands of mostly white, long-haired, blue-collar fans stormed a baseball field and started a riot. Or it is simply when the music began to suck (as early as 1976's "Disco Duck" by Rick Dees and His Cast of Idiots). By the last days of the 1970s, it was clearly over. But what killed it? Besides boredom and shoddy songwriting, the scene's demise was implicit in its anarchic spirit. The spiritual malaise that struck the scene centered on the fact that, despite anthems like "We Are Family," this was a solitary pursuit. It was the first African-American dance music in which it was permissible, even recommended, to dance alone. That concept would have been physically impossible when talking about the lindy-hop or other jazz dances.

Blacks had to deal with this fact first; for them, disco represented a seismic shift in outlook. The late 1960s and early 1970s saw the emergence of conscious soul: The O'Jays, Earth, Wind and Fire, Sly and the Family Stone, and Curtis Mayfield sang about black pride and unity. The subject of their music was "we." We are beautiful, we have unique gifts, we need to get together. Disco shifted the subject to "I." "Disco was the most hedonistic music I ever heard in my life," said disco impresario Nile Rodgers, leader of the seminal band Chic. "It was really all about Me! Me! Me! Me!"[13] After Sister Sledge released "He's the Greatest Dancer," their singer recalled countless men coming up to her in clubs and announcing, "I am the person you were singing about."[14] Goldman suggested that outside of every disco there should be erected a statue of the scene's "presiding deity." One would think of Dionysius or Eros, but Goldman in fact had another god in mind: Narcissus.

Narcissus ends up enraptured but alone, and that was the indictment leveled rather hysterically against disco: its self-absorption, its pursuit of the sensual, its emptiness. It hadn't taken long for many, especially women, to become disenchanted with the new sexual freedom, however. In *Looking for Mr. Goodbar*, Diane Keaton finds out what happens to nice, unattached girls who look for love in the discothèques; she meets self-absorbed hustlers like the one played by Richard Gere and floats in a limbo of meaningless attachments. The movie is like a tour of the disco underworld. In the late 1970s, the dark and lonely side of the sexual revolution began to reveal itself: not only what John Cheever called in *Falconer*, one of the decade's signature novels, "the utter poverty of erotic reasonableness," but more concrete things: the astronomic rise in STDs and divorces, the epidemic in drug addiction, the climb in abortions (made legal in 1973), the unbecoming

sight of aging playboys cruising into their fifties, the whole dank, cre-
puscular twilight of youthful dreams.

The black pimp could have predicted it all; he had been privy to this
knowledge for over a century. In his nonpareil study of southern life,
The Mind of the South, W. J. Cash traced the appearance of the black
pimp to the Reconstruction streetwalking laws that drove prostitution
into the hotels. There the black bellhops procured women for male
guests, and learned their tastes and their weaknesses.

> *The result was a rise of a horde of raffish blacks, full of secret, con-
> temptuous knowledge of the split in the psyche of the shame-faced
> Southern whites, the gulf between their Puritanical professions and
> their hedonistic practices—scarcely troubling to hide their grinning
> contempt for their clients under the thinnest veil of subservient
> politeness and, in the case of the bellboys, hugging to themselves with
> cackling joy their knowledge of the white man's women.*

Tinged as it is by racist anxiety, the passage still rings true. No less an
authority than Iceberg Slim, the former procurer and author of *Pimp*
and other classics, came across the same theory being expounded on
the streets of Chicago. A veteran hustler named Sweet told him about
the game's bylaws and secrets, known as "the book," and included this
thumbnail history of the profession:

> *The truth is that the book was written in the skulls of proud Niggers
> freed from slavery. They wasn't lazy. They was puking sick of pick-
> ing white man's cotton and kissing his nasty ass. The slave days stuck
> in their skulls. They went to the cities. They got hip fast.*[15]

This idea that procuring was, in fact, a form of resistance and dominance over white men runs through Slim's work. White pimps are
pathetic: "if they was black, they'd starve stiff." And white johns are
weak masochists who come to black whores to wallow in their own suffering. In contrast, the black pimp is a rock-hard "gutter god" who
dominates by sheer will and his knowledge of human weakness. He
knows every single product and sensation that the street offers.

In his autobiography, Slim learns for himself the tradeoff involved
in being king of the streets, which is loneliness and paranoia of an

intense kind: "A pimp lives his life with a stick of dynamite stuck up his rectum," as he so memorably put it in *The Naked Soul of Iceberg Slim*. As a nightlife historian, Slim knew about the noxious aspects of the life, the sexual infatuations of middle-class johns with certain whores ending in ruin and misery; the endless morning-afters; addiction and betrayal that is so common in his world as to be hardly worth mentioning. At the core of his wisdom was the realization that he could trust no one, a lesson Slim's mentor taught him right off the bat. "A pimp is the loneliest bastard on Earth," Sweet informed him. It was the lesson the secretary and the middle manager learned in the discos. Like Tony, they left the certainty of what they knew to brush up against a sexier, more alluring world; but few of them could handle its implications. Not to put too fine a point on it, disco gave mainstream Americans a taste of the existential demands of the high life: the knowledge that to be alone and fabulous in a hard world requires a coming to terms with the loss of faith in everything but a brief rapture.

The pimp can serve one final purpose in our look at the contributions of the 1970s. Step back again to examine one last time his famous wardrobe: the outrageous colors, the flamboyant tailoring, the alligator shoes, the rare leathers and furs, diamonds in stickpin, tooth, and pinky ring—it was all a study in hyperbole. It dared you to point out that this paragon of masculinity really dressed very close to Liberace in his peak years. But it was all premeditated. The over-the-top style summed up the pimp's credo: I am so far beyond masculine that I can appear feminine. I am so beyond square that I can appear foppish. I am not and can never be touched by mainstream standards. The pimp was bigger than life, and he carried along with him the revenge of the ghetto personality: the compressed memory of thousands of petty humiliations that demanded an outlandish response. While in prison, Iceberg Slim thought about his place in the world once he was released; he dreamed of getting and using power. Power for the black community? No—for himself.

The [dreams] were fantastic. I would see myself gigantic and powerful like God Almighty. My clothes would glow. My underwear would be rainbow-hued silk petting my skin. My suits were spun-gold shot through with precious stones. My shoes would be dazzling silver. The toes were as sharp as daggers. Beautiful whores with piteous eyes groveled at my feet. . . . The whore's painted faces would be wild in fear. They would wail and beg me not to murder them on those sharp steel stakes. I would laugh madly.[16]

The 1970s adopted enough of this mad narcissism that the results began to grate. Norman Mailer, in Zaire for the Ali-Foreman fight in 1974, reflected on his evolving attitudes toward blacks back home. He was nettled by their cultural ascendancy, and he could have spoken for many an American.

So much resentment had developed for Black style, Black snobbery, Black rhetoric, Black pimps, superfly, and all that virtuoso handling of the ho. The pride Blacks took in their skill as pimps! . . . [He] felt a private fury at . . . that eternal emphasis on centrality—"I am the real rooster of this block, the most terrible cock, the baddest fist. I'm a down *dude. You motherfuckers better know it."[17]*

Of course, Mailer was a prime offender when it came to just such self-absorption, but his charge stood the test for many whites and some blacks. If America felt liberated by black influence, it also felt increasingly haunted by the black show-off (soon followed by the white show-off), the strutting, the cakewalking, the "attitude," and the intensification of public and private personality they represented. It was no accident that Mailer had these thoughts covering an Ali fight. The fighter had seemed an oddity in the 1950s with his beautifully honed egomania, but now it seemed that he was not a charming aberration but a model for the future. Ali earned his conceit—if anyone deserved to be enamored of himself, it was him—but in the 1970s it seemed that ordinary Americans in all walks of life were attracted to the same kind of display. One could quote Andy Warhol on fame here, and certainly the exploding importance of the media and its need for celebrities figures in to the general scene. But the shift had occurred that went beyond celebrity to how Americans viewed what made up a significant life.

Black men did not, of course, invent public vanity. Many different forces converged to give us the Me Decade: the rise of television and its need for personalities; an exhaustion with serious people and serious subjects; the 1960s contempt for traditional ideas of the good life. But in the 1970s, blacks just seemed better at it. Take the small but representative case of Billy "White Shoes" Johnson of the Houston Oilers. In 1974, Johnson was a rookie punt returner, until his arrival a fairly lowly occupation in the National Football League. A five-foot-nine "midget" (in the words of the Oilers coach) picked in the fifteenth round, he was a nobody from an obscure Division III school. But his speed earned him a place on the roster and in one of his first professional games, after running a reverse for a touchdown against the Pittsburgh Steelers, Johnson stood in the end zone and did something unprecedented: he handed the ball to the referee and then for no reason at all *broke into a dance*. Black nightlife aficionados quickly recognized the dance as the Funky Chicken, but what was Johnson doing performing it on the football field? "The end zone became Apollo Theater," recalled writer Bill Shefski.

White Shoe's behavior was shocking in ways that are hard to recapture; in the androgynous carnival of the 1970s, football was the last refuge of masculinity. It was a sport populated by the likes of Jack Lambert and Mean Joe Greene, both of whom happened to be on the field that day and who took pains to "menacingly" brush past Johnson after his outburst. Lambert and Greene and players like them were stoics who never smiled on the field, let alone danced in their spikes. But now this punt returner, this *showman*, had taken it upon himself to perform an arm-flapping, knee-crossing vaudeville routine in the end zone, an act that soon expanded week by week to include other current dances and which eventually became a highly touted traveling show that Johnson took on the road from Philadelphia to L.A. It's no surprise that Johnson once admitted that "Muhammed Ali was my idol."

Houston and the national media adored Johnson, but for others, he was an abomination, actually evil. It was not only white jocks and fans who despised his transformation of the game; many black Americans were appalled, including "Deacon" Jones, the legendary defensive end. "Every time we meet at a banquet or some other function, he threatens me with violence," Johnson said in 2001. Calling him "you little actor," the Deacon regularly and quite seriously accused Johnson of starting "all that mumbo-jumbo."[18] Jones spoke for everyone who regretted the passing of old school ways.

The 1970s abounded with such temporary personalities, black and white: from "Rockin'" Rollen Stewart, the attention-starved loon in the rainbow-colored wig who began jumping into television shots in 1976 (only later to include a biblical message in his routine) to the beloved egomaniac Evel Knievel to a thousand other forgotten "celebs." But there was a feeling that the bar had been raised by black men from Ali onward. The volume of American society had slyly been thumbed upward: If you were going to be valued or value yourself, you were going to have to become louder, cockier, more exuberantly alive, more self-involved.

If there was any saving grace to this development—and many felt, and feel now, that there was not—it was brought home to the anonymous many in the world of the American Basketball Association. What Donna Summer was to disco, an obscure ABA forward was to 1970s sports.

The American Basketball Association came of age in the early 1970s, and it embodied the era more than any other sports organization; many times, it seemed like the last thing on the players' minds was the game itself. Josh Wilker remembered one ABA outfit:

> The best team in the league, the Indiana Pacers, had a front line that featured, in turn: A center who burst through the locker room door every day dressed like a cowboy, complete with sharpened spurs and gleaming, fully loaded six-shooter pistols; a roisterous power forward who brought his pet lion along with him when he went out for his nightly dose of revelry; and a small forward who was convinced he could mesmerize his defender by dribbling the multicolored ball a special way.[19]

There were many standouts in the ABA, but none came close to Julius Erving. With only spotty coverage of ABA games on television (these were the days before ESPN), Erving was at first a rumor, but a rumor that traveled from coast to coast. If you were a sports-mad teenager in those years, you heard about Erving before you actually saw him. And when you saw him, you knew the game of basketball had changed. In white neighborhoods everywhere, kids screamed out the name of a black star—"McAdoo!" in Buffalo or "Kareem!" in L.A.—as they attempted some unmakable shot, invoking the particular god of their local professional sports team. In the summer of 1976, more kids began yelling out "Dr. J" than any other single name.

Erving was the first wildly popular exponent of what might be called black style, which goes back through the Harlem Globetrotters and beyond. Black style versus white style is an ongoing debate in the sport. They are simplified and often misused ideas (particularly to accuse black athletes of being selfish or lazy), but if you spend two hours on a court anywhere in this country, you will at some point see the dialectic reveal itself. White style is epitomized in the play of, say, Indiana University: a highly structured offense where passing is the most valued weapon and unselfishness is demanded, combined with a ferocious hands-up defense to which one is required to sacrifice one's body. It could be said that Indiana basketball emerges out of a certain ideal of small-town midwestern life. Apocalyptic winters, floods, and Indian attacks rest deep in the communal memory, demanding an unquestioning devotion to teamwork and dependence on one's neighbor; flashiness of any kind is not only irresponsible but potentially dangerous. When an Indiana coach diagrams a complicated offense filled with intersecting lines of picks, rolls, back doors, and passes, he is drawing a portrait of small-town values in action.

For some basketball classicists, that style is how the game existed in its Arcadian past: disciplined, modest. Then came the onset of flash, trash-talking, 360-degree-behind-the-back gorilla slams. But they are wrong: Basketball began in the late 1800s as a pleasant outlet for white inner-city men, but almost immediately descended into near-anarchy. Even amateur games often became bloody scrums, during which the ball holders were pillaged from all sides and where, according to one of the players in the first basketball game ever played, in December 1891, "all of the players wanted to shoot." Ball-hogging, "jealousies and rivalries," and violence nearly ruined the game. The Ivy League colleges were as bad as anywhere; Charles Eliot of Harvard successfully moved to ban the game in 1909 because it had "become even more brutal than football," which in the days of regular, gruesome fatalities on the gridiron, was saying something. The Indiana philosophy was instead a hard-fought achievement, a slow rationalization of the game away from its roots in frenzied selfishness.

Black style is very different from the Indiana style. It is actually black inner-city style and it is epitomized by one move: the viciously unstoppable slash to the basket. In the black game, you must locate fear and exploit it. "When you play a guy, you know," said Michael Jordan. "You can see it in his eyes. He's scared. He's got no heart."[20] Basketball is a game of scarce resources: only one man can hold the ball at once. It is one man versus not only the five opponents standing between him and the basket, but one man versus nine, because the player's four teammates also want the chance to slice to the basket. One might say that signature move emerges out of the exigencies of ghetto life—the ethic of the lone young black male. The demand placed upon the point guard catching his breath at the top of the key, his eyes cool and almost dreamy as he surveys various routes through his enemies, is very different from one in the Indiana offense: he must create a solitary solution or risk his own self-respect. The inner city has produced one of the more extreme forms of individualism ever seen on the continent, and the basketball player works within its demands.

What emerged in the 1970s in the style of Dr. J and others was the realization that brute power will not get you from the top of the key through the maze of players hawking for the ball all the way to the basket, where your reward—respect, momentary awe, perhaps even a college scholarship—awaits you. White Americans had seen bone-crushing acts of will on the court and the gridiron before; Dr. J was not inherently tougher than white heroes such as football's Dick Butkus. What was new in Dr. J's game was a realization: the key to devastating opponents was not intensity or maniacal strength, but an artfulness that made everyone else on the floor look slow, brutal, and stupid. For evidence, review the archival photos of Dr. J pulling off his classic moves on the court. He always seems to be soaring past or jumping clear over some poor defender, the man's shoulders twisted in the opposite direction of his hips, his hands lunging after a ball that passed by a second before, and his mouth distorted in exhaustion and horror. These are friezes depicting the arrival of a new epoch in sports, and whites welcomed it and emulated it. Even a basketball fan like Woody Allen succumbed to one of Erving's forerunners, the great Earl Monroe: "Some kind of diabolical intensity comes across his face when he has the ball," Allen said. "And yet he has enough wit in his style to bring off funny ideas when he wants to."[21]

For whites, the diabolical intensity was expected; what else did Hollywood and local rumor bring back from the black neighborhoods except stories about how life there was hard and unforgiving? By the 1970s, white Americans acknowledged that blacks who grew up in the ghetto were tested in ways they had not been, and anyone who emerged whole gained their respect. Working-class ethnic whites, with their immigrant stories, can relate directly to the rise from poor origins. But Dr. J responded to the sick intensities of the ghetto not with crude displays of power but with a deadpan artistry that immediately enlarged the idea of grace under pressure. It was as if black athletes like him had taken two near-extremes of the American personality—iron will and a certain cool flair—and bent them until they touched. This amazed the white player and the white audience, just as it confirmed for the black audience the riches of their own tradition.

Dr. J was not a product of the ghetto. In fact, neither he nor the two players of genius who followed him in the role of NBA hero, Magic Johnson and Michael Jordan, came from the ghetto; all three emerged from intensely strong, supportive, and relatively well off families with tremendous work ethics. But they were educated in black style, and beneath their winning smiles there was the attitude of a killer. Dr. J prided himself on his stone-faced coolness on the court; he later said he had "programmed himself" to act in a certain way. The turning point had come at the death of his father, an experience that taught him that emotion could unman you. And Erving did not want to be unmanned, ever:

I went to the cemetery the first few days after he was buried and I cried each day. . . . I was really brought to my knees and made to feel

*helpless and powerless. It was like I no longer had control. . . .
[Then] I told myself I wasn't going to cry anymore, ever . . . I
became fearless.*[22]

Erving's mental toughness was a reaction to experience; he would
let nothing touch him. (In that way, of course, he arrived at the same
point as the pimp did—belief in a hard-core individuality.) Michael
Jordan's toughness was seemingly inborn. Jordan's will and his feral
need to compete and to win in even the smallest areas of life, often
spilling over into brutal mocking of teammates and opponents, was
legendary in the NBA. He is accurately described by his teammate Luc
Longley in one word: "predator." As for Magic Johnson, his fellow
Laker Mychal Thompson provided this intimate evaluation:

*Forget Magic's smile. That's not who he was. He was like Ali, and
Ali smiled a lot too. But what they both wanted was nothing less than
to kill you.*[23]

This is not to say that these three most important black NBA styl-
ists were cold or maniacal. In fact, they were the exact opposite—their
charm as public figures was unmatched in contemporary sports. But
what is often missed by the casual fan is the fact that their charm disguised an intent to destroy everything that stood in their way. Their
"creativity" was a response to certain pressures in black life, to which in
solitary moments Dr. J and the others had devised a response. If some
of the ghetto's poison—the contagious monomania of the ghetto, as
embodied by the pimp—had flowed irreversibly into the American
mainstream during the decade, Erving took it and distilled it into a
something that was immediately understood in the white ghettos with
which we began: an eccentric beauty.

The 1970s infatuation with street life ended in bitterness and a right-
ward shift in the culture. To put it crudely, the Brooks Brothers look
replaced the 125th Street look; that awful term "nesting" replaced
nightlife; and in many ways a newly challenged and invigorated sense
of white male tradition—Wall Street, the Ivy League, the Masters of
the Universe and all their followers, now amped up to new levels of
forcefulness—met and defeated the black male challenge to represent

the social ideal. The customers in the bars we began with shed their discowear and became Reaganites, almost to a man. But one can hardly in good faith regret the experience. This more than mild flirtation made America louder, but also more sensual; less decent, but perhaps more free. What Erving and Summer brought to American life—a rigorous and joyful approach to the old American creed of individualism—is with us still.

An Afrika Bambaataa concert. Crazy for new sounds, sampling from every culture
within its global reach, hip-hop is a triumph of mulatto culture.
But at its heart lies a contradiction.
By David Corio. Courtesy of David Corio.

11

THE DEATH OF COERCION

THE PHONE COMPANIES don't keep records precise enough to measure the statistic, but the place and time from which the highest number of cell phone calls are made every weekday may be the southwest corner of 45th and Broadway in Times Square, beginning at 3:30 EST and lasting for an hour and a half. If you stand on the corner for those ninety minutes, you will see perhaps every fifth caller—many of them young teenage girls who are exquisitely made up, cheeks dabbed with tiny plastic sparkles, ready for their close-up—pulling out their phones with hot-pink and lime-green faces and fingering a memorized number, the number of home or a best friend. They are calling all over the world; you hear the girls speaking in Japanese and Arabic and midwestern American English. But in all their chatter one acronym is always recognizable: "TRL." MTV's *Total Request Live* broadcasts from a studio one story up.

You can't really see that much from the street. The positioning of guest stars and host Carson Daly is indicative: their faces point toward the cameras, their asses toward the crowds below. And apart from the occasional screaming, it is a quiet and divorced experience: when Carson announces a video and the studio audience vaults into the air, one cannot hear a sound. But for the fans it's enough to be here, close to the lights and the stars, the warm center of their own world.

This is where the young international tourist insists on coming; it is their New York City landmark, as the Statue of Liberty or the Met belongs to their parents. Once here they pack into a thin cordon marked off by blue NYPD barricades and patrolled by cops who bait them pleasantly in the New York manner. ("Sure, it's free to go in," one cop tells a couple trying to exit the cordon, "but it's a hundred bucks *to leave*. You didn't know?") The tourists respond as best they can, sometimes with a little style borrowed from hip-hop lyrics; as another cop approaches, one thin white teen nudges a friend. "Uh-oh," she whispers. "*The po-po.*" They are, of course, black and white and Asian and Latino and their language, their intonation, their body posture, their clothes (puffy down jackets in pink and powder blue are everywhere this year) are nearly identical. Today they are here to see Justin Timberlake of N'Sync and Elton John, who play what appears to be some kind of quiz game with Carson. When the duo appear at the window, a terrifying keening so perfectly modulated that it seems rehearsed bursts in the air above the crowd like a mortar round, the girls launching from silence to arrive full-throated at the same high note.

Pop culture really does seem to rule the world. And race cannot hold a candle to it.

A look at the Christmas concert sponsored by a local radio station that features a host of TRL regulars shows how outmoded a word like "integration" has become. "Z100's Jingle Ball 2001" featured Enrique Iglesias, the Latino pop heir to his father's throne, who mixes black R & B with blue-eyed pop and salsa rhythms; Alicia Keys, the biracial Harlem wonderchild who in concert plays Beethoven's Fifth and her own soul vamps; Pink, a Philly white girl with issues who borrows Elvis's curled lip and sings a mixture of hip-hop, dance music, and pugnacious rock; the pop/R & B boy band O-Town—four white, one black—assembled on MTV during a prime-time show; and Lenny Kravitz, the black/Jewish guitarist who mixes funk with Jimi Hendrix-style rock. There are a few other acts who keep their music more stylistically pure, such as Jay-Z, the superb hip-hop MC. And there is

Jewel, who sings pretty folk-rock without breaking into Latin percussion or rapping at all. But most of the lineup cannot claim anything close to a style—an identity, really—that does not borrow from at least two disparate musical traditions with roots in different ethnic communities. The Jingle Ball celebrates a culture far more incestuous and mongrelized than that of Sodom at its height, and it sells hundreds of millions of records every year in every corner of the world, to all kinds of people, who profess to love it.

In the pop world, one's ethnicity is not very important; it is mostly an element of style. It is displayed for a tantalizing second, savored, before being whipped into the mélange, adding its particular mild flavor but never allowed to dominate the palate. It is considered rude and old-fashioned to be too black, too white, too Latino, or to refuse to assemble your style from among the ethnic buffet.

MTV's idea of roots, ethnic and otherwise, can perhaps best be appreciated online. At the TRL website, one must create a profile before one can chat about Pink's personality or how cute Lenny Kravitz is. One is asked to pick a "species" that one belongs to, and there are twenty-four life-forms to choose from: "none, male, female, extraterrestrial, punk rocker, dogg, playa, human, carnivore, herbivore, angel, devil, rock star, diva, dude, freak, hacker, princess, dj, rapper, baller, geek, people person, clown." The locations from which one will be posting are just as rad, if slightly less numerous: "home, mi casa, my crib, my mansion, my school, the love shack, Nirvana, the hood, a padded room, the trailer park, my personal hell, Da Big House, Monkey Butt, my Mom's basement, a hole in the wall, stanktown, anytown, a parallel universe, area 51, the catwalk, an undisclosed location." The fact that a kid in a Bed-Stuy project can choose "the trailer park" or "my mansion" and not be called on it, while his coeval in Beverly Hills can opt for "da hood," is not important; requiring no commitment, the choices bear little weight in the actual world or even the virtual world. What sticks in one's memory is the fact that the very basis of one's identity, person and place, are seen as unfixed, made up out of catchphrases, the *National Enquirer*, band names, and, of course, songs. In pop, who you are depends mostly on who you want to be. Here is where essentialism—the nineteenth-century philosophy that the races have certain hardwired capabilities and traits—breathes its last.

Whether or not you like MTV or current pop music is irrelevant; it is being sucked into the salty pores of adolescents along with their experiences in years 12-18, and that will be its chief function. In ten or twenty years, those songs will be played on the radio and they will draw up from the memory banks of the grown-up fan the input from the year 2002 that has chemically attached itself to the sound of O-Town. It will be the bond between the scenes that pass through the minds of Latino, Asian, black, and white girls. And it is not only the songs that are eerily alike, but the clothes, the values, the attitudes toward life displayed by its performers and fans. Each ethnic group contributes some swatches of clothes, some slang, some bars of music. MTV mixes the concoction thoroughly; and then each person scoops out the final product.

On TRL, race has been vanquished as a divisive factor. Pop music has revealed itself as the common language that Paul Robeson drove himself mad looking for. In the peaceful valley of MTV, the black child and the white child walk hand in hand together through a landscape full of sneaker ads and bare midriffs. Despite the make-believe atmosphere and the heavy corporate presence, it is a rather breathtaking achievement.

Having come through the dramas and excitements of the Christian revivals, of jazz and Dorothy Dandridge's final days, however, the historian feels compelled to ask a simple question: Is this what we're left with? A good pop song or video is a tonic for the spirit, an up-to-the-second snapshot of the culture; and the cleverness with which they sew opposing strands of American life together is underappreciated. But one has to ask: Can this really be the promised land?

Not quite. The worshipping that goes on at the corner of 45th and Broadway is just the most public face of a wider phenomenon: not the multicultural society, in which blacks represent blacks, Asians Asians, like delegates at the UN, but the society of the multicultural self, in which one assembles an identity out of the widest possible cultural materials. Americans of all colors have never been so free or so doomed to follow their hearts, and not simply their ethnic traditions, in seeking out what delights and shapes them.

Ralph Ellison was the poet of such things. In *Shadow and Act*, he wrote of his 1920s Oklahoma boyhood, where he and his close circle of friends were secretly involved in searching the world for models and styles:

> *We fabricated our own heroes and ideals catch-as-catch-can, and with an outrageous and irreverent sense of freedom. Yes, and in complete disregard for ideas of respectability or the surreal incongruity of some of our projections. Gamblers and scholars, jazz musicians and scientists, Negro cowboys and soldiers from the Spanish-American and First World Wars, movie stars and stunt men, figures from the Italian Renaissance and literature, both classical and popular, were combined with the special virtues of some local bootlegger, the eloquence of some Negro preacher, the strength and grace of some local athlete, the ruthlessness of some businessman-physician, the elegance in dress and manners of some headwaiter or hotel doorman.*

Whites (at least affluent whites) have been freer to pursue such a program for centuries, and, as we have seen, black culture has been one of their chief resources. The rap music that so many white teenagers grow up with is only the latest chapter in an old story. What is most intriguing is the emerging black ability and desire to follow Ellison's example.

Until fairly recently, few black men and women have been encouraged to do what Ellison did; for hundreds of years, white society forced them back relentlessly upon the idea of their color. And especially in the 1960s and 1970s, blacks themselves maintained in and out lists for the race. Modeling your worldview on a Third World thinker like Mao was in. Modeling it on, say, Michelangelo (one of those "figures from the Italian Renaissance" that Ellison presumably looked to) was most definitely out. There was a freedom struggle to be waged, and it demanded purity.

But today, even that mandate is fading. "Acting white" is now a curse tossed at bright inner-city students by classmates, not a taunt in the general black population; "sellout" is heard less and less often and is less and less meaningful. Only "Uncle Tom," an accusation that one has betrayed the race, qualifies as fighting words. For many decades, black life was cordoned off by barriers and limitations. But today most black Americans not hampered by poverty or prejudice take for granted their right to study Italian, listen to Britney Spears or opera, play in the NHL, eat Thai food, live anywhere, work anywhere, play anywhere, read and think and say anything. So does it even make sense to search for the final meeting point between black and white culture, when the entire society is one vast mating ground that encourages them to merge?

To answer that, it might be best to begin with the last great hold-out to the trend; perhaps the final major rearguard action in black American life to the impulse toward full cultural freedom. It is not, as one might think, Afrocentricity. It is hip-hop.

We are now only a decade past the last great spasm of racial tension in the United States. In the 1980s and 1990s, dramas such as the Howard Beach murder and O.J. and Amadou Diallo made the newspapers garish with race. Looking back, it was an era in which public violence was necessary to appease the level of anger and frustration: Diallo, Denny, Michael Griffith of the Howard Beach murder, Yankel Rosenbaum in Crown Heights. Only a few years afterward, it seems incredible that at the center of the racial debate, people bled and died.

That kind of rage now seems impossible to attain again, anytime soon. Race no longer charges the air with electricity as it once did. America is more tolerant, fairer, more preoccupied with other things. That is not to say that the inner city is a bootstrapping paradise now, or that history—evil, really—did not have a hand in placing blacks in urban or rural ghettos, where they too often lead unacceptably miserable lives. It did. But the mental and physical world that the inner-city resident wakes up to is not primarily conditioned by race; it is conditioned by depression, bad faith, poor nutrition, poverty, and self-doubt. The young black kid growing up in Bed-Stuy has far more in common with the Arab kid growing up in Paris or the Irish kid growing up in a Dublin housing project or even the white Appalachian teen than he does with a black middle-class homeowner anywhere in this country. He often doesn't get the *chance* to be discriminated against; if only he could. He lives and dies miles from such dilemmas as affirmative action and glass ceilings; racial profiling makes little sense when *all* your neighbors are black and Latino and when you rarely venture outside a four-block radius. History is irrelevant to his daily life; history's relevance lies with the national responsibility to such lives.

What the poor black youth got in the post–civil rights era instead of solutions to his problems was hip-hop. Hip-hop became in the two decades at the end of the century more than an industry; it became something between a culture and a religion, one that revealed its major themes in record time. It produced in two decades its founding fathers (Herc, Grandmaster Flash, Afrika Bambaata); its sacred texts (the early masterpieces of Public Enemy, Eric B. and Rakim, Nas, Jay-Z); its martyrs (Biggie, Tupac, and countless local dead legends); its heretics (leaders of lost tribes such as Grandmaster Caz, enemies of the faith such as C. Delores Tucker); its schisms (of which East versus West was only the most publicized); and an obsession with death and the afterlife.

But what really gave hip-hop its religious intensity was its twin promises of deliverance. The first promise was to the talented, who could pursue a record contract and an exit out of the ghetto. Inner-city kids act on this promise: they are ceaselessly turning their experience into art and hoping to turn their art into commerce. They chant out lyrics as they walk down the street, bag groceries, sit on stoops waiting for a girlfriend or just for the day to end. They aren't the first musicians to dream of getting rich quick. There have been plenty of rock, jazz, gospel, and R & B artists who wrote songs expressly for that purpose, but that purpose was almost always hidden. Rock's songs were about love, cars, revenge, whatever. ("Money, That's What I Want"—a 1960 hit co-written by who else, Berry Gordy—was an exception.) Not in rap. There the artist tells you what his sales figures are, about his empire, his clothing wing, the cars in his garage, his protégés, his failing competitors. The rap song is a mind-boggling piece of capitalist art; it states that its function—not its pleasant, unintended result, but its *function*—is to make the artist rich. The rap song's honesty about its intention is brutal in a way only the poor could invent.

The second promise is to the fan: hip-hop will provide you with answers. For every situation a youth in the ghetto faces, a rapper has rhymed about it and that rhyme comes unbidden to the true believer at the proper moment. Like all religions that emerge out of desert conditions, hip-hop's edicts can be harsh. It provides difficult lives with a way to understand the world through the obedience of severe masculine codes. And its lessons extend to every aspect of life. The adjective "hip-hop" actually means something: there is a hip-hop way to dress and walk, to conduct a friendship, to drive a car (slouched waaaay back, left arm locked on the wheel, eyes at windowsill level like a shark cutting across the water's surface). One cannot say intelligibly, "He did it country-and-western style." It expresses nothing, because country-and-western is a musical style, not a code. That someone did it "rock and roll style" is only a bit less opaque. But when Jay-Z recounted last year how his mother had called him on his cell phone to chastise him about a crack he made about archrival Nas, the Queens rapper laughed and told reporters: "It wasn't a very hip-hop way to handle the situation." Hip-hop gives the believer a value system that should apply to all situations and that provides rules, joy, meaning.

So, like disciples of other religions that require memorization of the sacred text, the true believer walks down the street chanting the verses that promise the wisdom that allows him to transcend his situation. For the religious believer, the text gives spiritual deliverance from the world of men; for the hip-hop believer, it is deliverance from powerlessness. Economically, through his own verses; psychologically, through the sacred verses.

The culture can make the poor rich, the ugly beautiful, the dangerous more theatrically dangerous, the unrespected respected. But it comes at a price. Witness the case of perhaps the greatest MC ever, Brooklyn's own Notorious B.I.G. In becoming Biggie, the erstwhile Christopher Wallace lost to his street-king persona a great deal of his true personality: his goofy humor, his mother's Caribbean moral strictness, his sweetness, and his peaceable nature, none of which earned him anything on the street. The myth he created about his early life— "you either sling crack rock or got a wicked jump shot," a famous line from his debut album, *Ready to Die*—was true, but edited; with his sterling grades in school and his mother's work ethic, Wallace could have become an accountant or a lawyer and moved to the suburbs, which was his dream in the first place. That would have been a serious loss to American culture, but Biggie is the exception; many less talented youths make the same sacrifice to the rap code without producing anything of interest. Biggie's deal with hip-hop was reflected in his verses; eventually he would outdo every American detective writer with his ability to compress the language into hardbitten syllables, where all extraneous language, all unnecessary emotion, has been excised. Hip-hop encourages its stars and its fans to do the same with their own lives. This is where it divorces itself from modern expansiveness, the world of Ellison. In rap, there are unthinkable thoughts, impermissible emotions—things from the mainstream culture that cannot be allowed in.

The limits that rap sets are not ethnic or racial, but emotional and behavioral. Hip-hop is mostly fair: it accepts white fans and white performers. When in the early 1990s an unknown Detroit kid named Eminem entered a battle-of-the-MCs contest, one of his black opponents mocked him for being white. The largely black crowd ripped into Eminem's challenger for that; skills, not color were what counted. Eminem did encounter serious racism from blacks on his way up, but he eventually won deep respect in the culture. But, as far as what you are allowed to think or feel, the culture tends to lend power but take away range. It is as if rap tells its believers: I will make you bigger, deffer, rawer, tougher, more arrogant, and wickedly funny—but less curious, less tolerant and openhearted, more cynical, harder, narrower. Of course, these are the same demands the ghetto makes on any kid trying to survive it; it was perhaps a lot to ask of hip-hop to defy them. And for the most part, it didn't.

There are many brilliant exceptions, of course, from the impossible-not-to-love Slick Rick, a British dandy dropped into the wilds of the Bronx, to comedians like the Fat Boys to the unclassifiable Outkast. But beginning with gangsta rap in the early 1990s, the culture increasingly emphasized a stripped-down, hardboiled outlook on life that spread quickly to youth culture around the world. Hip-hop excels in exteriors: loving descriptions of the latest cars, sneakers, homes, fashions, which—far from being frivolous examples of materialism—tell you more about the life of the poor than any sociological tract: *to be poor in America is first and foremost to desperately wish not to be poor.* Rarer in hip-hop are masterpieces about interiors, portraits of the mind of the young man (or, rarely, woman) alone in the life. Hip-hop is the reverse of doo-wop, which talked about emotional states—mostly, being crazy in love—until the listener wanted to scream. Now, one must hide those things away. It took serious courage for Tupac Shakur to bring out the deep-feeling "Dear Mama," and as Benj DeMott has written,[1] for LL Cool J to write the breathy chant "I Need Love." Both those artists were larger than their rap personas: Tupac, with his troubled, miles-deep eyes and art-school past, who picked out a thug persona that fit his darkest moods and eventually got him killed; and Cool J, who had to become an actor and a rap elder statesman before he could begin flashing his smile and his full personality.

And it takes courage, for example, for a Jay-Z to release the recent "Song Cry," which exhibits the tensions in current hip-hop. It's a classic I-got-everything-I-wanted-but-lost-you song, placed in a rap context. Jay-Z could speak for Biggie or any other homely young black male who made it out of the ghetto with a good woman by his side. In the song, which is addressed to his lover, Jay-Z talks about how the girls he wanted before he became a star called him ugly "and wouldn't touch me." Then came the cash, the nice cars, and all the rest. Suddenly, he was awash in groupies, and his woman was crowded out. It's an old story, an old love song—but this is hip-hop, which means certain rules must be observed. MCs don't cry, so Jay-Z, his voice a little husky, lets the sound of the female soul singer moaning behind him carry the emotion. I can't drop the pose, Jay-Z says, so I have to make the "song cry." He's forced to express love without actually mentioning its name. At the end of the song, his lover wants to leave and it's killing him. If Jay-Z were a heartbroken player like Sam Cooke in "Bring It On Home To Me," he'd snap out of it and scream at her to come back. But this is 2003 and the rules in hip-hop are stricter than soul. All Jay-Z will allow is that, behind the mask, things ain't right: "Deep inside a nigga soooo sick."

Most kids not from the suburbs can inhabit those lyrics for a moment, and then go out and break the taboo; they aren't bound by rap's codes. But that taboo is still operative in many black kids' lives, telling them that the street will not tolerate certain things: softness of any kind, fidelity to women, idealism or naïveté.

But at least hip-hop belonged to them, as nothing else did.

MCs took their early material from the black ghetto, but they quickly looked around the nonblack world with a ruthlessly discerning eye and chose certain things to add to the culture: the bug-eyed violence and the moral logic of Hollywood gangster films; the incredible speed of kung fu actors and the dynasties of their plot lines; the language of the upper class ("proper" was hot for a while), as well as their wardrobes (one remembers fondly the polo-leisure craze of the early 1990s, with those matching outfits ripped out of a Harvard class of '22 picture) and their cars (the Bentley). But hip-hop uses all these things for its own purposes: it sees itself as the dominant culture, the more authentic one. One can have a Learjet and party in Monaco with Italian designers, but one must still remain true to the faith.

Outside life is sampled and brought into the culture carefully, and with a twist. When Jay-Z took a song from the Broadway show *Annie* and rapped over it for his first mainstream hit, "Hard Knock Life," he was being ironic. In the chorus he sampled from the show, Annie and the other white ragamuffins sing about their rotten lives. How they get tricks instead of treats, and kicks instead of kisses.

Annie is a nostalgic, Broadway version of ghetto; Jay-Z is the real thing. Importing the sound not only added a fresh sound, but background humor: What do those little white girls know about the hard-knock life? *Please!* White culture (apart from the Mafia and the jet set, both of which get major respect for their hard-core pursuit of their own ends) is most often used as a straight man for hip-hop's hard-core stories. Rap's deepest instinct is not to integrate with the world, but to conquer it on its own terms.

Of course, the main reason hip-hop believers feel this way is that the culture's first home, the ghettos, were largely abandoned by the larger society years ago. Hip-hop's question is not James Baldwin's in the civil rights era—"Why integrate into a burning house?"—but a more poignant one: "Why integrate into a house that never wanted us?" Hip-hop produced an empire out of nothing, and it retains a strong taste of its roots. It began as the art of the throwaway child.

In the post-gangsta era, commercial hip-hop has adapted to the global market. Not only has it grudgingly accepted white rappers—including one genius, Eminem—into the fold, it has lost a good part of its outsider's stance. Former underground stars like Ja Rule now do love songs with R & B stars; the midwestern phenom Nelly guest-starred on an N'Sync single. Love songs, sad songs, happy songs—super-commercial rap has joined the old showbiz tradition that goes back to Tin Pan Alley. That is, it has become just another musical style, rather than a culture that gazes on the mainstream from across an unbridgeable gap.

It still has its glorious holdouts, like the very grimy DMX, a hardcore traditionalist from Yonkers. DMX will never do a duet with Justin Timberlake, and he may go on TRL, but he will never be *of* TRL. His 2002 hit, "Who We Be," restated hip-hop's core stance. The song is a portrait of ghetto life, mostly just nouns strung together, rat-a-tat images; what's being described is too jagged and crazy for the comfort of verbs. The words—"the bullshit," "the armor," "the thugs"—pile one on top of the other. Ghetto life is just so bananas, DMX implies, that he can't even form a coherent sentence out of it. Besides, his audience can fill in the blanks: Each word by itself can call up moments from their biographies.

This is the stuff that hip-hop was built on, and that the underground still survives on. Its attitude toward the world—mostly the white world of cops, judges, lawyers, all collected under the name "they"—arrives in the chorus. Backup singers moan, "They don't know / who we be". The Ebonics is pointed. Then DMX steps in and states the message even more clearly. Speaking directly to his hard core, he tells them that "they" (you know who your are) have absolutely no idea "who we are." It's like the past 40 years never happened.

For white fans, it was cuts like "Who We Be" that made you go quiet the first time you heard it. No longer was the voice of black youth—that mysterious, scowling figure that you knew only through the evening news—channeled through literary mediums or garbled by political ones. It was as if society's mute had suddenly sat bolt upright and broken into strange verses. Whoever heard the opening of rock-hard masterpieces like Ice Cube's *AmeriKKKa's Most Wanted* or Public Enemy's *Fear of a Black Planet* can never forget the shock. Here was an immediate new standard for so many things: crisply tailored rage, verbal delight, honesty, raw power of expression. Hip-hop made the ghetto kid the final critic of what was both cool and hard.

But is black culture leaning DMX's way, or TRL's way? Is it really prepared to accept Ellison's challenge to create oneself out of all the world offers? One place to look is in the raft of black novels, the most popular art of the new black middle class that emerged in the last two decades.

Begin with the most ambitious recent black novel: Colson Whitehead's 2002 novel *John Henry Days*. In it, a wised-up young black New York journalist travels to West Virginia for a celebration of the larger-than-life black railwayman John Henry, whom legend has it, outworked a steam drill and then died. Whitehead's narrator, J., is nervous about his trip south; footage of old atrocities keep flashing into his head. On his way to one event with some other journalists, the tape seems to leap into the present when a pickup overtakes their van on the archetypal country road. Somewhere in his heart, J. always knew it was going to come down to this, and he allows himself one last racial freak-out.

> *Peering through the windshield he sees the vehicle trying to run them off the road, the red pickup truck of his nightmares. So much depends upon a red pickup truck, filled with crackers.... Here it comes, J. thinks, this is how it goes down. The van capsized in a ditch. Open the door, I said open the damn door. What chew all doin' ridin' with nigruhs? We don't abide no consortin' with nigruhs in Summers Country.... Then the ropes, the guns, the fire. The South will kill you.*

The pickup turns out to contain not Kluxers out for blood but just another freelancer, rushing to catch up. Whitehead is, of course, invoking history—here, the murders of Schwerner, Chaney, and Good-man—for comedic purposes, and it's not the last time. J. has more bad moments: as he ravenously scarfs up some beef at a free buffet, a way-ward chunk goes astray and he begins to choke; he gestures toward his throat as his white tablemates stare at him. As he dies, J. squeezes off one last malediction at their pale faces: "All these crackers . . . know how to watch a nigger die." His final realization turns out not to be quite final: A white stamp collector jumps in and performs the Heim-lich. But J. is unconsoled: any one of them—or better yet, all of them in cahoots together—just might be planning a midnight visit to his room. The paranoia is fitful and hardly central to the story, and there is humor in the fact that whites' bumbling innocence can inspire J. to Stokely Carmichael–style rants. (Whitehead, one thinks, does want to elicit laughter at J.'s distrust, but nervous laughter.) In the end, the South, filled with knickknacks, strip malls, and polite, overweight white people, consistently proves a disappointment in the area of racial profundity. The iconic age of John Henry is dead; the iconic age of the civil rights era as well. J. must live his life like everyone else, basically unmolested, in an era of pop crap.

J.'s flashbacks are seen again and again in very different works, the mass-market black novels that coalesced into a major phenomenon in the late 1980s. Many characters in black pop novels have jabbing doubts about whites in general. In *And This Too Shall Pass* (1996) by the superstar author E. Lynn Harris, an African-American lawyer who has failed the bar exam twice has recurrent dreams in which a "heavyset white man" with flowing hair sits behind a bench, gavel in hand, while she takes the test for the third time. When she hands this ominous fig-ure her completed exam, he breaks into laughter and, without even glancing at her answers, pounds the gavel on the test. Flunked again. In *Meeting of the Waters*, Kim McLarin's 2001 novel about the L.A. riots, a black journalist hears her mother tell of a white woman she had—almost—befriended. "I liked Connie, but I always knew, in my heart, if it came down to it she would stand me on that auction block and sell me down the river," she is told. "I never forgot that. You better never forget it either." And in 1998's *Singing in the Comeback Choir* by best-selling author Bebe Moore Campbell, TV producer Maxine finds the elevator is out in her building and climbs the stairs to the twentieth floor, where she encounters a locked door. Panicking, she pounds on it and is eventually let in by a white colleague. Accident—*or not?* "[Maxine] wondered then if despite their caring expressions the white people around her were glad that she'd been locked out, if, indeed, that lock had been put there just for her." These frissons of middle-class black doubt are as common as the shadows in *film noir*, and they serve the same function: most likely, they hide nothing, but one can never be quite sure. There are shapes lurking there that might be delusions or might be the outline of a hood or a secret wish.

White characters in black pop literature occasionally do serve a more concrete purpose. In *Your Blues Ain't Like Mine* (1992), Moore Campbell is remarkably successful in entering the lives of her white characters, including Lily, the put-upon wife of a racist killer. Lily is, above all, weak: "She felt frightened and weak when he was away from her," Moore writes. "It was as though she didn't exist when he was absent." This theme of what might be called ghostliness runs through Moore's work. "[Lily's] voice sounded frail, as though the words and the person speaking them could be broken into tiny little pieces and scattered all over." Another white character, Clayton, is a newspaper editor and son of a powerful and dominating white businessman; his relationship with his father is a cold one. When he tips off a northern newspaper about a lynching, he imagines his father's reaction:

> He could picture his father, his face apoplectic with rage, his breath coming in heaving waves. He would probably hit me, Clayton thought, and he couldn't help smiling. His father hadn't hit him in a very long time; they hadn't stood within arm's reach of each other in years.

Apart from tone, inflection, tastes in food, the black characters are not very different in their interior lives—even at the height of the 1990s culture wars, no pop black author was suggesting that. But they are, on this point of physical realness, wholly different. In *Blues*, the black parents of the murdered boy meet in a psychiatric ward where the memory (and his drinking) has driven the father, Wydell. Delotha is furious with him, but their bodies communicate:

> Again the rusty laughter. Right here in Wydell's arms, she was giggling and gasping for breath, her head so close to his chest that she

*could hear his heartbeat. His thin white hospital gown suddenly
turned wet from her tears. . . .*

*". . . Why they have to do that? Why?" She began sobbing, her
breasts heaving, her fingers splayed out across Wydell's chest, which
was full and powerful and familiar. His arms roped around her.
They cried together for a long time before she realized that she had
been lulled by Wydell's warmth, by their communion of tears. Being
in his arms was like a second funeral, full of mourning and sweet
release.*

In Moore's 1994 novel, *Brothers and Sisters*, set in modern-day L.A., the
theme continues. White characters—not just the villains—are described
as "soft," "wooden," "weak," "slippery," "pleading." Caucasians are foils
that make blacks more human, more alive, and more black.

In such adjectives one feels there is a larger implication. Whites are
not quite of this world the way blacks are; their history in America is
too ruthless to have been carried out by warm, natural people. In this
sense, the lack of black style becomes rather sinister; whites lack not
only soul but *a* soul. This rumor has led, variously, to the "ice people"
theory of nationalist loon Leonard Jeffries, the Black Muslim idea that
whites are a mutant race created by a mad scientist, and a million other
rumors and conspiracy theories that have their foundation in the idea
that whites are capable of anything because they are somehow inau-
thentic.

But in these novels, the idea that whites are some kind of killer
wraiths is fading, a touchstone from the past. In *Comeback Choir*, Maxine has her suspicions, but her job as producer of a mainstream talk
show requires her to think beyond her race. As her staff discusses a
future episode on the subject of Las Vegas showgirls, Maxine interjects:
"I'm a thirty-two-year old white single mother on welfare. I'm a fifty-
year-old black woman on vacation. I'm a twenty-three-old white man
who works the late shift. Why should any of us care?" And, although
the novels are shot through with annoyance at white women stealing
black men and uptight Caucasians in general, the writers express an
exhaustion with the old formulas. In Terry McMillan's latest (and best)
novel, *A Day Late and a Dollar Short*, a mother takes a hard look at her
ne'er-do-well son, Lewis.

He blames everybody except Lewis for his personal misery. Can't find no job: "I'm a threat to the white man," he says. "How?" I ask. "You more of a threat to yourself, Lewis." He huffs and puffs. "I'm a victim." And I say, "I agree. Of poor-ass planning!"

What one senses in the novels is that color is no longer of sufficient reliability in judging character or intent. In *A Day Late and a Dollar Short*, a character is ruminating about Viola, the book's cantankerous mother, and her friendship with her white neighbor Loretta.

She don't take nobody's feelings into account except her own. Say the first thang that come out her mouth, which is why she ain't got but a roomful of friends. Loretta ain't no threat, that's why she's so nice to her. Plus she white. I thank Viola is either scared of white people or feel like she gotta prove she just as good as they are. But Loretta don't want nothing. She just downright friendly. Decent. She came with offerings, her palms turned up.

Black style, black tradition, black suffering, the black story: all are as vital and real as one's blood type. But "race" in the abstract—that unseen presence that defined one's essential place in the world—has lost most of its terrors and its charms.

If race is really fading, leaving its last true subjects stranded in the ghettos and in forgotten rural hollows, what has replaced it? The society, the market, nothing? There is one movement that demonstrates how fast and how far the nation has moved past color into other obsessions. It is led by a black woman and has millions of adherents. Its flagship endeavor—the *Oprah* show—airs alongside TRL every weekday afternoon.

The therapeutic movement—the self-help revolution, the Oprahfication of America, whatever you will—has its immediate predecessors in the religious enthusiasms that blossomed in the 1970s: EST, TM, Taoism, and others. As people turned away from the old-line monotheistic religions, they sought the answers in a bouillabaisse of traditions. The old gods had been revealed as corrupt: the men who ran the war in Vietnam were, after all, mostly Protestants in good standing. So the generation tended to shop around, to take what it liked from religion X and blend it with religion Y. The future New Age author Marianne Williamson tried damn near everything:

> *As my pain deepened, so did my interest in philosophy: Eastern, Western, academic, esoteric. Kierkegaard, the I Ching, existential-ism, radical death-of-God Christian theology, Buddhism and more.*[1]

Black men and women in the 1970s mostly passed on such things and pursued black nationalism and old-fashioned middle-class security. But in the thirty years since, black women especially have flocked to the movement that developed out of such explorations. Almost lily-white in its beginnings, it is now fully mixed in its leadership and following.

Iyanla Vanzant's story is representative. The African-American author and speaker (who was launched to national prominence on *Oprah*) was, in the 1970s, in very bad shape. She had gone through hell: low to no self-esteem (triggered by years of child abuse by a relative), drinking, bad marriages, brushes with the law, financial mismanage-ment, and suicide attempts. In desperation, she was initiated as a priestess in the African Yoruba religion and began to write about the classic themes of the therapeutic movement. Her earliest work was specifically aimed at women of color; her early book *Interiors* was dedi-cated to "all African American women, Latin American women, Native American women, and Caribbean women." But Vanzant's trajectory describes what happened to mainstream black culture in general. By 2000, Iyanla had become an institution, with her own books, speaking tours, spiritual guidance workshop center, and a television show. And by then, she had clearly broadened her outlook:

> *Maybe you're a corporate executive or a Kansas City housewife, but there are certain universal truths that connect us all. And at some level that Kansas City housewife is not going to deal with her broken marriage any differently from the way the corporate executive would.*[2]

Certainly, the market spoke to Iyanla, as it had to Sam Cooke and any other black entrepreneur who wanted to cross over. But common sense and the society's slow progress toward true equality also played a role. At some point, black American women, especially, found racial

questions overtaken by issues that demanded immediate attention: trifling men, self-doubt, overeating, bad marriages, financial disaster.
When journalist Tamara Jeffries attended a Possibility of Woman
course, a four-day workshop given around the world that aims at
mending "unbalanced, disjointed and unfulfilled lives," she learned
that she was jealous of her younger sister and prone to self-sabotage.
Her revelations occurred in a mixed group of similarly afflicted
women. "I cry with women whose names I don't know," she wrote.
"White women, grandmothers, people with whom I thought I had
nothing in common."[3]

In the therapeutic movement, the personal trumps the social and
the historical. The movement's focus is constantly on the journey of
the individual: this is not only a device to hook viewers into a difficult
subject, it *is* the subject. Iyanla had the moment of clarity after many
tragedies: "Then and only then," she wrote later, "could I have understood that all the paths were leading me to the road of self."[4] What she
discovers is that the world exists only as a kind of cunning but rational
maze at whose center lies a great treasure. "My journeys along all the
paths I have trod were mapped out for one purpose," she writes in *Interiors*. "To bring me to total, unconditional love of myself." This radical
solipsism leads to rather breathtaking reinventions of history and even
biology; in one memorable passage, Vanzant writes about her discovery
that one chooses one's parents; they are placed in one's life to provide
"the exact circumstances and situations we need to learn our own special spiritual lessons."[5] This idea combines the stance of the
eighteenth-century Irish philosopher Berkeley—who stated that nothing exists outside of our own perceptions—to Marty McFly's discover-
ies after his mother hits on him in *Back to the Future*, and it announces
the almost unlimited powers that the modern self has been granted in
the movement.

What is important to our story is that history and race have been
made to kneel and bow before the individual. Despite their horrors,
earthquakes, wars, plane crashes, plagues and racial prejudice are actually lesson plans for the soul. Suze Orman, a regular on Oprah's TV
show and a mainstay in the financial wing of the empowerment movement, addressed 9/11 in the December 2001 issue of *O* magazine. "I
believe," she wrote, "that for those of us who were spending ourselves

into credit-card debt oblivion—and that was many of us, my friends—this has been a wake-up call." The mind boggles, especially when Orman's voice drops an octave into the Churchillian gravity of "*and that was many of us, my friends.*" The traditional, objective understanding of history has been heaved out the window. The joining of selfless and completely admirable action to supernarcissism is peculiarly American and modern.

If the therapeutic movement has significantly increased the supply of nonsense in American society, it has also done enormous good: more people have probably changed their lives within the *O* empire than they do within many American churches or synagogues. Certainly, more women have left their abusers, lost weight, curbed their defeatism, and understood their depression through the practical advice offered on the show. (And not incidentally, more bigoted whites have watched the show and been converted than have been converted from America's pulpits.) It is a faith that, beneath the warm visuals, is fairly relentless in its demands. Possibilities must be fulfilled. The self, newly freed from the constraints of history, will be served. Americans now see themselves as too unique and too free to be dominated by race or any other remnant of history.

The black American was largely the creation of a community fashioning itself in response to brutal daily circumstances; but, in different times, it is more and more the individual who is left to carry the splintering tradition forward. It is Karl Marx, oddly enough, who best sums up the current situation; in 1845–1846, the philosopher wrote in *The German Ideology* that in his ideal world he would be free to be a farmer in the morning, a fisherman in the afternoon, a cattleman at dusk, and a social critic after dinner—and yet, presumably, to go to bed all, and none, of these things. (Marx, not much of a fisherman or a farmer, was speaking not for himself but for the ordinary worker.) Marx's happy man would be a multitude unto himself. Today, most (but not nearly enough) black Americans are within reach of Marx's dream, in a cultural sense; they can be Afrocentrists in the morning, corporate workers at noon, Europeans in the afternoon, and shameless pop consumers after dinner. Often, they are *required* to be all these things, in order to function in American society.

That is not to say that negritude is fading from black life. There are still gut-strong connections between the black individual in Brooklyn and the black individual in Seattle, though they've never met; between both of them and the unfolding African-American story, which they feel themselves intimately a part of; between the middle-class doctor and the ghetto child. (Even Oprah is a race woman, one in a long tradition.) Still, the black American has been mostly freed from one part of being black in America: coercion. That coercion does come into play when a security guard follows her around a department store for no good reason; or when a real estate agent fails to show her houses in a certain neighborhood; or when he seeks a job as a head coach in the NFL or a governorship or promotion in a modern company with old-boy cabals; or when a black friend criticizes him for dating a white woman or listening to *Carmen* instead of Luther. Increasingly, African Americans live in a world of post-black possibility. The details of his or her life are often black; but his mind is free to flash between black and mulatto and white and Latino shades. Choice has defeated coercion.

For their part, whites live in a world where cultural integration is taken for granted. Most white children reach their late teens having brushed up against black life in a fairly significant way, through hero worship of Dr. J's successors, or through music or a black novel assigned in high school. Too often, it is a virtual experience. Most white kids know Method Man better than they know the quirks of an actual, breathing black peer living a mile away. Culturally, some of the dangerous frissons that mark white explorations into black territory are fading: hip-hop took the white fan into the ghetto, the last truly undiscovered place in black America. And the Huxtables made black middle-class life a familiar bore. What one gains in justice, one often loses in excitement.

The mulatto present can be a disconcerting one. In Ellison's and TRL's and Oprah's world, which increasingly looks like the modern American world, you never quite settle to Earth; you are borne aloft on a series of electrical storms—the newest idea, the latest book, the next band or diet or sensibility—that sweep you constantly over familiar and unfamiliar landscapes. Even the old racial myths, as comforting as they were wrong, are on the way out. Today one arrives at a final idea of what makes up a significant life and takes a long breath, only to have that idea torn apart by a new wind from the east or north. At times, one recognizes old places: the town where one grew up, the country of one's ancestors, even a book one read as a child or a young person that was, at that time, the sum of the world. These glimpses create a strong desire to live simply, as people did in the past, when one's place in the world was fixed from birth. But that is, increasingly, a rare achievement: in America today, only the devout and the incurious live in certainty.

The mulatto instinct in American life, that desire to discover what the Other was thinking, has played a part in all this. The white slave dissolved confidence in the immutability of blood; jazz musicians laughed at the very idea that life was simple or fated, and in the process gave the national culture a new kind of honesty; the black pop singers and early white rockers pilfered sounds they had repeatedly been asked not to mess with, and thus boosted young Americans over the razor-wire fences built around racial styles. The pioneers of this history ignored laws and pseudo-science, obeying instead the promptings of pleasure, taste, daring, and grandiose ambition. In this way, mulatto culture was really the fugitive expression of a moral truth. Its singer and writers broadcast the lonesome truth of American equality long before the nation honored it.

NOTES

CHAPTER ONE

1. Paxton Hibben, *Henry Ward Beecher: An American Portrait* (New York: George H. Doran Company, 1927), 133.

2. Henry F. May, *Protestant Churches and Industrial America* (New York, Octagon Books, 1963), 67.

3. Wm. C. Beecher and Rev. Samuel Scoville, *A Biography of Rev. Henry Ward Beecher* (New York: Charles L. Webster & Co., 1888), 292.

4. Ibid., 293.

5. Hibben, *Henry Ward Beecher*, 134–135.

6. Abbott, *Henry Ward Beecher*, 394.

7. William G. McLoughlin, *The Meaning of Henry Ward Beecher* (New York: Knopf, 1970), 201.

8. Niles *Register*, June 9, 1851. Quoted in Rogers, *Sex and Race*, vol. 2 (New York: self-published), 206–207.

9. William Chambers, *American Slavery and Colour* (London & New York: W. & R. Chambers/Dix and Edwards, 1857), 3.

10. Quoted in Carol Wilson and Calvin D. Wilson, "White Slav-

ery: An American Paradox," *Slavery and Abolition*, vol. 19, no. 1, April 1998, 5.

11. Ibid., 7–9.

12. Ibid., 14.

13. Holm, John James, *Holm's race assimilation; or, The fading leopard's spots; a complete scientific exposition of the most tremendous question that has ever confronted two races in the world's history* (Naperville, Ill.: J. L. Nichols, 1910), 347.

14. Lydia Maria Child, *Anti-Slavery Catechism* (Newburyport, Conn.: C. Whipple, 1839), 16–17.

15. Bourne, *Picture of Slavery in the United States of America* (Boston: I. Knapp, 1838), 145.

16. Parker Pillsbury to William Lloyd Garrison, *National Anti-Slavery Standard*, Nov. 12, 1853.

17. *Anglo-African Magazine*, vol. 1, no. 10, October 1859, 336.

18. Levi Coffin, *Reminiscences of Levi Coffin, the Reputed President of the Underground Railroad* (New York: Arno Press, 1968), 28–31.

19. Rogers, *Sex and Race*, 210.

20. Ibid., 210.

21. Ibid., 208.

22. Ariela Gross, "Litigating Whiteness," *Yale Law Journal*, October 1998, 1.

23. Ibid.

24. Frederick Law Olmstead, *The Cotton Kingdom*, vol. 2 (New York: Mason Brothers, 1962), 210.

25. Charles Mackay, *Life and Liberty in America; or, Sketches of a Tour in the United States and Canada* (New York: Johnson Reprint Co., 1971), 317.

26. James Annesley, *Memoirs of an Unfortunate Young Nobleman* (London: Printed for J. Freeman, 1743), 55.

27. Quoted in *Anglo-African Magazine*, vol. 1, no. 11, November 1859, 368.

28. Rogers, *Sex and Race*, 368.

29. Quoted in Chambers, *American Slavery and Colour*, 2.

30. David Herbert Donald, *Lincoln* (New York: Touchstone, 1995), 187.

31. Stephen B. Oates, *The Approaching Fury: Voices from the Storm,*

1820–1861 (New York: HarperCollins, 1997), 166–167.

32. Richard Hildreth, *The Slave: Or Memoirs of Archy Moore*, vol. 1 (Boston: Bela Marsh, 1848), 1.

CHAPTER TWO

1. John W. Blassingame, *The Slave Community* (New York: Oxford Univ. Press, 1972), 136.

2. Eugene Genovese, *Roll, Jordan, Roll* (New York: Vintage, 1976), 17.

3. Lawrence Levine, *Black Culture and Black Consciousness* (New York: Oxford Univ. Press, 1977), xiii.

4. Genovese, *Roll, Jordan, Roll*, 583.

5. Ibid.

6. Peter Wood, *Black Majority: Negroes in Colonial South Carolina from 1670 to the Stono Rebellion* (New York: Norton, 1974), 133.

7. Frank Lambert, *Pedlar in Divinity: George Whitefield and the Transatlantic Revivals, 1737–1770* (Princeton, N.J.: Princeton Univ. Press, 1994), 16.

8. Quoted in Darrett Rutman, ed., *The Great Awakening: Event and Exegesis* (New York: John Wiley & Sons), 93.

9. Ibid., 43.

10. Ibid., 35.

11. Quoted in Lambert, *Pedlar in Divinity*, 155.

12. Ibid., 205.

13. Ibid.

14. Mechal Sobel, *Trabelin' On: The Slave Journey to an Afro-Baptist Faith* (Princeton, N.J.: Princeton Univ. Press, 1988), 69.

15. Clifton H. Johnson, ed., *God Struck Me Dead* (Cleveland Pilgrim Press, 1993), 109.

16. Riggins R. Earl, Jr., *Dark Symbols, Obscure Signs: God, Self and Community in the Slave Mind* (Maryknoll, N.Y.: Orbis Books, 1993), 119.

17. Curtis Johnson, *Redeeming America: Evangelicals and the Road to Civil War* (Chicago: I. R. Dee, 1993), 77.

18. Milton Sernett, "Black Religion and American Evangelicism" (Ph.D. diss., Univ. of Delaware, 1972), 29.

19. Ibid., 31.

20. Riggins, *Dark Symbols, Obscure Signs*, 41.

21. Blassingame, *The Slave Community*, 44.

22. Quoted in Levine, *Black Culture and Black Consciousness* (New York: Oxford Univ. Press, 1977), 3.

CHAPTER THREE

1. George M. Fredrickson, *The Black Image in the White Mind: The Debate on Afro-American Character and Destiny, 1817–1914* (New York: Harper & Row, 1971), 262.

2. James Hugo Johnson, *Race Relations in Virginia and Miscegenation in the South, 1776–1860* (Amherst: Univ. of Massachusetts Press, 1970), 166.

3. Elise Virginia Lemire, "Making Miscegenation: Discourses of Interracial Sex and Marriage in the U.S.," 1790–1865 (Ph.D. diss., Rutgers, 1996), 169.

4. Lerone Bennett, *Before the Mayflower: A History of Black America*, 6th rev. ed. (Chicago: Johnson Pub. Co., 1982), 302.

5. Martha Hodes, *White Women, Black Men: Illicit Sex in the Nineteenth-Century South* (New Haven: Yale Univ. Press, 1997), 19.

6. Beth Day, *Sexual Life Between Blacks and Whites: The Roots of Racism* (New York: World Press, 1972), 56.

7. Hodes, *White Women, Black Men*, 138.

8. Rogers, *Sex and Race*, 170.

9. Quoted in Bennett, *Before the Mayflower*, 179.

10. Quoted in Lemire, *Making Miscegenation*, 52.

11. Martha Hodes, ed., *Sex, Love, Race: Crossing Boundaries in North American History* (New York: New York Univ. Press, 1999), 200.

12. Ibid., 205.

13. Angela Davis, *Women, Race and Class* (New York: Vintage, 1983), 26.

14. Joel Williamson, *New People: Miscegenation and Mulattoes in the U.S.* (New York: Free Press, 1980), 3.

15. Quoted in Sidney Kaplan, "The Miscegenation Issue in the Election of 1864," *Journal of Negro History*, vol. 34, no. 3., July 1949, 276.

16. Quoted in J. M. Bloch, *Miscegenation, Melaleukenation, and Mr. Lincoln's Dog* (New York: Schaum, 1958), 5.

17. Ibid., 1.

18. Kaplan, "The Miscegenation Issue," 296.

19. Bloch, *Miscegenation*, 47.

20. Ibid., 41.

CHAPTER FOUR

1. Leon Litwack, *Been in the Storm So Long* (New York: Knopf, 1979), 101.

2. Ibid., 252.

3. Eric Foner, *Reconstruction* (New York: Harper & Row, 1988), 288.

4. Litwack, *Been in the Storm So Long*, 165.

5. Foner, *Reconstruction*, 91.

CHAPTER FIVE

1. W. E. B. Du Bois, *The Autobiography of W. E. B. Du Bois* (New York: International Publishers, 1968), 87.

2. Quoted in Errol Hill, *Shakespeare in Sable: A History of Black Shakesperean Actors* (Amherst: Univ. of Massachusetts Press, 1984), xxii.

3. David Levering Lewis, *W. E. B. Du Bois: Biography of a Race* (New York: Henry Holt and Company, 1993), 260.

4. Henry Lee Swint, *The Northern Teacher in the South, 1862–1870* (New York: Octagon Books, 1967), 72.

5. Litwack, *Been in the Storm So Long*, 472.

6. Robert C. Morris, *Reading, 'Riting and Reconstruction: The Education of Freedmen in the South, 1861–1870* (Chicago: Univ. of Chicago Press, 1981), 178.

7. Henry Lee Swint, *The Northern Teacher in the South*, 89.

8. W. E. B. Du Bois, "The Meaning of All This," *W.E.B. Du Bois: A Reader* (New York: Henry Holt and Company, 1995), 162.

9. David Levering Lewis, *W.E.B. Du Bois*, 162.

10. Ibid., 282.

CHAPTER SIX

1. Quoted in David Levering Lewis, *When Harlem Was in Vogue* (New York: Knopf, 1981), 82.

2. Quoted in *Hear Me Talkin' to Ya: The Story of Jazz as Told by the Men Who Made It*, Nat Shapiro and Nat Hentoff, eds. (Rinehart & Co., 1955), 53.

3. Kathy L. Ogren, *The Jazz Revolution: Twenties America and the Meaning of Jazz* (New York: Oxford Univ. Press, 1989), 28.

4. Quoted in Alan Lomax, *Mister Jelly Roll: The Fortunes of Jelly Roll Morton, New Orleans Creole and Inventor of Jazz* (New York: Duell, Sloan and Pearce, 1950), 15.

5. Ogren, *The Jazz Revolution*, 16.

6. Ibid., 88–89.

7. Ibid., 89–90.

8. Marshall and Jean Stearns, *Jazz Dance: The Story of American Vernacular Dance* (New York: Da Capo, 1994), 148.

9. Ibid., 153.

10. Ibid., 96.

11. Richard M. Sudhalter, *Lost Chords: White Musicians and Their Contributions to Jazz, 1915–1945* (New York: Oxford Univ. Press, 1999), 190.

12. Ibid., 153.

13. Quoted in Lewis, *When Harlem Was in Vogue*, 99.

14. Quoted in Neil Leonard, *Jazz, Myth and Religion* (New York: Oxford Univ. Press, 1987), 79.

15. William Howland Kenney, *Chicago Jazz* (New York: Oxford Univ. Press, 1993), 101.

16. Richard M. Sudhalter and Philip R. Evans, *Bix: Man and Legend* (New Rochelle: Arlington House, 1974), 310.

17. Ibid., 268.

18. Jay D. Smith and Len Guttridge, *Jack Teagarden: The Story of a Jazz Maverick* (New York: Da Capo Press, 1988), 58.

19. Sudhalter and Evans, *Bix: Man and Legend*, 185.

20. Nathan Irving Huggins, *Harlem Renaissance* (New York: Oxford Univ. Press, 1971), 260.

CHAPTER SEVEN

1. Donald Bogle, *Toms, Coons, Mulattos, Mammies and Bucks*, 3rd ed. (New York: Continuum Publishing Group, 1994), 6.

2. Al-Tony Gilmore, *Bad Nigger! The National Impact of Jack Johnson* (Port Washington: Kennikat Press, 1975), 40.

3. Ibid., 38.

4. Allan Keiler, *Marian Anderson: A Singer's Journey* (New York: Scribner, 2000), 212.

5. Ibid., 213–214.

6. Lena Horne, *Lena* (Garden City: Doubleday, 1965), 65.

7. Keiler, *Marian Anderson*, 146.

8. Martin Duberman, *Paul Robeson: A Biography* (New York: Knopf, 1988), 417–418.

9. Ibid., 23.

10. Ibid., 265.

11. Quoted in Neil A. Wynn, *The Afro-American and the Second World War*, revised ed. (New York: Holmes & Meier, 1993), 79.

12. Duberman, *Paul Robeson*, 281.

13. Ibid., 162.

14. Ibid., 520.

CHAPTER EIGHT

1. Tony Douglas, *Lonely Teardrops: The Jackie Wilson Story* (London: Sanctuary Publishing Ltd., 1997), 109.

2. Daniel Wolff, *You Send Me: The Life and Times of Sam Cooke* (New York: William Morrow, 1995), 21.

3. Ibid., 112.

4. Ibid., 76.

5. Charlie Gillett, *Sound of the City: The Rise of Rock and Roll* (New York: Pantheon, 1983), 5.

6. James T. Patterson, *Grand Expectations: The United States 1945–1974* (New York: Oxford Univ. Press, 1996), 19.

7. Ibid.

8. Mary Wilson, *Dreamgirl: My Life as a Supreme* (New York: St. Martin's Press, 1986), 11.

9. Quoted in Patterson, *Grand Expectations*, 28.

10. Anthony J. Gribin and Matthew M. Schiff, *Doo-Wop: The Forgotten Third of Rock 'N' Roll* (Iola, WI: Krause Publications, 1992), 88.

11. George White, *Bo Diddley: Living Legend* (Chessington, Surrey:

Castle Communications, 1995), 20.

12. Phil Groia, *They All Sang on the Corner: Black R&B Vocal Groups of the 1950s* (Setauket, N.Y.: Edmond Pub. Co., 1973), 95.

13. Bill Millar, *The Drifters: The Rise and Fall of the Black Vocal Group* (London: Studio Vista, 1971), 5.

14. Quoted in Gribin and Schiff, *Doo-Wop*, 50.

15. Gerald Early, *One Nation Under a Groove: Motown and American Culture* (Hopewell, N.J.: Ecco Press, 1995), 117.

16. Quoted in Millar, *The Drifters*, 46.

17. Berry Gordy, *To Be Loved: The Music, the Magic, the Memories of Motown, an Autobiography* (New York: Warner Books, 1994), 53.

18. Quoted in Rob Bowman, *Soulsville U.S.A.: The Story of Stax Records* (New York: Schirmer Books, 1997), 182.

19. Ibid., 182.

20. Quoted in David Ritz, *Divided Soul: The Life of Marvin Gaye* (New York: Da Capo, 1991), 30.

21. Ibid., 34.

22. Chuck Berry, *Chuck Berry: The Autobiography* (New York: Harmony Books, 1987), 116.

23. Ibid., 90–91.

24. Quoted in Gribin and Schiff, *Doo-Wop*, 84.

25. Bowman, *Soulsville U.S.A.*, 65.

26. Wilson, *Dreamgirl*, 211.

27. Wolff, *You Send Me*, 157.

28. Stephen B. Oates, *Let the Trumpet Sound: The Life of Martin Luther King Jr.* (New York: Harper & Row, 1982), 296–297.

CHAPTER NINE

1. Oates, *Let the Trumpet Sound*, 254.

2. Nicolaus Mills, *Like a Holy Crusade: Mississippi 1964—The Turning of the Civil Rights Movement in America* (Chicago: I.R. Dee, 1992), 67.

3. Quoted in Howell Raines, *My Soul Is Rested* (New York: Putnam, 1997), 180.

4. Diane McWhorter, *Carry Me Home: Birmingham, Alabama. The Climactic Battle of the Civil Rights Revolution* (New York: Simon & Schuster, 2001), 223.

5. Robert Coles, *Children of Crisis: A Study of Courage and Fear*

(Boston: Little, Brown, 1967), 147–152.

6. Ibid., 113.

7. McWhorter, *Carry Me Home*, 366.

8. David Halberstam, *The Children* (New York: Random House, 1998), 75.

9. James Farmer, *Lay Bare the Heart: An Autobiography of the Civil Rights Movement* (New York: Arbor House, 1985), 133

10. Coles, *Children of Crisis*, 129.

11. Anthony Lewis and The New York *Times*, *Portrait of a Decade: The Second American Revolution* (New York: Random House, 1964), 40–42.

12. Willie Morris, *North Toward Home* (Boston: Houghton Mifflin, 1967), 22.

13. *Mademoiselle*, September 1963, p. 116.

14. Quoted in Studs Terkel, *Race* (New York: New Press, 1992), 42.

15. Mills, *Like a Holy Crusade*, 43.

16. David Halberstam, *The Children*, 493–494.

17. Bob Blauner, *Black Lives, White Lives: Three Decades of Race Relations in America* (Berkeley: Univ. of California Press, 1989), 134.

18. Ibid., 51.

19. Terkel, *Race*, 33.

20. Oates, *Let the Trumpet Sound*, 397.

21. Lewis, *Portrait of a Decade*, 200–203.

22. Quoted in *Eyes on the Prize: A Civil Rights Reader* (New York: Penguin Books, 1991), 276.

23. Robert Weisbrot, *Freedom Bound: A History of America's Civil Rights Movement* (New York: W. W. Norton, 1990), 157.

24. Ibid., 158.

25. Joan Morrison and Robert K. Morrison, *From Camelot to Kent State: The Sixties Experience in the Words of Those Who Lived It* (New York: Times Books, 1987), 220.

26. Coles, *Children of Crisis*, 109.

CHAPTER TEN

1. David Frum, *How We Got Here: The Seventies, The Decade That Brought You Modern Life—For Better or Worse* (New York: Basic Books, 2000), 262.

2. Bruce J. Schulman, *The 70s: The Great Shift in American Culture,*

Society and Politics (New York: Free Press, 2001), 55.

3. Ibid., 58.

4. Michele Wallace, *Black Macho and the Myth of the Superwoman* (New York: Verso, 1999), 48.

5. Quoted in *Rolling Stone: The Seventies* (Boston: Little, Brown, 1998), 140–141.

6. John Heidenry, *What Wild Ecstasy: The Rise and Fall of the Sexual Revolution* (New York: Simon & Schuster, 1997), 275.

7. Ibid., 138.

8. Author interview with Badham, November 2001.

9. Quoted in Shelton Waldrep, ed., *The Seventies: The Decade of Glitter in Popular Culture* (New York: Routledge, 2000), 276.

10. Ibid., 275.

11. Interview, *Penthouse*, July 1979.

12. Ibid.

13. John-Manuel Adriote, *Hot Stuff: A Brief History of Disco* (New York: HarperEntertainment, 2001), 80–81.

14. Quoted in *The Seventies: The Decade of Glitter in Popular Culture*, 275.

15. Iceberg Slim, *Pimp: The Story of My Life* (Los Angeles: Holloway House Pub., 1987), 194.

16. Ibid., 77.

17. Norman Mailer, *The Time of Our Time* (New York: Random House, 1998), 907.

18. Bill Shefski, Interview for "Bill Shefski's Ageless Sports," agelesssports.com, 11 November 2001.

19. Josh Wilker, *Julius Erving* (New York: Chelsea House, 1995), 51.

20. Sam Smith, *The Jordan Rules* (New York: Simon & Schuster, 1992), 41.

21. Quoted in Nelson George, *Elevating the Game: Black Men and Basketball* (New York: HarperCollins, 1992), 172.

22. Wilker, *Julius Erving*, 43.

23. David Halberstam, *Playing for Keeps: Michael Jordan and the World He Created* (New York: Broadway Books, 2000), 276.

CHAPTER ELEVEN

1. Benj DeMott, "Back to Life," *First of the Month*, vol. III, issue 2, 69, 2 August 2000.

2. Marianne Williamson, *A Return to Love* (New York: Harper Perennial, 1992), xv.

3. Interview, *Essence*, January 2000, 78–124.

4. *Essence*, January 2001, 107–134.

5. Ivanla Vanzant, *Interiors: A Black Woman's Healing in Progress* (New York: Writers and Readers, 1995), 202.

6. Ibid., 401.

INDEX